Tourism and Crime:
key themes

Tourism and Crime: key themes

Edited by David Botterill
and Trevor Jones

(G) **Goodfellow Publishers Ltd**

(G) Published by Goodfellow Publishers Limited,
Woodeaton, Oxford, OX3 9TJ
http://www.goodfellowpublishers.com

British Library Cataloguing in Publication Data: a catalogue record for this title is available from the British Library.

Library of Congress Catalog Card Number: on file.

ISBN: 978-1-906884-14–7

 Design and typesetting by P.K. McBride, www.macbride.org.uk

Printed by Marston Book Services, www.marston.co.uk

Cover design by Cylinder, www.cylindermedia.com

Contents

Contributing authors

Esther Bott is a lecturer in the School of Sociology and Social Policy, Nottingham University

David Botterill is Professor Emeritus of Tourism Studies in the Welsh Centre for Tourism Research, University of Wales Institute Cardiff and Visiting Research Fellow at the Centre for Tourism Research, University of Westminster.

Paul Brunt is a professor of Tourism and Head of School of Tourism and Hospitality and Associate Dean in the Plymouth Business School, University of Plymouth.

Gordon Hughes is a professor and director of the Centre for Crime, Law and Justice in the School of Social Sciences at Cardiff University.

Trevor Jones is Reader in the Centre for Crime, Law and Justice in the School of Social Sciences at Cardiff University.

John Lennon holds the Moffat Chair in Travel and Tourism Business Development at Glasgow Caledonian University.

Rob Mawby is Visiting Professor of Criminology and Criminal Justice in the Centre for the Study of Crime, Violence and Disorder, University of Gloucestershire.

Heather Montgomery is a senior lecturer in the Centre for Childhood, Learning and Development at the Open University.

Helen Selby is Research and Analysis Manager at Merseyside Police.

Martin Selby is a senior lecturer in the Faculty of Education, Community and Leisure at Liverpool John Moores University.

Mike Shiner is a senior lecturer in Criminology at the London School of Economics.

Toine Spapens is a researcher in the Police and Gambling Research Group of Tilburg University Law School.

About the editors

David Botterill is a freelance academic, Research Fellow in the Centre for Tourism at the University of Westminster and Professor Emeritus in the Welsh Centre for Tourism Research, University of Wales Institute Cardiff. He has worked with a number of external and industry partners including the Higher Education Academy Network for Hospitality, Leisure, Sport and Tourism, Tourism Concern, the Wales Tourist Board and the Tourism Training Forum for Wales and held research leadership positions at UWIC for 15 years, most recently in the Cardiff School of Management. David is a reviewer for several publishing houses and external assessor of research quality for universities and research bodies.

Trevor Jones is Reader in the Centre for Crime, Law and Justice at the School of Social Sciences, University of Cardiff and Visiting Fellow at the Vrije University Amsterdam. He has published widely in the fields of policing, community safety and criminal justice policy-making. He has undertaken research and published widely on the subjects of policing, security and crime prevention. In recent years he co-edited a cross national comparison of developments in plural policing forms (*Plural Policing: A Comparative Perspective*, with Tim Newburn, Routledge 2006), and recently published a major comparative study of policy transfer in crime control (*Policy Transfer and Criminal Justice*, with Tim Newburn, Open University Press 2007). He is on the editorial board of the international journals *Policing and Society* and is a managing editor of the house journal of the British Society of Criminology, *Criminology and Criminal Justice*.

1 Introduction: Tourism Studies and Criminology

David Botterill and Trevor Jones

In this chapter we:

♦ Make the case for collaboration between tourism studies and criminology
♦ Sketch the emergence of both tourism studies and criminology in the academy
♦ Briefly review the key themes in both fields
♦ Suggest potential lines of analysis that arise from collaboration.

The ambition of this book is to begin a project that on the face of it might appear somewhat baffling. Holidays are surrounded by images that convey an escape; a promise of freedom from the pressures and problems of everyday 'normal' life. Be it idyllic seascapes, soaring mountains, luxurious therapies, adrenaline-pumping extreme rides, or monumental cultural icons, the images suggest that on holiday we are, primarily, getting away from all those awkward, uncomfortable, damaging and life-threatening bits of human existence that constrain the promised good life. The criminal 'underworld', on the other hand, is the bad life personified. Here the vilified perpetrators of the worst excesses of human depravity dwell. And, despite a voyeuristic fascination with the criminal world when kept at a safe distance through the mediation of the news, or popularised through literature and film, this dark side of human behaviour is necessarily cordoned-off, regulated, incarcerated or even extinguished from sight. Why then bring these two seemingly oppositional domains of the social world together?

It is not that the falsehood of the separation of holidays and crime go unnoticed. Most of us know that the seduction of the holiday bubble bursts when travel inconvenience, marital dispute, frightening encounters with 'other' strangers occur, or when unlawful actions maim and kill. We also know that crime is not cordoned off by tourism and can occur anywhere and at any time, but somehow this has yet to be reflected in the research agendas of tourism studies and criminology. It is as if we have internalised the popular images of holidays and crime and thus closed our collective sociological imaginations to this important interface.

This book intends to spark a debate and encourage the two subject communities to explore the interface of tourism and crime and how it might open new lines of analyses important to both subjects. We hope that the book will be a dialectical moment for both subject communities; an opportunity to address the absence of each other in their respective canons. There are substantive reasons why, as social scientists, we should do this. Tourism continues to grow as a human activity in both scale and significance. The voluntary mobility of a holiday uproots citizens from secure and known social and legal structures and exposes them, often unwittingly, to different legal and cultural environments, along with unanticipated dangers and temptations. This same condition of mobility, exercised by those with criminal intent, opens up new opportunities for criminal offending and ambiguously policed territories. Thus we hope that this book is just a beginning of what will become a more important area of academic enquiry for both subject communities leading to increased empirical work, theoretical development and contributions to policy debates.

We begin the task of dialogue by reporting the academic background, key themes and approaches to both tourism studies and criminology. This we hope will be helpful to the book's readers whom we assume will be new to one or other of the subjects. Inevitably, given space restrictions, these overviews can only touch broadly on the key themes of research and writing within each area of study. The overview of tourism studies will focus on tourist behaviour (holiday choice, destination image, perceptions of safety and risk, tourist behaviour and moral codes) and destination management (international and domestic tourism, tourism destination development, tourist enclaves, tourist policing). The overview of criminology will provide a brief outline of the development of academic criminology (focusing mainly on Britain). It will outline three central themes within criminological research that can be seen as particularly relevant in the context of this book. These themes are the measurement of crime patterns and trends; explaining the causes of crime; and societal responses to crime. The chapter concludes with a discussion of the potential benefits of cross-disciplinary collaboration between these areas of study.

The emergence of tourism studies

Tourism studies emerged through the influences of a multidisciplinary set of social sciences but particularly geography, economics, sociology and in more recent times, cultural anthropology and business and management studies. In the UK, the study of tourism at postgraduate level began in the late 1960s and early 1970s at different universities and in different academic contexts. At the University of Edinburgh, tourism became a topic of interest in geography as a part of the growing interest in the leisure and recreational use of land in the UK. This was further stimulated by academics and students at the University of Hull. In 1979, De Kadt published his seminal work, *Tourism: Passport to Development?* from the Institute for Development Studies at the University of Sussex and opened the debates about tourism development impacts on lesser-developed countries (De Kadt, 1979). At the University of Birmingham's Centre for Urban and Regional

Studies, academics were interested in the public policy implications for leisure and tourism of changes taking place in the 1960s/early 1970s in UK national and local government structures. By the mid-1970s, economists at Bangor University had produced the first studies of tourism's economic impact and at the Polytechnic of Central London (now the University of Westminster) the sociological analysis of leisure was extended to include tourism. Two of the earliest, dedicated, postgraduate courses in tourism were created in the early 1970s at the Universities of Strathclyde and Surrey within departments concerned primarily with the study of hotel and catering management. This development in the subject was underpinned by industrial economics.

It is noteworthy that the emergence of tourism higher education at postgraduate level began over 15 years before the establishment of the first named undergraduate degrees in tourism in UK higher education institutions in 1986/87 at Bournemouth, Northumbria and South Glamorgan (Cardiff) Institute. It was the subsequent growth in undergraduate students of tourism, however, and the formation of academic departments to support that provision that has fuelled the scholarship of tourism.

Tourism studies has emerged alongside a suite of other subject areas particularly the study of leisure, hospitality and sport. The social conditions in the 20th century that have fuelled the growth in academic interest in these subjects has largely followed a pattern across the nation states of Europe. The principal social concern in the early part of the century was to explore how to educate the masses for and about their leisure time and various moral panics about anti-social behaviour were a strong imperative. After the Second World War, nation states embarked upon modernist projects in leisure that were predicated on a belief in creating a better society. This resulted in an increase in applied research and a serious interest in the planning of, and for, leisure. Aligned with these 'welfare' notions about leisure an expansion of higher education opened the academy to new subjects and enabled the introduction of leisure and tourism studies into higher education. More recently there has been a shift in emphasis away from issues of leisure as citizenship to embrace the questions associated with leisure consumption including the business of holidaymaking.

In the USA, postgraduate study of leisure and recreation and subsequently of tourism emerged from a different mix of influences, albeit from the same preoccupation with leisure of the masses. The early 20th century concern for urban 'rational' recreation echoed the Western European tradition in leisure studies. These were expressed in the creation of urban parks and communal bathing facilities. A muscular Christian movement, not of course unique to the USA, fuelled the emergence of physical education and subsequently led to the creation of departments of health, physical education and recreation in several universities. The outdoor recreation movement with its focus on conservation and the recreational use of natural areas of forestry and open countryside grew in popular appeal, fuelled by the growth in road and rail networks, increasing affluence and the perceived need to escape urban life. A number of landmarks in US higher education occurred during the 1930s; the development of a national park management course at Colorado State College in 1934, a recreation and municipal forestry programme at Michigan State College in 1935, and both undergraduate and graduate courses in recreation education at New York University in 1936.

Tourism or travel, sometimes the preferred subject label, had been taught since the late 1960s, usually as a stand-alone or short series of optional modules, but awards in the subject were few and far between. Pioneers in the study of tourism became influential figures beyond the borders of the USA through their publications. However it wasn't until the early 1990s that many of the departments in which the teaching of tourism occurred, and which were created in this health/natural resource/recreation nexus referred to above, adopted the inclusion of tourism in their titles. (See for example Texas A&M University's Department of Recreation, Parks and Tourism Sciences.)

Tourism is now studied in virtually all parts of the world and at all levels of post-16 education; from vocational training to doctoral studies (Airey and Tribe, 2005). In the UK, annual undergraduate enrolments in universities had reached 4000 by the year 2000. The rich mix of subject influences within tourism studies can be seen in the current agenda of the anglophone tourism studies academy. In a recently published handbook (Jamal and Robinson, 2009), topics included the relationship of tourism to culture, the ecology and economics of tourism; special events, destination management and tourism; tourism and transport; tourism and heritage; tourism and post-colonialism; global tourist business operations. There is a dynamism that is typical of less mature domains of study that is necessarily uncomfortable with a strict 'canon' of ideas. Scholars consistently press for the inclusion of new topics of enquiry and the exploration of novel theoretical frames of explanation. From a tourism studies perspective it is this momentum that invites our current project to explore the intercepts of tourism studies and criminology as a contribution to critical tourism studies.

There is a developing literature of critical tourism studies that has been nurtured through a series of conferences. At the most recent, a critical tourism studies community of some 90 scholars from 27 countries met in June 2009 in Zadar for the third bi-annual conference. 'Critique', within this international community is not wedded to any particular ideological position but follows from numerous methodological, epistemological, theoretical and moral points of departure. It finds unification, however, around a commitment to reconfigure a new agenda in tourism studies. For example, the second conference held in Split in 2007 had as its purpose to explore, 'the potential of tourism theory and practice as a progressive force for engagement in and analysis of global social justice; the de-centering of and decolonization of tourism studies; the emotional dynamics of research relations and the personal, the political, and the situational nature of research journeys' (Pritchard and Morgan, 2007: 23).

One of the objectives of this book is to contribute to the further development of critical tourism studies. Specifically, by foregrounding an exploration of crime and tourism, the book challenges the striking absence of deviance in a field of study that draws heavily upon the disciplines of the social sciences but has eschewed the critical line of thinking that is common to those disciplines. With the notable exception of a very few studies of sex tourism, the tourism research literature largely reads as a version of 'middletown' holiday taking. It is devoid of any significant treatment of the abnormal, the dissenting and the deviant. Consequently, a dialogue with criminology promises much for the de-centring ambitions of the critical tourism studies community and the maturing of tourism studies as a domain of social science.

Key themes in tourism studies

The dynamism and diversity of tourism studies is not helpful however to those who are unfamiliar with it and the purpose of this section is to introduce the persistent themes and approaches within tourism studies. We begin with a division between on the one hand the evidence and concepts applied to the study of tourist behaviour and, on the other hand, those found in the literature about tourism destinations. This simplistic division reflects the influence of economics in tourism studies and the preoccupations of tourism researchers with the demand and supply sides of tourism or, taking an industry perspective, the markets and products of the tourism industry.

Tourist behaviour

Studies of tourist behaviour have become central to an understanding of tourism particularly in the tourist generating regions of the world. The extent and frequency of holiday taking is captured at a macro scale by large-scale surveys, usually funded by national governments. Surveys are conducted both at the level of the household, for example in the UK 'Social Trends' or the UK Tourism Survey (UKTS), and at points of departure and arrival in a nation state, such as the UK government's International Passenger Survey. Thus, tourist behaviour can be described in terms of frequency, duration, origin and destination. These data have consistently indicated that around half of the population of the UK take a holiday of four or more nights away from home each year.

Patterns of tourist behaviour are captured in terms of domestic holiday taking, that is by residents within their homeland, and in terms of international arrivals. For example, in 2008, UK domestic tourism accounted for 52 million holidays of one night or more and spending of £11.4 billion, 18.2 million overnight business trips and spending of £4.5 billion, and 44.1 million overnight trips to friends and relatives with spending of £4.8 billion (Visit Britain, 2009). Overseas visitors to the UK in 2008 reached 31.9 million with spending of £16.4 billion. In 2007, the

UK ranked sixth in the international tourism earnings league table behind the USA, Spain, France, Italy and China (Visit Britain, 2009). On a global scale, international tourist arrivals grew by 2% in 2008 to reach 924 million, up 16 million over 2007. International tourism generated US$856 billion in 2007, or 30% of the world's exports of services and the United Nations World Tourism Organization predicts 1.6 billion international arrivals worldwide by 2020 (WTO, 2009). Statistics of tourist behaviour at the macro level provide estimates of the economic value of tourism and facilitate the tracking of trends in tourism demand. They are of particular importance, therefore, to national governments who are concerned with the balance of trade in tourism and the economic and employment impacts of tourism. More recently the focus of attention has been in capturing these data in the form of tourism satellite accounts[1].

Micro level studies of tourist behaviour have attempted to capture the activities, experiences and motivations of tourists. Consequently, the influences of sociology, anthropology and psychology, particularly consumer psychology, are very evident here and studies of tourist behaviour reflect the diversity of research methods employed in the social sciences. Early sociological studies attempted to categorise behaviours along a tourist–traveller dichotomy. Greater sophistication in tourist behaviour taxonomies ensued, and continue, in the application of multivariate statistical analysis to determine, name and characterise segments of the tourism market. Anthropologists applied theories associated with 'pilgrimage' and 'rites of passage' to the behaviour of tourists where upon the concept of 'authenticity' became a central concern.

Explorations of social theory shifted the focus of study of tourist behaviour away from the individual tourist to the structures of power that surround the tourist. Most notably in John Urry's seminal contribution on the tourist gaze where he argued in a Foucauldian thesis that what tourists look for and see is not a matter of choice but is highly structured by powerful interests in the narratives of places (Urry, 2002). The theoretical framing of tourist behaviour continues apace with influences of feminism, consumption, mobility, post-colonialism and globalisation all now being employed. Alongside these explorations of social structure, studies of tourist 'agency' have continued in ever more sophisticated studies of tourist consumer behaviour.

Of particular interest here is the importance of destination image in consumer choice behaviour. The image of a destination is formed through both the activities of destination marketing organisations, public relation campaigns and 'official' consumer information sources such as guide books and the Internet. Additionally, and importantly, the image of a destination is notoriously difficult to manage. News media and the informal networks of blogs and social networking sites provide unauthorised destination imagery. A destination can be instantly knocked out

---

1 A tourism satellite account (TSA) is a set of data tables based around analyses of data on both expenditure by tourists, and on business sectors which serve tourists

of a consumers 'choice set' by the release of adverse or negative news or consumer feedback. The speed at which information about destinations now flows and the unlocking of the control of destination imagery has accentuated the importance of tourist perceptions of risk and safety in tourism research.

An increased awareness of the negative social and environmental impacts of tourism has led to the promotion of various 'codes of conduct' for tourist behaviour. These usually aim to reduce moral or religious offence and to reduce negative environmental impact. Scant attention has been given to deviant tourist behaviour until fairly recently. The rise of social movements associated with tourism has highlighted deviant tourist behaviour, particularly paedophilia, and through some high-profile journalism, the problems of alcohol consumption and explicit sexual behaviour in some tourist resorts have been exposed (see, for example, Andrews, 2009). Another recent, and small, shift in focus has been to examine non-participation and barriers to participation in tourist behaviour.

Tourism destinations

The naming of a geo-political space as a tourism destination can occur at varying scales from complete nation states to a local community or purpose built resort. Common to all destinations is the likelihood of some sort of destination management organisation or DMO. At the national level, a DMO is invariably created through government legislation and is likely to have both a promotion and a development function often with the power to provide financial assistance. At sub-national level a private–public partnership model is more likely and powers are likely to be limited to promotion and marketing. Here begins the complex relations between the public, private and voluntary sectors that surround the management, planning and development of tourism destinations. Additional complexity is introduced because DMOs seek to promote tourism in both international and domestic tourism markets and at the sub-national level the defined destination areas do not neatly fit into the administrative labels and boundaries of government. It is much more likely that they are defined by some theme or image associated with a place and consequently their boundaries are much more fluid.

The components that make up a tourism destination are generally agreed to be:

♦ Natural and cultural attractions

♦ Amenities such as hotels, shops, tour guide service

♦ Transport infrastructure

♦ Ancillary services such as visitor information, banking, medical facilities.

Again there is no simple mapping between the components of tourism and the ownership and control of them being vested in a particular sector. The complexity and fluidity of the structure of tourism present considerable managerial challenges and much of the research in this area has been targeted at achieving better co-ordination and more effective partnerships. In considering the tourism/crime nexus we can immediately see how the absence of clearly defined structures and the presence of multi-sector involvement in destinations present problems for policing. This has led some destinations to create specific tourist police units, for example in Greece, Mexico, Thailand, and Miami in the USA.

A particular model of development in response to these management challenges has been the creation of tourist resort enclaves where the tourist experience is comprehensively and physically contained. The separation of the tourists from the local environment affords greater managerial control but many researchers have argued that such resorts are by definition exclusionary in that they fail to fairly distribute socio-economic benefits (Shaw and Shaw, 1999). The concentration of tourists in one place has also resulted in increasing their vulnerability to terrorist attack (see, for example, Richter and Waugh, 1986 and various incidents over the past 20 years) and as Jaakson (2004) observes, cruise ship passengers on shore excursions are a target for petty criminals. Some resorts are open only to heterosexual couples and this has resulted in accusations of discrimination and in 2003, led to the removal of poster advertising from the London Underground. This model of development has reappeared as a model for housing in many of the tourism generating regions of the world and in common with its use in tourism destinations, the solution to policing enclave resorts or housing has involved private security companies.

The dichotomy of tourist behaviour and tourism destination we have used in this brief introduction certainly characterises many of the preoccupations within tourism studies. However it fails to account for a whole range of issues associated with voluntary mobility. In particular, it is unhelpful in understanding some of the ambivalences of identity associated with mobility at ports of entry and exit and in transportation by sea and air.

The emergence of academic criminology

To the layperson, the terms 'criminology' and 'criminologist' bring to mind the application of scientific expertise to the understanding and 'solving' of crime. A common assumption is that this expertise draws on investigative psychology or forensic science, and is applied in very practical ways. For example, it is often assumed that a key part of the job of a criminologist is to assist the police in the detection of serious crime, or prison/probation officials in the assessment and reform of offenders. Similar views about the nature and scope of criminology are frequently expressed by first-year undergraduates embarking on criminology degrees, and even by social science (and other) academics working in universities. However, whilst there are certainly experts in applied psychology and forensic science who would call themselves 'criminologists', most criminologists – in the UK at least – have very different intellectual backgrounds and identities.

'Criminology' is a particular brand of research and inquiry about crime that is distinct from, but related to, a range of scholarly discourses. Indeed, it has been described as a 'rendezvous subject' (Downes, in Heidensohn, 2006) because of its conceptually and methodologically eclectic nature. Criminology draws upon the perspectives of a number of longer established academic disciplines such as law, psychology, political science, history, anthropology and sociology and brings them to bear on the study of 'crime' and responses to it. Criminology emerged, in tandem with the new 'human sciences' during the 19th and 20th centuries as 'scientific' forms of reasoning about crime increasingly challenged formerly dominant moral and religious discourses. These scientific approaches were linked to new forms of governing and the expansion of institutional sites in which 'deviants' were separated, classified and controlled. Thus, criminology was closely connected to the development of the modern penal state, and in particular growth of the prison in industrial societies. The prison provided a captive research population, amenable to observation, classification and statistical measurement. In Britain, the late 19th century saw a growth in psychiatric and related research which sought to identify and classify various forms of mental disorder among convicted offenders. This work set the tone for academic enquiry about crime for the next few decades, which continued in tradition of medical-psychiatric research into the early part of the 20th century. The 1920s saw a growing focus on research outside of the penal system, exploring factors associated with the development of 'delinquency' among young people (Garland, 2002).

The teaching of criminology at postgraduate level in universities began to spread from the 1940s onwards, with a key focus on training recruits for social services and probation. In 1941, a Department of Criminal Science was established in Cambridge University (eventually to become the influential Institute of Criminology, and the host of the *British Journal of Delinquency*, forerunner to the current leading journal in the UK, the *British Journal of Criminology*). Three distinguished European academics – Hermann Mannheim at the LSE, Leon Radzinowicz at Cambridge, and Max Grunhut at Oxford – all émigrés from Nazi-occupied countries – were appointed in leading British universities during the 1930s and 1940s. These individuals played a central role in the establishment of criminology as an area of academic enquiry in the UK. During the 1950s, government funding for research on crime and justice grew rapidly with the establishment of the Home Office Research Unit in the late 1950s, and the founding of the Cambridge Institute of Criminology. The growth of public funding for criminological research reflected growing concerns in official circles about increasing rates of criminal offending. Much of the research effort focused on finding more effective methods of reform and rehabilitation of offenders. This clear policy focus, along with a dependence on government funding, attracted criticism. In particular, it was suggested that this governmentally-oriented 'administrative criminology' (Vold, 1958) was largely atheoretical and subservient to governmental agendas.

The late 1960s saw a growth of radical thinking in criminological circles as well as the academy in general. A group of influential young academics established the National Deviancy Conference in 1968 with the explicit intention of challenging the theoretical assumptions about causes of crime and the dominance of governmental research agendas. One of the key impacts of this shift in academic thinking was to change the focus of criminological study away from the supposed 'causes' of offending, and towards a more critical approach to what constitutes crime, and attempts to gain a better understanding of processes of state control. This period coincided with the expansion of the university sector in the 1960s and 1970s, a time that saw a significant growth of academic criminologists in British universities along with growing numbers of postgraduate students. Academic growth continued during the 1980s and 1990s, increasingly at the expense of related social scientific areas such as social policy and sociology. During the 1990s, most new universities established undergraduate criminology degrees which proved extremely popular. In recent years, there has been a growth of single honours undergraduate criminology courses in a number of the older universities. Partly reflecting a wider social and political obsession with crime and its control, the popularity of undergraduate courses has continued to grow, even when other social science disciplines have faced stagnation or contraction of applications.

Although some debate remains about whether criminology should actually be described as a 'discipline' (see Newburn, 2007) there is no doubt that criminology now has many of the institutional elements that constitute a distinct disciplinary identity. It has its own professional associations with large memberships and their own well-attended annual conferences, as well as a plethora of more specialist groups and associations with their own programmes of meetings and conferences. There is also a large number of peer-reviewed journals in which criminologists (and academics in related disciplines) publish. There are criminology full or half degrees at undergraduate level in at least 70 British higher education institutions, along with 40 masters courses in criminology or related subjects, usually based in social science, social policy or law departments. The British Society of Criminology (BSC) has almost 1000 members, and its annual conference attracts 400–500 delegates. But although criminology has many of the institutional trappings of an academic discipline, the intellectual case for conferring disciplinary status remains strongly contested. Many criminologists themselves are doubtful that criminology has the necessary commonly-held conceptual 'domain assumptions' (Gouldner, 1970) to be seen as a discipline in its own right.

Much of the above discussion has focused upon the development and core features of British criminology. Whilst there is insufficient space to discuss in detail the development of criminology in other countries, it is important to recognise two key contrasts with the character of criminological enquiry in other national contexts. First, compared with dominant approaches in the USA, academic criminology in the UK remains profoundly 'sociological' in nature, and dominated by qualitative methods of social enquiry. Most of the leading names in UK criminology in recent decades emerged from a sociological tradition, one that seeks to explain (and respond to) crime with reference to social structures external to the individual. There remains considerable scepticism among many UK criminologists about the contribution of psychology to a rounded understanding of crime. However, psychological approaches have undoubtedly expanded in importance in recent years, not least due to the work of David Farrington and colleagues (see for example, Farrington, 2007). These approaches have also gained increasing currency with politicians and policy-makers, particularly in the field of offender management. Notwithstanding these developments, the quantitative and psychological approach to criminology still remains substantially underdeveloped in the UK when compared with the current dominance of such perspectives in the USA. Second, when contrasted with the predominant approaches towards the study of crime in many continental European countries, UK criminology conversely appears as a relatively pragmatic and empirically-driven enterprise, with an avowedly policy-oriented focus (see Edwards and Hughes, 2005 for a discussion of these contrasting traditions of criminological enquiry).

Key themes in criminology

The wide-ranging and eclectic nature of academic criminology is clear from the excellent summary provided by David Garland (2002: 15):

> Criminologists…address themselves to a wide range of research topics which somehow or other relate to crime and its control. Major areas of work include research on the incidence and distribution of criminal behaviour, inquiries about the causes or correlates of criminal conduct, clinical studies of individual delinquents and ethnographies of deviant groups, penological studies, victim studies, the monitoring and evaluation of criminal justice agencies, the prediction of future criminal conduct, crime prevention studies, research on criminal involvement, careers and desistance, the study of processes of social reaction, and historical work on changing patterns of crime and control. The list of 'central' topics is long and diverse, and each topic breaks down further into numerous sub-topics and specialisms.

Given the impossible task of providing details about all these areas of research, this section will focus on a few important strands in criminological thinking that have a particular relevance to dialogue with tourism studies. They should thus be seen as examples of where criminological thinking may have relevance to tourism studies, rather than be taken as an exhaustive list.

Defining and measuring 'crime'

Criminology is defined by its substantive focus, in that what is shared by scholars from a range of contrasting disciplinary backgrounds is their shared interest in the matter of 'crime'. However, one of the problems of criminology is that its central subject matter is 'essentially contested'. Most criminology textbooks will begin with a discussion of 'what is crime?'. At its most basic level, crime is defined as an infraction of the criminal law. But this 'black letter law' approach to studying crime avoids awkward questions about how certain harmful behaviours, and not others, come to be defined as criminal, and furthermore, concerning the fact that only a tiny fraction of potentially 'criminal' issues ever come to be processed by the formal criminal justice system. In particular, crime is not a concrete or universal category, and has different meanings at different times and places. Behaviours that are considered perfectly acceptable in some cultures are deemed criminal in others. Furthermore, what counts as 'criminal' changes over time. For example, prior to the late 1960s the act of sexual intercourse between consenting adult men, abortion, etc. were considered to be criminal offences that could be sanctioned with long prison sentences. Thus, 'crime' is not a concrete and universal phenomenon, but is a social and political construct whose meaning varies between different times and different places. This book includes chapters that discuss behaviours undertaken (or experienced) by tourists that may incur social disapproval (such as drug-taking, pressure selling, homophobic discrimination, or certain kinds of sexual activity) but are not necessarily always and in all places 'crimes' in the strict legal sense. Contemporary criminology continues to draw upon a long and distinguished tradition in the 'sociology of deviance' that focuses on a broad range of 'rule-breaking' activities rather than narrow legal categories defined by the criminal law. 'Critical criminologists' – see below – challenge the very foundations of criminology, arguing that what they see as its restrictive focus on legally-defined 'crimes' should be replaced with a broader focus on 'social harm'. We will return to these definitional disputes below, but for now it should be clear that the intersection of tourism studies and crime provides an opportunity to focus upon the ephemeral and contingent nature of criminology's core subject matter.

Leaving aside definitional issues, there is a vast body of work that attempts to measure levels of, and trends in, different types of crime – as defined by the criminal law. Much of the early work on this utilised the main source of statistical information about crime levels and trends; officially recorded statistics. However, starting in the 1970s, criminologists were increasingly sceptical about taking police-recorded crime statistics at face value, because of their contingent and socially-constructed nature. Rather than reflect a concrete reality, police-recorded crime statistics are incomplete and biased in some important ways. The emergence of crime victimisation surveys during the 1970s, which asked representative samples of the population about their experience of crime during the past year (rather than rely on those crimes recorded by the police), provided a more complete and less slanted picture of levels and patterns of crime. The development of this methodology eventually led to the establishment of the British Crime Survey, funded by the Home Office, in the early 1980s, and this has become seen as the authoritative source of information about trends in and patterns of crime in the

UK. Victimisation surveys demonstrated, in a number of ways, the problems with police crime statistics. First, there is a huge 'dark figure' of unreported crime, with only around a half of crimes reported in victim surveys actually being reported to the police. Second, even where crimes are reported to the police, factors such as the attitudes of individual officers and organisational imperatives around performance measurement, can result in offences being 'no-crimed' and taken out of the police statistics. Third, proactive policing is focused upon particular kinds of crime in particular kinds of places, and, of course, particular kinds of suspect. If the police decide to focus on, say, drug dealing in inner cities, this will lead to an increase in recorded offences in this category and greater number of arrests of young working class men (see Maguire, 2007). 'Critical' criminologists (see below) have argued that if the police were required to place a similar focus on the crimes of the wealthy, then police-recorded statistics would include a greater proportion of, for example, fraud, tax evasion and other 'white collar' crimes. Despite these problems with official crime statistics, and attempts by government and others to publicise alternative sources of information such as the British Crime Survey, there remains a considerable media and public focus on the police-recorded crime statistics.

Explaining the causes of crime

For much of the history of criminology, criminological research has been driven by the question; what causes crime? In brief, we can distinguish two key elements within the 'positivist' tradition of applying scientific principles to the study of crime causation. The earliest tradition, but one which survives today (not least in public imaginations of what criminology is) concerns individual explanations of crime, with reference to the biological or psychological dispositions of individual offenders. One of the most celebrated, or infamous, early attempts of this kind of criminology was the work of Lombroso, whose comparison study of Italian convicts and army recruits led him to claim the discovery of a 'born criminal' – a biological 'type' marked out by particular genetic dispositions. Whilst such crude genetic determinism is now widely rejected, there remains a tradition of biological criminology that seeks to explain offending behaviour with reference to a person's inherited genetic characteristics. A more mainstream form of individual positivism is found in the psychological explanations of offending with reference to the individual offender's faulty reasoning abilities, which result in, for example, an inability to defer gratification, exercise self-control, or think about consequences of one's actions for oneself or for others. Whilst crude psychological determinism is roundly rejected by many criminologists, psychological explanations of offending resonate strongly within both the wider public views about crime causation, but also within official circles. Psychological studies have been important in promoting the use of 'cognitive behavioural therapy' with offenders, and also, more broadly, in recent developments of 'risk factor' research, which links adult offending to various individual risk factors that are present during the childhood years. In contrast to this way of explaining crime, there is a major tradition of 'sociological positivism' within both British and US criminology. Rather than look inside the individual – to their genetic or psychological dispositions – for explanations of offending behaviour, sociological positivists looked at the pressures exerted by the social contexts within which offenders find themselves. Important strands within this way of thinking include the emphasis of the Chicago School on the impact of social disorganisation in high crime inner city areas, the development and transmission of 'deviant' subcultural values within deprived groups of urban youth, and the anomic 'strain' between the pressure to 'succeed' via financial gain and the limited legitimate opportunities for this in capitalist societies. In some studies, sociological positivists prioritised social 'causes' of crime in terms of inequality, unemployment, poor housing and poverty, rather than in forms of individual pathology.

Responses to crime

The central focus of the criminological enterprise for the first part of the 20th century was 'criminals', the causes of their behaviour, and how best to prevent or reform them. From the late 1960s onwards, however, this was challenged by the emergence of 'labelling' perspectives that demonstrated the socially constructed nature of crime (Becker, 1963; Lemert, 1964). These new approaches analysed crime and deviance as the product of complex interactions between individuals and the social audience. From this 'interactionist' viewpoint, the operation of criminal justice agencies – and particularly the police – was absolutely vital. In order to fully comprehend the problem of crime and its construction, criminologists needed a detailed knowledge and understanding of police interactions with members of the public, the factors that shape police attitudes and behaviour, and the ways in which organisational policies are formed and translated (or not) into practice (Reiner, 1997). Subsequent developments in critical criminology also placed policing centre stage to analyses of crime and deviance, this time as a key weapon deployed by the capitalist state to control the working classes, demonise marginal groups, and maintain the existing system of class relations (Hall *et al.*, 1978). Much water has passed under the bridge since these heady radical times, but there remains a vibrant body of self-ascribed 'critical criminologists' who actively oppose what they see as collaboration in the governmental project of crime control. Although such views are not dominant amongst academic criminologists, the project of studying the operation of the state's institutional responses to offending remains a central part of contemporary criminology, and is considered in the third part of this book. In particular, there is a huge sub-discipline of 'police studies' that examines, among other things, the occupational cultures and everyday practices of police officers, the organisation and accountability of the police, and the emergence of new 'nonstate' forms of policing such as the private security industry. The operation of the courts and sentencing has also been the focus of a large body of work, looking at such things as consistency and disparity in sentencing trends, judicial discretion and sentencing policy, and the differential treatment of ethnic minority and women offenders in the courts. Another important theme within criminological research on responses to crime concerns the probation and prisons sector. The 'what works' debate has continued to focus on evaluation of probation and the effectiveness of its interventions with offenders. Prisons research remains vibrant with criminologists exploring the impact of prison regimes upon inmates' behaviour within the prison setting and upon post-release offending. An important contemporary theme within both probation and prisons research concerns the concepts of risk and dangerousness, with a key focus upon the assessment and management of risk for public protection purposes. Finally, a relatively recent development within criminological research on societal responses to crime has concerned the areas of crime prevention and community safety, reflecting the emergence of an institutional framework of crime control beyond the traditional criminal justice system of 'cops, courts and corrections'. This research explores new methods of crime prevention, and the operation of these relatively new institutional forms such as community safety partnerships.

Tourism studies and criminology: initial meeting points

We believe that even this brief review of the subject areas of tourism studies and criminology brings to mind numerous possibilities for fruitful collaboration and dialogue. In this final section, we discuss some key examples of themes where both subject areas can potentially learn from and subsequently enhance each other's approaches. They are set out as examples of the kind of thinking we wish to encourage, rather than a comprehensive manifesto for future research. We aim to set out a more detailed framework for a future collaborative research programme in the final chapter. For now though, we can identify three areas of overlap between tourism studies and criminology, and possible fruitful foci of collaborative research.

First, in terms of conceptual and theoretical developments, we can reiterate the point made above about the contested nature of the core subject matter of criminology – crime itself. A focus on crime and deviance as committed by and against tourists, and the social responses to such acts, provides some particularly interesting opportunities to explore further some of the foundational questions of criminological theory. In particular, what acts or behaviours constitute 'crime' or 'deviance' in different legal and cultural contexts, and how do such acts come to be so defined? What theoretical approaches might best explain different forms of offending by and against tourists, and how might the body of work on tourist behaviour and tourist destinations inform and develop criminological theorising about offending and victimisation?

Second, we feel that both subject areas have much to learn from each other in terms of research methods. As noted above, criminologists now deploy an impressive range of methodological approaches, from sophisticated statistical analyses of large data sets on the one hand, to in-depth ethnographic studies on the other. Criminologists have often been divided over conceptual and methodological approaches, sometimes bitterly, but one outcome of this atmosphere of debate and questioning has undoubtedly been a willingness to innovate in terms of research methods. Criminology also draws this methodological vitality from its nature as a 'rendezvous' subject, bringing in concepts and methodological approaches from a range of related disciplines. This methodological vitality has much to offer the area of tourism studies. In return, tourism studies can help criminology to address one of its methodological and conceptual limitations. It has been noted elsewhere that criminology is 'strikingly uncomparative' (Downes, 1988). Partly related to legalistic approaches to defining its subject matter, the attention of criminologists has often been within-jurisdiction. The lack of cross-national comparison in criminology – although it is beginning to be addressed – remains a problem (Jones and Newburn, 2006). Tourism studies has much to offer criminology here, as cross-national (and other) forms of comparative approach are 'built-in' to the subject matter.

Third, in terms of policy agendas, there is much potential for productive cross-fertilisation between the two subject areas. Criminology has been criticised in recent decades for being too 'policy-focused', but there is no doubt that the practical and applied nature of the subject is a key defining feature of what criminology is, particularly in the United Kingdom. Whilst conceptual and theoretical work remains important, much criminological research is focused upon informing and improving public policy. Applied, policy-relevant, research is of course also an important element of tourism studies. To date, however, there has been little crossover between the two areas, despite the existence of a growing number of 'policy audiences' for applied research on tourism and crime. These include national and local governments in countries/regions where tourism makes a central contribution to the economy; the various elements of the increasingly globalised 'tourist industry' including hotels and holiday resorts, travel agents, and all the attendant businesses who rely for their existence upon tourism; criminal justice agencies who are charged with preventing, investigating, and punishing crime by and against tourists; and finally, tourists themselves who may find themselves victimised, criminalised or both. All these audiences have a clear interest in the intersection between crime and tourism, and stand to benefit from rigorous, theoretically-informed but policy-relevant research on the subjects of tourism and crime.

We see this book as the first stage in an ongoing project. In part, this is because it is highly likely that attention to crimes against and by tourists will increase. From the perspective of tourism studies, the incidence of crime for tourists is likely to increase as long as the growth of tourism continues as predicted. We see no reason to suggest that the world will become a safer place for tourists. While volume growth is by no means certain due to a number of risk factors – increased political instability in the world as a result of global warming and terrorist activity; taxation pressures on the transportation industry to reduce carbon emissions and thus increased costs of transportation; the diminishing supply of fossil fuels – volume growth is not the only demand determinate. Thus far the industry has proved remarkably resilient to such risks and continues to be central to the expansion of capitalism. In the thirst for new and ever more exotic destinations, tourists are accessing more remote and challenging spaces not just in unpopulated rural areas but also in densely populated urban locations. Innovations in information technology provide tourists with consumer information that enables more independent travel outside the protection of the package tour bubble or tourist resort enclave. Risk of danger and criminal opportunity increase in intensity and the call to take the interface between tourism and crime seriously becomes more and more urgent. We hope that the chapters included in this volume will be an important step in the growing dialogue between these two areas of study.

References

Airey, D. and Tribe, J. (eds) (2005) *An International Handbook of Tourism Education*, Oxford: Elsevier.

Andrews, H. (2009) '"Tits out for the boys and no back chat" – gendered space on holiday', *Space and Culture*, **12** (2), 166–182.

Becker, H. (1963) *Outsiders: Studies in the Sociology of Deviance*, New York: Free Press.

de Kadt, E. (ed.) (1979) *Tourism – Passport to Development? Perspectives on the Social and Cultural Effects of Tourism in Developing Countries*, New York: Oxford University Press.

Downes, D. (1988) *Contrasts in Tolerance: Post-war Penal Policy in the Netherlands and England and Wales*, Oxford: Oxford University Press.

Edwards, A. and Hughes, G. (2005) 'Comparing the governance of safety in Europe: a geo-historical approach', *Theoretical Criminology*, **9** (3), 345–363.

Farrington, D. (2007) 'Childhood risk factors and risk-focused prevention', in M. Maguire, R. Morgan and R. Reiner (eds), *The Oxford Handbook of Criminology*, 4th edn, Oxford: Oxford University Press, pp. 602-640.

Garland, D. (2002) 'Of crime and criminals' in M. Maguire, R. Morgan, and R. Reiner (eds), *The Oxford Handbook of Criminology*, 3rd edn, Oxford: Oxford University Press., pp. 9-50.

Gouldner, A. (1970) *The Coming Crisis in Western Sociology*, New York: Basic Books.

Hall, S., Critchley, C., Jefferson, T., Clarke, J. and Roberts, B. (1978) *Policing the Crisis*, London: Macmillan.

Heidensohn, F. (2006) 'Contrasts and concepts: considering the development of comparative criminology', in T. Newburn and P. Rock (eds), *The Politics of Crime Control: Essays in Honour of David Downes*, Oxford: Clarendon Press., pp. 173-196.

Jaakson, R. (2004) 'Beyond the tourist bubble? Cruise ship passengers in port', *Annals of Tourism Research*, **31** (1), 44–60.

Jamal, T. and Robinson, M. (eds) (2009) *The Sage Handbook of Tourism Studies*, London: Sage.

Jones, T. and Newburn, T. (eds) (2006) *Plural Policing: A Comparative Perspective*, London: Routledge.

Lemert, E. (1964) 'Social structure, social control and deviation', in M. Clinard (ed.), *Anomie and Deviant Behavior*, New York: Free Press, pp. 57-97.

Maguire, M. (2007) 'Crime data and statistics', in M. Maguire, R. Morgan and R. Reiner (eds), *The Oxford Handbook of Criminology*, 4th edn, Oxford: Oxford University Press. 99. 241-301.

Newburn, T. (2007) *Criminology*, Cullompton: Willan.

Pritchard, A. and Morgan, N. (2007) 'De-centering tourism's intellectual universe or traversing the dialogue between change and tradition', in I. Ateljevic, A. Pritchard and N. Morgan (eds), *The Critical Turn in Tourism Studies: Innovative Research Methodologies*, Oxford: Elsevier, pp. 11–28.

Reiner, R. (1997) 'Policing and the police', in M. Maguire, R. Morgan and R. Reiner (eds), *The Oxford Handbook of Criminology*, 2nd edn, Oxford: Oxford University Press, pp. 980-1033.

Richter, L.K. and Waugh. W.L. Jr (1986) 'Terrorism and tourism as logical companions', *Tourism Management*, **7**, 230–238.

Shaw, B.J. and Shaw, G. (1999) '"Sun, sand and sales": enclave tourism and local entrepreneurship in Indonesia', *Current Issues in Tourism*, **2**, 68–81.

Urry, J. (2002) *The Tourist Gaze*, 2nd edn, London: Sage.

Visit Britain (2009) http://www.tourismtrade.org.uk/MarketIntelligenceResearch/KeyTourismFacts.asp, accessed on 16 July 2009.

Vold, G. (1958) *Theoretical Criminology*, Oxford: Oxford University Press.

World Tourism Organization (2009) http://www.unwto.org/index.php, accessed on 16 July 2009.

Part I:

Tourists as Victims

2 Property Crime and Tourists

Rob Mawby

This chapter includes:

♦ A summary of the key themes in the research literature on the victimisation of tourists by different forms of property crime

♦ A discussion of the various methodological approaches to studying tourism and property crime, including those that draw upon official statistics and victimisation surveys

♦ A discussion of particular types of property crimes experienced by tourists

♦ An account of the ways in which particular criminological theories – in particular, routine activities theories, opportunity theory and rational choice theory – can help improve our understanding of patterns of property crime against tourists.

Introduction

This chapter[1] addresses the extent to which tourists are at risk of property crimes. It starts with a discussion of the difficulties of measuring crime risk that largely replicate those in mainstream criminology, but with the additional problem that the number of tourists – in the general population or who are victimised – is rarely distinguished. Accepting these limitations, police statistics, victim surveys, newspaper data, and offenders' accounts of their preferred targets are used to confirm that tourists are indeed overrepresented among the victims of property crime. This seems to apply across different offence categories, such as burglary, vehicle theft, robbery/theft from the person, and fraud. The final section attempts to explain the findings. Combining routine activity theory, opportunity theory and rational choice theory, four dimensions are identified that help explain why tourists constitute a high risk category: rewards, justifiability of target, guardianship, and accessibility.

---

1 This chapter uses, in an updated and modified form, some of the material from Mawby, Barclay and Jones (2009).

Tourist victimisation

Although property crimes far exceed crimes of violence, victim surveys show that in Western industrial societies only a minority of people suffer property crime in any one year. In England and Wales, for example, the British Crime Survey (BCS) suggests that about 17% of households experienced a property crime in 2008/09 (Walker *et al.*, 2009). Equivalent figures for the USA are slightly lower (Rand, 2009). However, these overall rates hide marked variations. Risk varies according to a number of variables: where within a country one lives, age, gender, ethnicity, etc. Explaining these patterns, victimologists have focused on citizens' behaviour and the way that the routine activities of victims lead to an increase or decrease in risk. As tourism becomes a more significant feature of modern-day living, it is therefore surprising that criminologists have largely ignored the extent to which temporary status as a tourist affects risk. Unlike tourism researchers, for whom crime and deviance appear to hold considerable attraction (Ryan, 1993; Pizam and Mansfeld, 1996; Brunt and Hambly, 1999; Mansfeld and Pizam, 2006), criminologists have, with a few notable exceptions, avoided discussions of tourist victimisation. Yet, intuitively, it would appear that the behaviour of tourists would affect their risk of crime. Where, for example, the 2004/05 International Crime Victim Survey (ICVS) found that residents of Rome were nearly five times as likely as those living in Sydney, Australia, to have their vehicle stolen (van Dijk *et al.*, 2008), we might anticipate that tourists visiting Rome (as opposed to Sydney) would also experience relatively greater risk of car theft. However, which country – or which city – tourists visit is only one aspect of the 'routine activities' (or tourist activities) people adopt on holiday. The nature of the tourist resort which they choose, and precisely where and how visitors spend their time while away from home could affect risk.

This suggests that further consideration of tourist victimisation is important for at least two reasons. First, it might have a theoretical relevance in adding to criminologists' understanding of the relationship between lifestyle and risk. Second, it might have a practical importance in helping to inform the tourist industry and therefore help it adopt crime reduction initiatives that are relevant to tourists. To this end, this chapter is divided into three key sections. The first two focus on what we know about tourists' vulnerability to property crimes, and in particular, burglary, vehicle-related crime, robbery/theft from the person and fraud. The third relates these findings to criminological theories and attempts to explain why tourists appear to experience relatively high risk of property crime. Before addressing these issues, however, the following section considers different research approaches to identifying tourists as crime victims.

Alternative research approaches

In considering the extent to which tourists are victimised, at least three research strategies might be considered: analysis of police data; interviews with known offenders; and surveys of the general public or tourists, known as victim surveys. Each approach has limitations.

Despite the problems associated with official statistics (Coleman and Moynihan, 1996; Maguire, 2007), most of the research by tourist academics has relied on them (see, for example, Chesney-Lind and Lind, 1986; Schiebler et al., 1996). Whether or not a crime is recorded and subsequently becomes part of official statistics usually depends on the willingness of the victim to report it to the police and the willingness of the police to record incidents as crimes. Some property crimes, such as car thefts and successful burglaries, are likely to be reported in most cases, especially where the victim intends to make an insurance claim, and this applies to tourists. However, tourists may be deterred from reporting even serious crimes, if the 'cost' of reporting exceeds the gains: for example if reporting eats into precious vacation time, or if there are language difficulties. In Spain, where non-Spanish speaking victims may be required to hire an interpreter in order to get their crime recorded, the disincentives are clear. Other types of property crime are reported only in exceptional circumstances: for example, attempted burglaries or where little or nothing is stolen. In other cases, such as some frauds (see below), victims may not realise a crime has taken place until they return home. Fraud is also a good example of a crime where victims, including tourist victims, may be reluctant to report if they feel embarrassed or partly culpable. Additionally, changes in police responses may affect levels of recorded crime. For example, if the police respond to a perceived 'crime problem' that may be adversely affecting tourism by cracking down on street crime, recorded crime may increase irrespective of any changes to actual crime levels.

In such cases, using police statistics on tourist victims shares many of the problems identified in a wider context by criminologists. An additional problem, though, arises where the police record the crime, but it is difficult to distinguish tourists from local victims. My own research in Cornwall illustrates this (Mawby, 2008). Unless crimes against tourists are 'flagged up', the only way to disaggregate them is by victim's address. But in many cases the police may record the holiday address rather than home address. Even if they did the latter, however, it would be difficult to quantify risk because figures on the numbers of tourists in an area, and their length of stay, are rarely available.

Given these problems, a more common approach adopted by criminologists is to compare police data with alternative sources. One option involves asking known offenders to choose between potential targets and justify their choices (Maguire and Bennett, 1982; Bennett and Wright, 1984). However, this approach, particularly common among burglary researchers, has at least two disadvantages. First, most studies depend on interviews with *arrested* offenders, where it might be that more successful offenders (i.e. those who have not been caught) would reveal a different pattern, or with surrogates, such as students, who may make decisions on very different criteria. Second, subjects may not be entirely honest in their declarations, not necessarily because they set out to mislead the researcher but because they may exaggerate the extent to which they make rational and informed decisions. That said, research, particularly more recent studies using hi-tech equipment (Lee and Lee, 2008), has much to offer.

The additional problem with applying this approach in the case of tourism, however, is that unlike, say, household burglary, it is difficult to identify a group of offenders who specifically target tourists. For example, there is no evidence of a subgroup of offenders who specialise in caravan park or hotel burglary. Consequently, researchers might be reliant upon the perspectives of offenders in general, which may be of limited value, albeit there is some evidence from interviews with robbers and pickpockets on their reasons for targeting tourists (see below).

One popular alternative is to use victim surveys of the general public, such as the BCS, U.S. National Crime Victimization Survey (NCVS) and the ICVS, that involve interviewing large samples of the public about crimes they have experienced. However, while such surveys generally exclude temporary residents, and provide few details of crimes against respondents that occur away from their home area, it is rare to conduct general population surveys that concentrate on crime experiences on holiday, primarily because of the costs involved in including those who never or rarely take vacations.

An alternative is to interview tourists either during their holiday – raising difficulties associated with identifying tourists near the end of their vacation (necessary to maximise exposure time) – or at their point of departure. The latter is in theory possible, if not straightforward, where there are a limited number of points of egress (airports, ferry terminals etc.),[2] but less practical where tourists travel by car or do not have to cross border checkpoints, as on much of mainland Europe. An obvious alternative is to survey samples of tourists about their previous holiday experiences. However, as we (Mawby *et al.*, 1999) discovered, gaining access to sampling frames via tour operators can be difficult where companies are reluctant to acknowledge the negative aspects of tourism. Consequently, our research was based on readers of *Holiday Which?*, a sample that excluded most 'non-tourists' but which was inevitably rather skewed, in terms of age and social class.

Finally, researchers may interview or otherwise collect data on samples of tourists identified from police records or other sources. This tells us little about the *extent* of victimisation, but may help our understanding of the crime and reaction of

---

2 A method used successfully by Bellis et al. (2000, 2003) in surveys of tourists' offending patterns in terms of the drug-taking habits of young tourists visiting Ibiza. For tourist victims, see Hauber and Zandbergen (1996), who interviewed foreign visitors to the Netherlands, either arriving at or leaving Schiphol airport.

police and other agencies. A good example here is Cohen's (1996) study of tourist victims of fraud in Thailand (see below), where he drew his sample from newspaper reports, notably from the *Bangkok Post*.

Tourists as victims of property crime

Bearing in mind these constraints, what do we know about crime against tourists?

As already noted, a number of studies by tourism specialists have used police data. Perhaps the most comprehensive of these was an early study by Chesney-Lind and Lind (1986) in Hawaii. Having noted the difficulties experienced by earlier researchers in distinguishing between crimes against local residents and visitors, they used police data on the residential status of crime victims in two areas of Hawaii – Honolulu and Kauai County – during the late 1970s and early 1980s, and related these to the average daily tourist and resident sub-populations. They derived annual average crime rates per 100,000 population for residents and tourists in Honolulu (1981–82) and Kauai (1978–80) and demonstrated markedly higher rates for tourists in the former. The rate of property crime against tourists in Honolulu, for example, was higher than the overall crime rate in all but one US city with a population of 500,000–1,000,000, the exception, notably, being Orlando, itself a centre of tourism. In a later study in Barbados, de Albuquerque and McElroy (1999) discovered that tourists had higher rates for acquisitive crime victimisation but lower rates for non-acquisitive violent crimes. Most recently, Michalko (2004) noted the predominance of foreign tourist victims, especially Germans, in Hungary, with risks from property crime particularly high.

All of these studies were dependent upon police statistics. In one of the few victim surveys undertaken, Stangeland (1998) compared tourists interviewed at the end of their holiday with local residents of Malaga and foreign owners of properties on the Costa del Sol. He found that tourists' rates of victimisation during a fortnight's (average) holiday were often not that much lower (and sometimes higher) than those of the other groups over a whole year. Similarly, Hauber and Zandbergen ((1996) estimated that foreign visitors had a rate of victimisation 8–10 times that of local people. Our victim survey of *Holiday Which?* subscribers reached similar conclusions (Mawby *et al.*, 1999; Brunt *et al.*, 2000; Mawby 2000). Respondents were asked whether or not they had been the victim of any from a list of seven offences while on their last holiday. Overall, 92 incidents were cited by 50 respondents. This translates to an approximate incidence rate[3] of 18% and a prevalence rate of 10%, extremely high for what was, on average, a two-week holiday. This can be presented as a rate per 10,000 respondents/households per two weeks and

---

3 This total includes violent crimes. Since people were only asked to record whether or not they had experienced any of the seven incidents, the incidence rate excludes cases where respondents suffered more than one crime from any one category.

a crude comparison drawn with conventional victim survey data from the British Crime Survey (BCS) (Mirrlees-Black *et al.*, 1996) by dividing the latter's incidence rates by 26.[4] This is, of course, only an approximation. However, the differences between traditional victim survey rates and these tourism victim survey rates are so great as to make such qualifications superfluous. The unequivocal conclusion to be drawn from this is that people generally experience considerably more crime as tourists than they do while at home. The findings for specific types of property crime, while not unanimous, tell a similar story.

Victims of specific types of property crime

Taking burglary first, Chesney-Lind and Lind (1986) found that Honolulu had a burglary rate of 1407 per 100,000 population for residents and 2045 for tourists, although in Kauai, a less-developed tourist area, tourists were less likely to suffer a burglary. Stangeland's (1998: 66) findings were even more dramatic, with 2.3% of his Malaga sample and 2.3% of his Costa sample having been burgled in the preceding year, compared with 3.9% of tourists who had been burgled during their holiday! Similarly, our survey of subscribers to *Holiday Which?* concluded that among this relatively middle-aged, middle-class sample, burglary was the most common offence cited. The rate for burglary (excluding attempts) over two weeks, at 467 per 10,000 households, for example, far exceeded the BCS estimated rate of 32 for burglary (including attempts).

Unfortunately, none of the studies to date have compared the burglary rates among tourists according to the type of accommodation in which they were staying. However, there is some evidence that tourists staying on caravan parks are vulnerable to burglary. Our ongoing research at 16 caravan parks in Cornwall, for example, has found that burglaries accounted for the largest crime category of crimes recorded by the police (Mawby *et al.*, 2008). Research on hotel crime, both in the USA (Zhao and Ho, 2006; Ho *et al.*, 2009) and England also suggests that hotel guests are particularly at risk of burglary.

Our own research in two holiday resorts in Devon and Cornwall (Mawby and Jones, 2007), for example, was funded to evaluate a hotel burglary reduction programme that aimed to tackle the disproportionate amount of burglary in hotels. Official crime statistics confirmed the extent of the problem, with burglary of guests' rooms accounting for 44.0% and 37.6% of recorded hotel crimes in the two resorts studied. In contrast, break-ins to other parts of the hotels (communal areas or staff rooms) was far less common, accounting for 6.2% and 5.5% of recorded crimes, respectively. While interviews with owners and managers of the hotels suggested that burglaries made up a far lower proportion of all (reported or non-reported) crime, it still appeared to be a significant problem. For example,

---

4 Data from the 1998 BCS is not strictly comparable, but rates were generally lower, so the differences reported here would have been greater.

22.1% and 23.2% of respondents from the two areas said that in the previous 12 months they had experienced burglary/theft of guest property,

Findings on vehicle-related crime suggest a similar pattern, although the pattern is obscured by the twin facts that many tourists do not hire cars and that different countries have varying levels of car ownership. One finding that perhaps illustrates the former is Ho *et al.*'s (2009) study of victims staying in Miami Beach hotels. They found that crimes against guests who lived in Florida were more likely to be vehicle-related, with crimes against foreign guests at the other extreme. The most likely explanation for this, quite simply, is that Florida residents are likely to drive to Miami, while tourists who fly in may not hire a car! Similarly, Michalko (2004) found that half the crimes reported by foreign victims in Hungary involved motor vehicles, with the proportion even higher among those from neighbouring countries, like Austria and Germany, who might have been expected to take their car with them, and relatively low among US and British victims. Thus, while our survey of *Holiday Which?* readers found vehicle-related crimes to be relatively uncommon, the rates per car user far exceeded those for respondents to the BCS (Mawby *et al.*, 1999).

The fact that offenders target tourists' vehicles is further demonstrated by a spate of crimes, including murder, in Florida in the early 1990s, where offenders were able to identify hire cars through their distinctive number plates (Brayshaw 1995; Schiebler *et al.*, 1996). A raft of new policy initiatives, including measures to make hire cars less obviously recognisable, was effective in reducing the problem.

The third category of property crimes to be discussed covers robbery and theft from the person. Acquisitive crimes that involve some contact between victim and offender, whether this involves force or the threat of force (robbery) or not (theft from the person) are discussed here, although it should be stressed that many national victim surveys, such as the BCS, include these with violent crime under the heading 'personal crimes', distinguished from household property crimes. Where these are disaggregated, either as robbery or pickpocketing, the picture again suggests that tourists are more susceptible to such offences than are local residents. For example, Stangeland (1998) found that 1.4% of tourists had been robbed during a fortnight's (average) holiday, more than foreign residents experienced over the preceding year (1.1%) and a third the annual rate of local people (4.3%). Similarly, Chesney-Lind and Lind (1986) found that the estimated annual recorded rate for robbery in Honolulu was 256 per 100,000 population for tourists compared with 157 for residents. While rates were lower in Kauai, there the rate of robbery against tourists was over four times that for locals. Similarly in Barbados, de Albuquerque and McElroy (1999) found the risk of a tourist being the victim of a robbery to be 4–6 times that of local residents.

Interviews with convicted pickpockets and robbers add weight to these findings. Inciardi (1976), for example, in an early study involving interviews with 20 pickpockets from Miami, noted that the professional pickpocket, or *class cannon*, specifically targeted tourists. This applied on three levels. Pickpockets would migrate into Florida during the peak tourist season, work the crowded areas such as the race tracks, fairgrounds and beach, that tourists frequented, and then identify their 'mark': 'The primary factor to the Miami *cannon* is whether his potential *mark* is a tourist', identified through attitude, dress and behaviour (Inciardi 1976: 449). Similarly, Dusquesne's (1995) research on pickpocketing and purse snatching in France in the 1988–93 period identified tourists as one of the targets of the thieves. Harper (2000, 2006), a tourism researcher, provides a similar picture vis-à-vis choice of targets by New Orleans' street robbers. Examples of tourists' experiences of acquisitive contact crime are contained in Box 2.1.

Box 2.1 Robbery and theft from the person

Targeting tourists in Bangkok

Many tour and travel companies in Thailand offer alternative rides to the provinces. Visitors prefer these air-conditioned vehicles to the usual buses that ply the regular routes; here they can sit comfortably, and feel safe. Or so they think. Many of these passengers have reported that, lulled by the night journey, they fall asleep and find that they have been robbed. The next morning, their cash, credit cards, cameras, and ornaments are gone. Not all of the visitors are as lucky as English tourist Leon Mason, or Japanese tourist Shi Yo Shi Maeda. They were travelling from Surat Thani to Bangkok on the night of 16 May this year when a gang robbed them. With the help of the Thai tourist police, the two got everything back. The two later learned that they and other tourists were "sold" to the gang by bus operators at a price of 10,000 baht. In exchange, the bus driver allowed gang members to rob the tourists.

Source: www.jamiemarr. org/caution/bus-theft.html, accessed 12 September 2007

The flower sellers of Tenerife

'We have just returned from a week's holiday in Playa de las Americas on Tenerife. We were constantly harassed on the street by people selling timeshare and recommending restaurants, but we were totally unprepared for the two South American flower-sellers whom we struggled to pass to enter a restaurant...My husband had been wearing his T-shirt over his bum-bag. Yet, in two seconds flat, one of the girls must have unzipped it, removed all the money and zipped it up again...'

Mrs Mary Schen in letter to the Daily Telegraph (Telegraph Travel, 3 March 2001)

Finally, we can consider the risk of fraud. Although fraud is not commonly included in victim surveys, there are indications that many fraudsters target tourists. In some cases, the con may have a direct bearing on tourism, such as the sleight of hand practised by Eastern European street currency exchangers during the Communist era or the timeshare or holiday club touts who operate in many European resorts (see also Chapter 4). On the other, it may build on the naivety and arrogance of the tourist, as in the case of the 'three shell trick' (Box 2.2).

Box 2.2 The three-shell trick

The conman sets up a table on which he places three shells, one of which has a nut under it. He reveals the nut, then moves the shells around rather clumsily before asking his accomplice to bet on where the nut is, which the accomplice does easily. Money exchanges hands invitingly, suggesting that it's easy to take money off the rather stupid native. Enter the arrogant tourist, soon to be a poorer tourist as he discovers the nut is never under the obvious shell...

A detailed case study of a rather different confidence trick prevalent in Thailand is provided by Cohen (1996). He suggests that fraud is the most common type of tourist-oriented crime in Thailand, and that while locals are also subject to confidence tricks, 'conning of tourists is relatively much more common' (Cohen 1996: 80). In such cases, the conman builds up a friendly relationship with the tourists, posing as a businessman proud to show the local attractions to the visitors. At the end of the week he casually mentions that he knows of a good jeweller where one can buy quality diamonds at local rather than tourist prices. It is normally only when the marks return home and have the jewellery valued that they realise that it is practically worthless. Even in exceptional cases where the tourist returns to confront the jeweller with the con, however, Cohen suggests that the Thai police are reluctant to act against the fraudsters, seeing the victims as partly culpable through their own greed.

The findings thus suggest that tourists experience relatively high levels of property crime and that this generally applies for different offence types. There is also some evidence that offenders choose to target tourists. The next section discusses how such findings might be explained.

Explaining differential risk

One approach to explaining variations in risk is routine activity theory (Cohen and Felson, 1979; Felson and Cohen, 1980). Routine activity theory attempts to explain the incidence and distribution of crime in terms of three sets of actors: potential victims, potential offenders, and law-enforcement agencies and other 'capable guardians', where the routine activities of victims interrelate with those of offenders and capable guardians. Opportunity theorists, in contrast, have emphasised the extent to which offenders take advantage of the behaviour of citizens to commit property crime. For example, Lynch and Cantor (1992) identified four dimensions of the interaction of victims' behaviour and 'policing' and the impact on offenders' target choices, namely:

♦ *Target exposure* – the visibility and accessibility of the home;
♦ *Guardianship* – the extent to which the home is protected;
♦ *Target attractiveness* – value of property that might be stolen;
♦ *Proximity* – distance of target from potential offenders.

A slightly different emphasis is adopted by rational choice theorists such as Cromwell *et al.* (1991) who address the processes by which an offender chooses a criminal career, selects targets, and carries out criminal acts. They subsequently identify three types of cues used by burglars in assessing risk:

♦ *Surveillability:* the extent to which premises are overseen by passers-by and neighbours;

♦ *Occupancy:* as suggested by the presence of a car, noise, lights, etc.;

♦ *Accessibility:* including the presence or absence of window locks, an alarm, open windows, etc.

 In considering the relationship between tourists and victimisation, we must therefore ask what it is about tourists and the ways that they behave that makes them attractive targets? Four aspects appear important: rewards; justifiability of target; guardianship; and accessibility.

Rewards

All other things being equal, we might expect offenders who commit property offences to target affluent citizens rather than poorer people. Thus in countries where tourists are affluent relative to the indigenous population, we might expect them to be especially at risk. More generally, tourists tend to have in their possession valuable and easily transportable items that might attract offenders: cash, credit cards, passports, hi-tech equipment, etc. This was the main reason why Inciardi's (1976) *cannons* specialised in stealing from tourists and why Thai conmen, especially the more professional among them, preferred to target foreign tourists. Even backpackers, who tend to travel on relatively modest budgets, carry with them considerable wealth in the form of cash and high-tech equipment. Finally, a high turnover of tourists means that offenders may return to the same location (e.g. a caravan) a week or two later and find it replenished with the latest visitor's valuables, adding a new dimension to the concept of repeat victimisation.

Justifiability of target

Tourists may be considered justifiable targets, when offenders are able, following Sykes and Matza (1957), to neutralise their right to be considered 'victims'. On the one hand, tourists may be seen as affluent and/or covered by insurance, and therefore unlikely to be badly affected. On the other, they may be seen as outsiders who exploit the country, ignore local traditions, etc. and therefore abdicate any right to being classed as 'deserving victims'. For example, Cohen (1996) argues that behind the friendly and polite façade many Thais hold Western tourists in contempt.

Guardianship

Third, tourists might be more at risk due to low levels of guardianship. This applies on at least three levels: self-guardianship, community guardianship and formal (public or private) policing. In terms of self-guardianship, tourists in general display far less concern to minimise risk than they would at home. For example, they display little anxiety about crime (Mawby *et al.*, 2000) and spend more time out after dark, leaving their accommodation unprotected from burglary and themselves open to robbery. This may be partly due to ignorance of high risk environments (Gallivan, 1994), partly to a 'culture of carelessness', with the assumption that crime is something that only occurs at home (Ryan, 1993; Harper, 2006), and partly a naivety based on the assumption that friendly, polite locals must be trustworthy (Cohen, 1996). Alternatively, the ability of tourists to rely on others to provide guardianship and policing is restricted. On the one hand, a large number and high turnover of tourists within a resort, and a lack of affinity between them, will reduce the willingness and ability of neighbours to act as guardians, a point stressed by Stangland (1998). On the other hand, tourists may be outside the routine policing arrangements adopted by the public police. Despite the introduction of specialist tourist police in some countries (Muehsam and Tarlow, 1995; Tarlow, 2000), local police may give low priority to crimes against tourists (Cohen, 1987, 1996). Indeed, offenders may target tourists because the chance of a conviction is minimal. Chesney Lind and Lind (1986) noted that even when perpetrators of crimes against tourists were detained, they were likely to be released without charge, partly due to the reluctance of tourists to change their travel plans and make themselves available to appear as witnesses in court.

Accessibility

Accessibility refers to the extent to which the offender is afforded easy access. It may be physical (e.g. barriers restricting access) or social (e.g. offender lives some distance from potential target). In both senses, the accessibility levels relating to tourists are in stark contrast to the home-owner who may deploy a range of social, physical and technological forms of protection. Holiday accommodation may not incorporate safes or security locks on doors. Our research on hotel burglary, for example, confirms the lack of security afforded in many hotels (Mawby and Jones, 2007), while security of caravans, tents, etc. is even more limited. In hot weather, for example, caravans may be left unoccupied with windows open so that they are relatively cool when the tourists using them return. This reflects back on the culture of carelessness described above, but in other cases, holiday accommodation cannot be secured, which may prompt their occupants to carry valuables on their person or in their cars, increasing the risk of street crimes or thefts from vehicles. One notable finding from Michalko's (2004) Hungarian study is that there appeared to be an inverse relationship between burglary and vehicle-based crime: visitors from countries that experienced high proportions of burglary experienced less vehicle crime, and vice versa. Moreover, tourists may be more accessible targets because their routine activities bring them into crime hotspots (Sherman *et al.*, 1989) and/ or into close proximity to offenders. To a large extent, this may be a matter of choice: prioritisation of leisure facilities and the night-time economy, or the desire to purchase alcohol or drugs. Lack of awareness is an additional factor. Tourists are often unaware of the predatory hot spots for crime and may undertake risky activities such as frequenting nightclubs and bars at late hours, or accidentally venturing into areas that locals consider 'unsafe'. In this context, for example, Gallivan (1994: 42), interviewed a Miami police officer who claimed that much crime was the result of new arrivals to the country who were reluctant to pay road tolls, subsequently driving off the highway into a high crime 'zone of body shops, used car lots and working-class housing'.

These four dimensions of routine activity theory help us to explain why tourists are at high risk of experiencing property crime. However, not all tourists behave in the same way. The 'average tourist' does not exist. The different holiday activities of different subgroups of tourist may increase or reduce their levels of risk. Elsewhere we have speculated about the extent to which different subgroups of tourists may experience different victimisation rates (Mawby et al., 2009), but this is only speculation. The next stage of research on tourists' crime risks needs to move on from comparisons between tourists and local residents, and assess differences *within* the tourist population.

Discussion

There has been little research on tourists as victims, and that which has been carried out is largely the work of tourism researchers rather than criminologists. This may, to some extent, be because both official crime statistics and victim surveys rarely distinguish between tourists and local people, but it is probably more that criminologists and victimologists have rarely considered this an interesting topic. This is regrettable, not least because the evidence suggests that tourists are at considerable risk of victimisation, but paradoxically worry little about issues of insecurity and danger. This poses considerable challenges for crime reduction policies in tourist resorts, where the tourist industry may already be reluctant to publicise risk. Nevertheless, what evidence there is shows conclusively that tourists experience relatively more property crime than do local people, and this seems to apply across a range of offences. Interviews with pickpockets and robbers, moreover, indicate that tourists are often specifically targeted. Considering the relationship between victims, offenders and capable guardians, at least four dimensions seem to be important: rewards; justifiability of target; guardianship; and accessibility. Tourists experience higher levels of risk because on average they offer potentially higher rewards to the offender, their victim status can be discounted, guardianship of their property is limited, and accessibility is relatively easy.

This chapter has described research findings to support this. However, it is equally likely that the same factors can be used to explain why particular subgroups of tourists will experience different levels of risk, and here there is an even greater paucity of research. Few researchers have focused on differences between subgroups of tourists, much less the extent to which such differences impact on risk.

I would suggest that this is a fertile area for future research. Just as victimisation appears to vary by lifestyle, such that, for example, citizens who spend more time out, particularly in the evenings, experience higher levels of property crime than those who rarely go out, so we might expect tourists attracted to resorts offering a nightlife based around cheap alcohol and the club scene to be more at risk than those attracted to family resorts or green tourism. Young tourists attracted to 'sun, sex and sand' in Cornwall's Newquay may be more vulnerable than retired tourists seeking a quiet holiday in the same resort out of peak season. The same grey tourists opting for a winter break in Eastbourne may be even less at risk. There is, however, little or no empirical evidence to support this hypothesis. While this chapter has summarised the current literature, it will, hopefully, encourage a new generation of researchers to focus on the risks experienced by different subgroups of tourists and the extent to which these are influenced by their different vacation routines.

References

Albuquerque, K. de and McElroy, J. (1999) 'Tourism and crime in the Caribbean', *Annals of Tourism Research*, **26** (4), 968–984.

Bellis, M.A., Hale, G., Bennett, A., Chaudry, M. and Kilfoyle, M. (2000) 'Ibiza uncovered: changes in substance use and sexual behaviour among young people visiting an international night-life resort', *International Journal of Drug Policy*, **11**, 235–244.

Bellis, M.A., Hughes, K., Bennett, A. and Thomson, R. (2003) 'Role of an international nightlife resort in the proliferation of recreational drugs', *Addiction*, **98** (12), 1713–1721.

Bennett, T. and Wright, R. (1984) *Burglars on Burglary*, Aldershot: Gower.

Brayshaw, D. (1995) 'Negative publicity about tourism destinations: a Florida case study', *Travel and Tourism Analyst*, **5**, 62–71.

Brunt, P. and Hambly, Z. (1999) 'Tourism and crime: a review', *Crime Prevention and Community Safety: An International Journal*, **1** (2), 25–36.

Brunt, P., Mawby, R.I. and Hambly, Z. (2000) 'Tourist victimisation and the fear of crime on holiday', *Tourism Management*, **21**, 417–424.

Chesney-Lind, M. and Lind, I.Y. (1986) 'Visitors as victims: crimes against tourists in Hawaii', *Annals of Tourism Research*, **13**, 167–191.

Cohen, E. (1996) 'Touting tourists in Thailand: tourist oriented crime and social structure', in A. Pizam and Y. Mansfeld (eds), *Tourism, Crime and International Security Issues*, Chichester: Wiley, pp. 77–90.

Cohen, E. (1987) 'The tourist as victim and protégé of law enforcement agencies', *Leisure Studies*, **6** (2), 181–198.

Cohen, L. and Felson, M. (1979) 'Social change and crime rate trends: A routine activities approach', *American Sociological Review*, **44** (4), 588–608.

Coleman, C. and Moynihan, J. (1996) *Understanding Crime Data*, Buckingham: Open University Press.

Cromwell, P.F., Olson, J.N. and Avary, D'A. W. (1991) *Breaking and Entering*, Newbury Park, CA: Sage.

Crotts, J. (1996) 'Theoretical Perspectives on Tourist Criminal Victimization.' *Journal of Tourism Studies* 7(1):2–9.

Dijk, J. van, Kesteren, J. van and Smit, P. (2008) *Criminal Victimisation in International Perspective: Key Findings from the 2004-2005 ICVS and EU ICS*, The Hague: Boom Legal Publishers, http://rechten.uvt.nl/icvs/pdffiles/ICVS2004_05.pdf, accessed 12 November 2009.

Dusquesne, V. (1995) *Les vols a la tire*, Paris:l l'Institut des Hautes Études de la Sécurité Intérieure (IHESI).

Felson, M. and Cohen, L.E. (1980) 'Human ecology and crime: a routine activity approach', *Human Ecology*, **8** (4), 389–405.

Gallivan, J. (1994) 'Looking for trouble with the Miami police department', *The Guardian*, 22 January, p. 42.

Harper, D.W. (2000) 'Planning in tourist robbery', *Annals of Tourism Research*, **27** (2), 517–520.

Harper, D.W. (2006) 'The tourist and his criminal: patterns in street robbery', in Mansfeld, Y. and Pizam, A. (eds), *Tourism, Security and Safety: from Theory to Practice*, Oxford: Butterworth-Heinemann, pp. 125–137.

Hauber, A.R. and Zandbergen, A.G.A. (1996) 'Foreign visitors as targets of crime in the Netherlands: perceptions and actual victimization over the years 1989, 1990, and 1993', *Security Journal*, **7** (3), 211–218.

Ho, T., Zhao, J. and Brown, M.P. (2009) 'Examining hotel crimes from police crime reports', *Crime Prevention and Community Safety*, **11** (1), 21–33.

Inciardi, J.A. (1976) 'The pickpocket and his victim', *Victimology*, **1** (3), 446–453.

Lee, K-H. and Lee, J-Y. (2008) 'Cross-cultural analysis of perceptions of environmental characteristics in the target selection process for residential burglary', *Crime Prevention and Community Safety*, **10** (1), 19–35.

Lynch, J.P. and Cantor, D. (1992) 'Ecological and behavioral influences on property victimization at home: implications for opportunity theory', *Journal of Research in Crime and Delinquency*, **29** (3), 335–362.

Maguire, M. (2007) 'Crime data and statistics', in M. Maguire, R. Morgan and R. Reiner (eds), *The Oxford Handbook of Criminology*, 4th edn, Oxford: Oxford University Press. pp. 241–301

Maguire, M. and Bennett, T. (1982) *Burglary in a Dwelling: The Offence, the Offender and the Victim*, London: Heinemann Educational Books.

Mansfeld, Y. and Pizam, A. (eds) (2006) *Tourism, Security and Safety: from Theory to Practice*, Burlington, MA: Butterworth-Heinemann.

Mawby, R.I. (2000) 'Tourists' perceptions of security: the risk–fear paradox', *Tourism Economics*, **6** (2), 109–121.

Mawby, R.I. (2008) 'Understanding and responding to crime and disorder: ensuring a local dimension', *Crime Prevention and Community Safety*, **10** (3), 158–173.

Mawby, R.I. and Jones, C. (2007) 'Attempting to reduce hotel burglary: implementation failure in a multi-agency context', *Crime Prevention and Community Safety*, **9** (3), 145–166.

Mawby, R.I., Brunt, P. and Hambly, Z. (1999) 'Victimisation on holiday: a British survey', *International Review of Victimology*, **6**, 201–211.

Mawby, R.I., Brunt, P. and Hambly, Z. (2000) 'Fear of crime among British holidaymakers', *British Journal of Criminology*, **40** (3), 468–479.

Mawby, R.I., Mcintosh, W. and Barclay, E. (2008) 'Burglary geographies: applying theories from domestic burglary to caravan park crime', paper presented at the British Society of Criminology Conference, Huddersfield, July.

Mawby, R.I., Barclay, E. and Jones, C. (2009) 'Tourism and victimization', in S.G. Shoham, P. Knepper and M. Kett (eds), *International Handbook of Victimology*, Boca Raton, FL: Taylor and Francis.

Michalko, G. (2004) 'Tourism eclipsed by crime: the vulnerability of foreign tourists in Hungary', *Journal of Travel and Tourism Marketing*, **15** (2–3), 159–172.

Mirrlees-Black, C., Mayhew, P. and Percy, A. (1996) *The 1996 British Crime Survey: England and Wales*, London: HMSO (HO Statistical Bulletin 19/96).

Muehsam, M.J. and Tarlow, P.E. (1995) 'Involving the police in tourism', *Tourism Management*, **16** (1), 9–14.

Pizam, A. and Mansfeld, Y. (1996) *Tourism, Crime and International Security Issues*, Chichester: Wiley.

Rand, M.R. (2009) *Criminal Victimization, 2008*, Washington, DC: US Department of Justice, Bureau of Justice Statistics, www.ojp.usdoj.gov/bjs/pub/pdf/cv08.pdf, accessed 12 November 2009.

Ryan, C. (1993) 'Crime, violence, terrorism and tourism: an accident or intrinsic relationship', *Tourism Management*, **14** (3), 173–183.

Schiebler, S.A., Crotts, J.C. and Hollinger, R.C. (1996) 'Florida tourists' vulnerability to crime', in A. Pizam and Y. Mansfeld (eds), *Tourism, Crime and International Security Issues*, Chichester: Wiley, pp. 37–50.

Sherman, L.W., Gartin, P.R. and Buerger, M.E. (1989) 'Hot spots of predatory crime: Routine activities and the criminology of place', *Criminology*, **27** (1), 27–55.

Stangeland, P. (1998) 'Other targets or other locations? An analysts of opportunity structures', *British Journal of Criminology*, **38** (1), 61–77.

Sykes, G.M. and Matza, D. (1957) 'Techniques of neutralization: a theory of delinquency', *American Sociological Review*, **22** (6), 664–670.

Tarlow, P. (2000) 'Letter from America: a short history of tourism oriented policing services', *Crime Prevention and Community Safety*, **2** (1), 55–58.

Walker, A., Flatley, J., Kershaw, C. and Moon, D. (2009) *Crime in England and Wales 2008/09*. London: Home Office (HOSB 11/09), www.homeoffice.gov.uk/rds/pdfs09/hosb1109vol1.pdf, accessed 12 November 2009.

Zhao, J. and Ho, T. (2006). 'Are foreign visitors more likely victimized in hotels? Policy implications', *Security Journal*, **19** (1), 33–44.

3 Violent crime and tourists

Rob Mawby

This chapter includes the following elements:

♦ An overview of the key themes in the research literature about the violent victimisation of tourists in general

♦ Specific discussion of the research on particular sub-groups of tourist victimisation, including that against young people, homicides, and politically motivated attacks

♦ The application to violent crime victimisation against tourists of a model derived from a range of theoretical accounts of crime victimisation in criminology (routine activities theory, opportunity theory and rational choice theory). This allows a fuller understanding of how violent victimisation varies according to potential rewards for the offender, victim status, guardianship and accessibility.

Introduction

Given limitations of space, this chapter is restricted to a conventional legal definition of violent crime as involving harm or the intent to harm. Even using this restricted definition, though, violence can take many forms, varying for example according to motive or the extent of injury. Perhaps for this reason, evidence of an overall relationship between tourism and victimisation is less clear-cut than in the case of property crime. This chapter therefore focuses on three scenarios which involve tourists as the victims of violent crime:

♦ Teens and 20s holidays

♦ Homicide, especially but not exclusively against backpackers

♦ Politically motivated attacks against tourists and tourist centres.

Using the model introduced in the previous chapter, it is argued that disproportionate risk might be explained in terms of: rewards, victim status, guardianship and accessibility.

Risk of violent crime victimisation

As was demonstrated in Chapter 2, tourists have almost universally been found to experience relatively high risks of property crime. However, the evidence on violent crime is more equivocal. Some studies, including those by Chesney-Lind and Lind (1986) in Hawaii and our own *Holiday Which?* survey (Mawby *et al.*, 1999), have found tourists to suffer more violent crimes than locals. Others, including that by de Albuquerque and McElroy (1999) in Barbados, found that tourists had lower rates for non-acquisitive violent crimes. This may be partly explained by the variation of offences subsumed under the heading 'violent crime', some of which may be more closely associated with tourism than others. It may also relate to the point made in the previous chapter: that different subgroups of tourists may, through their contrasting vacation styles, attract different levels of risk.

On the first point, while some criminologists include within their definition, corporate crimes that result in harm to employees and consumers, including tourists (Tombs, 2007), and the media and policy-makers often use the term emotively to incorporate damage to property, here the focus is on conventional legal definitions of interpersonal violence involving physical harm or the threat of injury. Even using this restricted definition, though, violent crimes may be distinguished on a number of dimensions, including:

♦ Seriousness/harm done, ranging from threats to homicide

♦ Use of a weapon

♦ Relationship between victim and offender, with the British Crime Survey (BCS), for example, distinguishing between stranger violence and acquaintance violence (accounting for 40% and 33% of incidents respectively), and domestic violence (14%) and muggings (robberies and snatch thefts) (Walker *et al.*, 2009)

♦ Motive, including personal, political, racist/sectarian, sexual and economic.

The BCS suggests that males, younger people, single persons and those frequenting bars are most at risk, and that a high proportion of offenders are judged by victims to be under the influence of alcohol (47%) or drugs (17%) (Walker *et al.*, 2009). Given that tourists, especially younger adults, are more likely to spend evenings in bars and other entertainment venues, we might therefore expect tourists, younger ones in particular, to be more at risk of violent crime, especially where the offender is a stranger or casual acquaintance. On the other hand, domestic violence is less likely to increase among tourists.

In the previous chapter, routine activity theory, opportunity theory and rational choice theory were adapted to explain the almost universally accepted higher level of risk from property crime experienced by tourists. It was argued that tourists experienced above average levels of property crime because they offered potentially higher rewards to the offender, their victim status could be discounted, guardianship was limited, and accessibility relatively easy. Here the same model will be applied to three high profile scenarios pertaining to tourists and violent crime: teens and 20s holidays; homicide, especially but not exclusively against backpackers; and politically motivated attacks.

Teens and 20s holidays

The image of British youths creating chaos in holiday resorts can be traced back to Stan Cohen's (1980) seminal work on the 'Mods and Rockers' disturbances at South and East-Coast English resorts in the 1960s, but achieved an international profile in the late 1980s in Spain, with reports of excessive drinking among (predominantly) young, British, male holidaymakers, culminating in public disturbances, aggressive, noisy and violent behaviour (Ryan 1991: 159–160). Ryan concluded that the problem stemmed from a combination of four factors:

♦ A background culture that emphasised group cohesiveness, ethnocentrism, and what has subsequently been described as 'laddish' behaviour

♦ The freedom of being away from home with its conventional constraints

♦ Expectations of a 'good time' fuelled by images produced by both advertising and returning holidaymakers

♦ Mass tourism where the resort aims to create 'England abroad'.

Since then, the proliferation of a tourist market from operators like Club Med and Club 18-30, aimed at 'young singles', with the promise of sun, alcohol, and sex, has provided the basis for episodic media exposés, for example in Ayia Napa (Cyprus), Newquay (England) and Faliraki (Rhodes). A Foreign and Commonwealth Office (FCO) report in 2005 underlined this by suggesting that 'clubbing', involving alcohol, drugs and sex, was the main focus for young British holidaymakers abroad.[1]

It is, however, misleading to see this as an exclusively British 'problem'. The case of 'schoolie' celebrations in Australia, with the end of the school year seeing thousands of school leavers ('schoolies') descending on coastal resorts, and reports of public disorder, vandalism and violence making headlines, well illustrates this (Homel *et al.*, 1997).[2]

However, while the limited academic interest in the topic almost exclusively focuses on the crime and disorder problems created by young tourists, it is arguable that such tourists are also at high risk of victimisation themselves, whether from other

---

1 www.travelmole.com, accessed 12 November 2009.
  And see FCO, 2007, British Behaviour Abroad report at www.fco.gov.uk For more recent figures see www.fco.gov.uk. Both accessed 12 November 2009.

2 See for example: www.guardian.co.uk/world/2003/nov/29/australia.internationaleducationnews
  http://fighthangover.blogspot.com/2009/11/australia-anti-glassing-campaign-for.html
  http://schoolies.blogspot.com/ All accessed 12/11/09

tourists or local offenders, a point also underlined in FCO publications.[3] Our research in Cornwall, for example, showed that Newquay, the place in the UK where teenagers are allegedly most likely to go for their first holiday without their parents (Mawby, 2007), was a hotspot for crimes, particularly against young tourists. Faliraki is another case in point. In 2002 *The Guardian* featured under the headline 'Erotic Emma: drunk and at risk' a story about the risk of rape in Faliraki, repeating a Home Office warning to females holidaying there alone (Gillan, 2002). Rapes, involving both British and Greek perpetrators, appeared to have been relatively common, if rarely reported and even less commonly recorded (Gillan, 2002; McVeigh, 2003). Andrews (2009) makes a similar point about young female tourists on Mallorca. More generally, though, young tourists on teens and 20s holidays are frequently the victims of violence and property crimes committed by their peers, locals, or itinerant workers. Referring back to the four dimensions cited:

♦ *Rewards:* While the valuables carried by young tourists might not be excessive by home standards, in countries like Cyprus and Greece they may become attractive targets.

♦ *Justifiability of targets:* Their unruly or seemingly amoral behaviour might help define them as justifiable targets – girls 'asking for it' or boys 'needing to be taught a lesson'. While, according to the FCO, 'Drunken behaviour, ignorance of local laws and lack of respect in non-secular countries is contributing to the culture that is seeing more Brits are arrested and charged whilst on holiday,'[4] it may also provoke a reaction from local people who see them as deserving everything they get.

♦ *Guardianship:* In terms of self-guardianship, they spend considerable time out after dark, and high alcohol consumption makes them easy prey for robbery and sexual offences. The fact that their peers are behaving in a similar fashion makes community guardianship unlikely. And their behaviour means they will be afforded low priority for protection by the police.

♦ *Accessibility:* In terms of accessibility, they are likely to stay in poor quality accommodation, where it is easy to force access, and where safes are a rarity, leading them to carry valuables on their person. Moreover, the focus on drink and sex means they spend considerable time in nightlife areas, where they are likely to cross the paths of offenders attracted there by their presence or also there to party. For example, it had become common practice for holiday reps in Faliraki to organise bar crawls, billed as nights out to introduce newly arrived tourists to the local 'attractions'. These involved tourists paying in advance for the night and being taken to about ten pubs and clubs, where the drinks were provided 'free'. This puts young tourists at their most vulnerable in crime hotspots (see also Andrews, 2009, for Mallorca).

3 http://www.fco.gov.uk/en/news/latest-news/?view=PressR&id=2001567
  www.fco.gov.uk/en/news/latest-news/?view=News&id=20759995
  Both accessed 12 November 2009.

4 www.travelmole.com, accessed 25 March 2009.

In essence, these violent crimes parody those against young males in Britain, where a high proportion involve offenders who are no more than casually acquainted with their victim and where victims and/or offenders may have been drinking.

Homicide of backpackers and other independent travellers

Although some violent incidents against young tourists on 'drink and sex' packages can end in fatalities,[5] most reported homicide cases involving British tourists seem to be against backpackers or other independent travellers. Many of the more publicised cases have occurred in Australia, including the case of serial killer Ivan Milat (Box 3.1) in the early 1990s, the arson attack resulting in mass murder by Robert Long of backpackers staying in a Childers hostel in 2000,[6] the murder of Peter Falconi and abduction of his girlfriend Joanne Lees in 2001 (Box 3.2), and the robbery and murder of 19 year old British backpacker Caroline Stuttle in Bundaberg, Queensland, in 2002.[7] Elsewhere, British backpacker Tom Dawson was murdered during a robbery near the Great Wall of China in 2002,[8] while in 2006 the murder of 21-year-old Welsh backpacker Katherine Horton made the national headlines. Katherine was raped and then killed on the Thai island of Koh Samui by two local fishermen (Levy and Scott-Clark, 2006; Johns, 2007). At the time of writing (March, 2009), 15-year-old New Zealander Jahche Broughton has just been sentenced for the murder of Scottish backpacker Karen Aim in Taupo in 2008.[9]

Box 3.1 Backpacker serial killer

In 1996 Ivan Milat was found guilty of the murders of seven backpackers in the Belangelo State forest area of New South Wales, Australia. The first bodies, those of British backpackers Caroline Clarke and Joanne Walters, were found in September 1992, buried in an area known as Executioners Drop, some five months after they disappeared after leaving a Sydney hostel. In October 1993, the bodies of two German backpackers were discovered in the same stretch of forest. A detailed search of the area uncovered a further three bodies, belonging to German backpackers who had gone missing in 1991. The subsequent publicity led two other British backpackers to come forward, describing a man who had attempted to abduct them in separate incidents in 1990. and it was their evidence, supported by forensics, that led the police to Milat.

Source: http://members.tripod.com/ahrens/serial/miltmrdr.html, accessed 23 March 2009.

5 In Rhodes, for example, the rape and murder of 26-year-old Wendy Sullivan in 2000 (www.hri.org) and murder of 17-year-old Paddy Doran in 2003 (www.mirror.co.uk), accessed 14 March 2009.

6 http://news.bbc.co.uk/2/hi/asia-pacific/1872141.stm, accessed 24 March 2009.

7 www.independent.co.uk and www.abc.net.au, both accessed 24 March 2009.

8 www.timesonline.co.uk/tol/news/uk/article1169333.ece, accessed 24 March 2009.

9 www.timesonline.co.uk/tol/news/world/article5978416.ece, accessed 26 March 2009.

Box 3.2 The abduction of Peter Falconi and Joanne Lees

In 2001, Peter Falconi and Joanne Lees were backpacking across Australia when the camper van they were driving was flagged down on the Stuart Highway, Northern Territory, by Bradley John Murdoch, a known drug runner and firearms aficionado. Pretending there was a problem with flames coming from their exhaust, he enticed Falconi out of the van, allegedly shooting him as he bent over the rear of the vehicle. He then tied and gagged Joanne Lees with the apparent intent of raping her. Lees managed to escape and hide until she flagged down a road train the next day. Murdoch was eventually arrested and convicted of the killing, with DNA evidence proving decisive.

Extensively covered on the Internet. For example: www.guardian.co.uk/uk/2005/dec/13/australia.world and www.independent.co.uk/news/world/australasia/murdoch-found-guilty-of-falconio-murder-519315.html both accessed 24 March 2009.
See also Joanne Lees' (2006) book about the case.

The Milat and Murdoch cases subsequently formed the basis for an Australia-made film, *Wolf Creek*,[10] with both the crimes and their sensationalisation leading to claims and counterclaims about the safety of tourists in Australia. Backpackers' safety has certainly been a newsworthy issue in Australia. In a content analysis of Australian print media's coverage of backpackers from 1990–2005, Peel and Steen (2007) found that the subtheme 'backpackers as victims' received far more coverage than any other single subtheme. In Britain, the deaths of those visiting Australia has also been headline news, in some cases being perceived as a threat to the tourism industry (Venditto and Mouzos, 2006). *The Times* and *Sun*, for example, pronounced Australia as an unsafe destination for British tourists. However, as reported in the *Sydney Morning Herald*,[11] a spokesperson for the Australian Tourism Corporation dismissed the allegations, arguing that 'incidents involving foreign nationals always make headlines in their home country' and that 'Australia is a safe place to visit'. Almost unprecedented, the Australian Institute of Criminology also produced a paper 'confirming' that tourists were indeed safe (Venditto and Mouzos, 2006). This conclusion must, however, be treated with caution. As well as being dependent upon victims' statuses as tourists being flagged in the National Homicide Monitoring Program (NHMP), it compared tourists who are in Australia for limited periods with data on Australian nationals who are in the country for almost the entire year. Additionally, it addressed risk for tourists as a whole, rather than backpackers. That said, no dedicated research on crime risk amongst backpackers has been carried out, albeit Israel (1999) has suggested that they experience relatively high rates of victimisation. This argument is persuasive (Mawby *et al.*, 2009). Referring back to the four dimensions identified earlier:

---

10 http://news.bbc.co.uk/2/hi/entertainment/4162385.stm
   www.outback-australia-travel-secrets.com/wolf_creek_true_story.html
   Both accessed 24 March 2009.
11 Sydney Morning Herald, 17 July 2001.

♦ *Rewards:* Backpackers frequently visit poorer countries where they appear affluent relative to the indigenous population. Moreover, there is considerable evidence that, despite a focus on minimising expenditure, backpackers carry with them considerable wealth in the form of cash and high-tech equipment. Homicides that are motivated by financial gain, such as the attacks on Caroline Stuttle, Tom Dawson and Karen Aim, illustrate the attractiveness of backpackers as targets.

♦ *Justifiability of targets:* Backpackers may be considered justifiable targets, where they are seen as symbols of Western capitalist values, especially where their moral values are questioned. Thus in Australia both Ivan Millat and Robert Long were described as having a perverted hatred of backpackers. In Thailand, Koh Samui, the site of Katherine Horton's murder, is described by Levy and Scott-Clark (2006) as a place where tourism has developed excessively, with little benefit to the indigenous population, leading to a resentment of foreign tourists who were targeted by locals committing offences of varying degrees of seriousness.

♦ *Guardianship:* Backpackers might be more at risk due to low levels of guardianship. In terms of self-guardianship, hitchhiking, or opting for cheaper travel and accommodation leaves backpackers exposed to the least desirable aspects of society. While the wider literature suggests that tourists in general display far less concern to minimise risk than they would at home, for example displaying little anxiety about crime and spending more time on the streets after dark, this may be even more the case among backpackers. Karen Aim, for example, was walking home alone in the early hours of the morning when she was attacked; Katherine Horton was walking alone along the beach at night. Drug and alcohol use also mean that the capability of self-guardianship is reduced. Alternatively, the ability of backpackers to rely on others to provide guardianship and policing is restricted. Independence allows more interactions with locals and other travellers and more opportunities for free travel or accommodation, but it also means that, backpackers lack the protection that travel packages offer. In Cohen's terms (1987), they exist outside the 'tourism bubble' that surrounds conventional tourists. The murders committed by Milat and Murdoch, for example, occurred in remote areas where the likelihood of the killer being disturbed was minimal. On the other hand, backpackers may be outside the routine policing arrangements adopted by tour companies/reps and the public police. Local police agencies may, moreover, give low priority to crimes against tourists, and especially non-conventional tourists (Cohen, 1972, 1973, 1987).

♦ *Accessibility:* Backpackers may also be highly accessible targets. To a large extent, this may be a matter of choice: prioritisation of leisure facilities and the night-time economy, the desire to purchase alcohol or drugs, and the prospect of sexual liaisons with strangers may put backpackers at increased risk (Allen, 1999; Israel, 1999). Lack of awareness is an additional factor, although it is likely that backpackers are more aware of unsafe locations through their communication with other backpackers, either in person or through the Internet.

Although there is little or no research available on backpackers and other independent travellers as homicide victims, the examples given here suggest that the pattern is somewhat different from that of homicides in England and Wales (Povey *et al.*, 2008). While attacks may be motivated by sexual desire or the financial attraction of victims, and the victim is often seen as a justifiable and easy target, most offences appear to be committed by locals with little prior connection to their victims.

Politically motivated attacks

Politically motivated attacks have been of particular interest to tourism academics because of the impact that the incidents have upon the holiday plans of tourists in general. However, many highly publicised incidents that impact upon tourism either are not specifically targeted at tourists or tourist centres or do not involve tourist victims: the Madrid train bombings, the July (2005) bombings in London (Moss *et al.*, 2008) and 9/11 being cases in point. Nevertheless, many terrorist groups do choose to target tourists and/or tourist areas.

Indeed, those killed in terrorist attacks comprise a significant proportion of all murdered tourists. Based on officially recorded data on Australian murder victims overseas, for example, Venditto and Mouzos (2006) found that no less than 99 of the 158 Australian visitors to other countries who were murdered between 1995–2003 were the victims of terrorism.[12] The Bali bombings in October 2002 accounted for the majority of these. Bali, one of Indonesia's many islands, is also its main tourist centre, attracting 2.5 million tourists in 2001. About half of these were foreign tourists, with Japan and Australia the major markets. Tourism accounted for about 80% of the island's income and provided employment for some 40% of the population (Henderson, 2003). The bombs were detonated near two nightclubs in Kutar, one of the major tourist resorts, killing around 200 people including 88 Australians and 21 Britons. Over 300 other people were injured. The attacks were carried out by Jemaah Islamiyah, Islamic extremists linked to Al-Qaeda.[13] The same group were also responsible for three suicide bombings at tourist restaurants in Central Kuta and on Jimbaran beach almost exactly three years later, resulting in 20 fatalities and over 100 injuries.[14] Terrorist groups have targeted tourists in a number of other countries (Richter and Waugh, 1986; Ryan,

---

12 Not all of these, of course, were involved in incidents where tourists were specifically targeted. Note, also, that the figures are distorted by the 88 killed in the 2002 Bali bombings.

13 See also: http://news.bbc.co.uk/1/hi/world/asia-pacific/2330359.stm
  http://news.bbc.co.uk/2/hi/asia-pacific/2324047.stm
  http://news.bbc.co.uk/1/low/uk/2329841.stm
  All accessed 30 March 2009.

14 www.travelmole.com/stories/105262.php?m_id=619493&mpnlog=1
  http://en.wikipedia.org/wiki/2005_Bali_bombings
  http://news.bbc.co.uk/1/hi/world/asia-pacific/4300274.stm
  All accessed 30 March 2009.

1993a, 1993b; Sonmez *et al*., 1999), including: Egypt (Hall and O'Sullivan, 1996; Huddart,1997) (Box 3.3); Jordan; Turkey (Box 3.4); Sri Lanka; and Spain, where the armed Basque separatist group ETA regularly conducts a summer bombing campaign aimed at undermining the crucial tourist sector and the foreign second home market.

Box 3.3 Islamic militants in Egypt

Egypt has a recent history of terrorist attacks by Islamic groups loosely tied to Al-Qaeda. These began in 1992, following a warning from the Gama'a al-Islamiya (Islamic Group), that tourists should not visit the province of Qena, which includes some of Egypt's most famous Pharaonic temples and tombs. A number of attacks followed, largely directed at foreign tourists. Then in 1996 conflict escalated when gunmen massacred 17 Greek tourists outside a hotel in Cairo. Six German tourists were among nine people fatally shot outside the Egyptian Museum in Tahrir Square in September. The Luxor Massacre in November of that year, at Deir el-Bahri, an archaeological site, resulted in the deaths of 62 tourists at the hands of six terrorists disguised as security guards. There was then a period of relative peace, until 2004, when in October, a series of bombings in Sinai also targeted tourist hotels, with Israeli visitors the main targets, although over half the 34 fatalities were local people. Three attacks in Cairo in April 2005 also appeared to be directed at tourists, and in July that year a series of bombs were detonated in the resort city of Sharm el-Sheikh, on the southern tip of the Sinai Peninsula. Eighty-eight people were killed and over 150 were wounded by the blasts, making this the most serious terrorist incident in Egypt since 1981. While the majority of those killed were Egyptian, a number were foreign tourists, including 11 from Britain and six from Italy. Then, in April, 2006 a series of bombs exploded in another tourist resort on the Sinai Peninsula, Dahab. Over 20 people were killed and about 80 injured. Most were Egyptians, but tourists from abroad were among those killed or injured. In 2008 the militants apparently changed their tactics, with 11 tourists, along with eight Egyptians, abducted in a failed ransom attempt. However, a bomb in Cairo in February 2009, killing a French teenager and wounding at least 20 other people, mainly French tourists, suggested a return to earlier tactics.

Sources: www.usdivetravel.com/T-EgyptTerrorism.html
  http://en.wikipedia.org/wiki/Terrorism_in_Egypt
  www.timesonline.co.uk/tol/news/world/middle_east/ All accessed 30 March 2009.

Box 3.4 Kurdish separatists target tourist resorts in Turkey

Visitors to Turkey have often been targeted by Kurdish rebels. Two groups appear to be behind most of the attacks: the Kurdistan Workers' Party (PKK), whose leader Abdullah Öcalan is serving a life sentence, and the Kurdistan Freedom Falcons (TAK), also known as the Liberation Hawks, which also draws inspiration from Öcalan. Turkish officials consider TAK a front for PKK attacks on civilian targets, including tourists, while the PKK maintains that it is a splinter group over which it has no control. Justifying the targeting of tourists, TAK has argued that 'Foreign currency brought in by tourists is the greatest resource of the Turkish state in its attacks against the Kurdish people.'

The current round of attacks by PKK started in 1999, with the first bombing of tourist targets by TAK in 2004, when two small hotels in Istanbul were singled out. Since then there have been a number of sporadic attacks. In one incident, on 16 July 2005, in the Aegean resort of Kusadasi, five people, among them a young British woman and an Irish teenager, were killed and 13 others injured when a bomb explosion tore apart a minibus in an area popular mainly with British tourists. In 2006, TAK again targeted tourists through a series of bombings in resort areas, including Marmaris and Antalya. Other attacks have occurred since then, and government departments in a number of countries, including Britain and Australia, advise visitors to Turkey to adopt extreme caution, especially in the south east of the country.

Sources: www.guardian.co.uk/world/2006/aug/29/topstories3.turkey
www.spiegel.de/international/spiegel/0,1518,435494,00.html
www.militantislammonitor.org/article/id/811
www.nowpublic.com/world/british-tourists-wounded-turkey-three-killed-second-terror-attack
www.smartraveller.gov.au/zw-cgi/view/Advice/Turkey
www.fco.gov.uk/en/travelling-and-living-overseas/travel-advice-by-country/europe/turkey
All accessed 30 March 2009.

There are a number of reasons why tourists and tourism are targeted. First, nationalist or faith-based groups may consider tourism to be an evil impacting on their society and culture. ETA in Spain is a good example here, where tourism and second-home ownership are seen to threaten traditional values. Second, and more generally, tourists and the tourist industry may be seen as symbolic of Western capitalism; tourists may then be targeted because of their 'symbolic value as indirect representatives of hostile or unsympathetic governments' (Richter and Waugh, 1986: 235). The Bali bombings are perhaps an example of this, where foreigners were targeted because they represented Western values. Third, attacking tourists may be viewed as less likely to lose the dissidents support from the indigenous population than attacks on local people, although, as the Egyptian example illustrates (Box 3.3), local people are often among the casualties. Fourth, where countries depend on tourism financially, attacks on the industry that cause a decline in tourist numbers can cripple governments by reducing much needed foreign expenditure (Hall and O'Sullivan, 1996). This underpins the strategy of PKK and TAK in Turkey. Fifth, tourists may be seen as soft targets: the attack on Israeli tourists in Egypt in 2004 is an example of where Islamic militants considered Israeli visitors to be easier to target than launching an attack in Israel itself. Sixth, attacks on tourists generate worldwide publicity for the political or religious activists (Hall, 1996). Finally, terrorist groups may kidnap tourists for financial reasons, holding them until their government pays a ransom. The kidnapping of European tourists in Egypt in 2008 is an example of this strategy.

In so far as there is considerable evidence that tourism is adversely affected by such incidents, militant actions can be considered successful (Enders *et al.*, 1992; Wahab, 1996; Pizam, 1999; Pizam and Fleischer, 2002). For example, according to Hall and O'Sullivan (1996), attacks by Muslim extremists between 1992 and 1993 cut Egypt's tourism trade by almost half. In a review of terrorist incidents worldwide, Pizam and Smith (2000) noted a significant decline in tourism in 79% of cases, albeit in half these cases, the impact was short-lived. Similarly, Brunt and Cousins (2002), comparing the impact on tourism of terrorist attacks in 1997 in Israel, Sri Lanka and Egypt, argued that the incidents resulted in a fall in demand, especially in the case of the Luxor (Egypt) attack (see also Mansfeld and Pizam, 2006). Henderson (2003) also identified the impact of the 2002 Bali bombings on tourism. The effect on tourism is particularly severe where tourists and tourist sites are explicitly targeted, where fatalities occur and where terrorist incidents can be classed as examples of 'ongoing volatility' rather than being isolated incidents (Pizam, 1999; Pizam and Fleischer, 2002). Nor are the effects confined to the country where the attacks occurred. Neighbouring countries may also experience a decline in tourist numbers as holidaymakers react with uncertainty to the extent of the threat (Hall and O'Sullivan, 1996; Henderson, 2003). However, there is less evidence of such incidents being successful when success is measured in terms of effecting political change. Ironically, perhaps the best example of this is the (largely non-violent) airport protests in Thailand in 2008 that were influential in the resignation of the prime minister.[15]

Governments do not, moreover, react passively to politically motivated attacks. While in some cases they may adopt a low profile, and give as little publicity as possible to aggression against tourism,[16] in others they have reacted by price cutting, attracting different client groups, increasing security and marketing aimed at reassuring tourists that the area is safe again (Richter and Waugh, 1986; Hall, 1996; Wahab, 1996; Henderson, 2003). Egypt is perhaps the classic example of where increased security has dominated policy responses (Wahab, 1996). However, as Barker's account less than two years after the Luxor Massacre illustrates (Box 3.5), it raises the question of whether a saturation of visible security increases tourists' feelings of safety, or actually promotes heightened concern, an issue that has been raised in the criminological literature (Nelson, 1998).

Box 3.5 In Egypt, a change of the guard

'Are you out of your mind?' That was the general reaction of most of my friends when I told them I was going to Egypt on vacation. Wasn't I scared I'd end up like one of those tourists massacred near Luxor last November? And what about the threat of another war with Iraq?

I'm now back from Egypt...and am happy to report that we all had a super, and safe, stay.

The Nov. 17 temple attack by six gunmen killed 58 tourists and four Egyptians, including a guide, and exposed lax security measures at this and other popular tourist sights. Yet it also galvanised Egypt's secular, military-backed government, which since 1992 has been the target of a largely underground revolt by Islamic fundamentalists that has killed more than 1200 people on both sides.

---

15 www.travelmole.com/stories/1133386.php?mpnlog=1&m_id=_rdmbmn, accessed 30 March 2009.

16 www.eturbonews.com/3620/turkeys-brand-under-attack, accessed 30 March 2009.

Whereas only two police guards were on duty at the temple the day of the 'accident' – that's what most Egyptians call the massacre – it and other famed temple and burial sites as well as the country's capital and busiest museums are now crawling with security.

From the day my group landed in Cairo, about 310 miles north of Luxor, an armed guard was on our tour bus at all times. And not a piece of luggage was loaded onto it until the bag had been identified by its owner. There was only one way in to our various hotels: through the metal detectors at the main entrance. No suitcase was delivered to any room until it was identified again by the guest. At the Sphinx and Pyramids at Giza, there were more guards than vendors. Everywhere, there were soldiers or tourist police at entrance gates, soldiers in trucks, soldiers on cliffs or other high vantage points, even soldiers on camels.

Given all that was at stake, the Egyptian government moved swiftly. Mubarak and other officials visited the site of the massacre and immediately ordered new and increased security measures. Electronic security was improved and more tourist police were recruited. They are now better trained, better equipped and better paid, according to El-Abyad. Egypt's minister of tourism was dispatched to conventions in Berlin and Milan to reassure travel agents about the precautions being taken.

KarlynBarker, Washington Post, 3 May 1998, E01.

Source: www.washingtonpost.com/wp-srv/travel/index/stories/barker05031998.htm accessed 1 December 2005.

How far, then, do the four dimensions cited earlier help to explain politically motivated attacks? The answer is that they do, albeit the emphasis is slightly different:

♦ *Rewards:* Attacks on tourists may be viewed as low cost in that they are less likely than attacks on locals to lose the dissidents' support from local people. Second, attacks on tourists generate world-wide publicity for the political or religious activists, and are therefore more 'rewarding' than attacks on locals. Finally, kidnapping tourists may be profitable if their governments pay a ransom.

♦ *Justifiability of targets:* Nationalist or faith-based groups may dismiss tourists as an evil and corrupting influence rather than the 'innocent victims' portrayed in the Western media. More generally, tourists may be seen as symbols of Western capitalism rather than people. Where they can be condemned for their chauvinist or amoral behaviour they become even more justifiable targets.

♦ *Guardianship/Accessibility:* While less important, guardianship and accessibility apply where tourists are chosen because they are soft targets: for example, Israeli tourists attacked in Egypt in 2004 were both more accessible and less well guarded than Israelis at home.

Discussion

Although the evidence on the relationship between violent crime and tourist risk is inconclusive, this chapter focuses on three examples of violence that is frequently associated with tourists, namely: teens and 20s holidays; homicide, where the victims are backpackers and other independent travellers; and politically/religiously motivated attacks. Unlike 'conventional' violent crime in general, in none of these cases is the victim/offender relationship commonly a strong one. In the first type of situation, acquaintance violence may be common, but in the other two types the offender is usually a stranger. This suggests that violent offences committed by perpetrators who are not well known to the victim are particularly likely to occur on holiday.

In the previous chapter, a model to explain the higher level of risk from property crime experienced by tourists was developed, using routine activity theory, opportunity theory and rational choice theory. The same model was deployed here, distinguishing between rewards, victim status, guardianship and accessibility:

◆ *Rewards:* Those on teens and 20s holidays and independent travellers may not be particularly wealthy, but they are likely to carry valuables on their persons, and may appear relatively affluent compared with potential targets from the indigenous population. The influence of rewards is, however, particularly powerful in the case of terrorist attacks. Attacking tourists may be viewed as low cost/high gain in that: they are less likely to lose the terrorists support from the indigenous population; attacks on tourists generate worldwide publicity for the political or religious activists; and kidnapping tourists may be financially worthwhile.

◆ *Justifiability of targets:* Both those on teens and 20s holidays and backpackers may behave in ways that allow them to be defined as justifiable targets. In the case of terrorist attacks, it is not the *behaviour* of the tourists per se that is crucial, but their symbolic status as representatives of Western capitalism.

◆ *Guardianship:* Although low levels of guardianship may contribute to the targeting of tourists by terrorist groups, guardianship is particularly important in explaining risk for those on teens and 20s holidays and backpackers. In the former case, the 'tourism bubble' may afford some protection, but their vacation behaviour suggests low levels of guardianship: for example, high alcohol consumption makes them particularly vulnerable, also meaning that they often receive little sympathy or support from the police. Backpackers, outside the 'tourism bubble', share some aspects of the same leisure style, and are also particularly exposed by their isolation.

◆ *Accessibility:* Similarly, easy accessibility may be a factor in the targeting of tourists by terrorist groups, but it is scarcely the driving force. However, it exerts a much stronger influence on the victimisation of those on teens and 20s holidays or independent travellers. They are likely to stay in poor quality accommodation, where it is easy to force access, and where safes are a rarity, leading them to carry valuables on their person, and, particularly in the former case, the prioritising of drink and sex means they spend considerable time at night in areas that are crime hotspots. This may be a matter of choice, but lack of awareness is an additional factor.

The model developed in the previous chapter appears robust in explaining the apparent high risks experienced in the three scenarios described. However, it must be stressed that in respect of teens and 20s holidays and homicide involving independent travellers, this chapter is dependent upon relatively soft data. We should, consequently, reiterate the point made earlier: that there is a need for more research focusing upon the experiences of specific categories of tourist, including backpackers and those on teens and 20s holidays. In this latter case this can redress the balance where this subgroup has traditionally been perceived as a problem rather than as a group vulnerable to crime.

References

Albuquerque, K. de and McElroy, J. (1999) 'Tourism and crime in the Caribbean', *Annals of Tourism Research*, **26** (4), 968–984.

Allen, J. (1999) 'Crime against international tourists', *NSW Bureau of Crime Statistics and Research, Contemporary Issues in Crime and Justice*, **43**, www.bocsar.nsw.gov.au, accessed 23 March 2009.

Andrews, H. (2009) '"Tits out for the boys and no back chat": gendered space on holiday', *Space and Culture*, **12**, 166–182.

Brunt, P. and Cousins, K. (2002) 'The extent of the impact of terrorism on international travel and tourism at specific tourist destinations', *Crime Prevention and Community Safety*, **4** (3), 7–21.

Chesney-Lind, M. and Lind, I.Y. (1986) 'Visitors as victims: crimes against tourists in Hawaii', *Annals of Tourism Research*, **13**, 167–191.

Cohen, E. (1996) 'Touting tourists in Thailand: tourist oriented crime and social structure', in A. Pizam and Y. Mansfeld (eds), *Tourism, Crime and International Security Issues*, Chichester: Wiley, pp. 77–90.

Cohen, E. (1987) 'The tourist as victim and protégé of law enforcement agencies', *Leisure Studies*, **6** (2), 181–198.

Cohen, E. (1973) 'Nomads from affluence: notes on the phenomenon of drifter-tourism, *International Journal of Comparative Sociology*, **14**, 89–103.

Cohen, E. (1972) 'Towards a sociology of international tourism', *Social Research*, **39** (1), 64–82.

Cohen, L. and Felson, M. (1979) 'Social change and crime rate trends: a routine activities approach', *American Sociological Review*, **44** (4), 588–608.

Cohen, S. (1980) *Folk Devils and Moral Panics*, Oxford: Martin Robertson.

Enders, W., Sandler, T. and Parise, G.F. (1992) 'An econometric analysis of the impact of terrorism on tourism', *Kyklos*, **45**, 531–554.

Gillan, A. (2002) 'Erotic Emma: drunk and at risk', *The Guardian*, 22 June, 13.

Hall, C.M. (1996) *Tourism and Politics – Policy, Power and Place*, Chichester: Wiley.

Hall, C. M., and O'Sullivan, V., (1996) 'Tourism, political stability and violence', in A. Pizam and Y. Mansfeld (eds), *Tourism, Crime and International Security Issues*, Chichester: Wiley, pp. 105–121.

Henderson, J.C. (2003) 'Terrorism and tourism: managing the consequences of the Bali bombing', *Journal of Travel and Tourism Marketing*, **15** (1), 41–58.

Homel, R. Hauritz, M., McIlwain, G., Wortley, R. and Carvolth, R. (1997) 'Preventing drunkenness and violence around nightclubs in a tourist resort', in R.V. Clarke (ed.), *Situational Crime Prevention: Successful Case Studies*, 2nd edn, Guilderland, NY: Harrow and Heston, pp. 263–282.

Huddart, G., (1997) 'Egypt killings "little impact"', *Travel Trade Gazette, UK and Northern Ireland*, 24 September, p. 80.

Israel, M. (1999) 'The victimisation of backpackers', *Alternative Law Journal*, **24** (5), 229–232.

Johns, N. (2007) 'Tourism and sentencing: establishing status privileges', *International Journal of the Sociology of Law*, **35** (2) 63–74.

Lees, J. (2006) *No Turning Back*, London: Hodder & Stoughton.

Levy, A. and Scott-Clark, C. (2006) 'Danger in paradise', *The Guardian*, 8 April 2006 (also available at www.guardian.co.uk, accessed 23 March 2009.

Mansfeld, Y. and Pizam, A. (2006) *Tourism, Security and Safety: From Theory to Practice*, Burlington, MA: Butterworth-Heinemann.

Mawby, R.I. (2007) 'Crime, place and explaining rural hotspots', *International Journal of Rural Crime*, **1**, 21–43, at www.ruralfutures.une.edu.au, accessed 5 November 2009.

Mawby, R.I., Barclay, E. and Jones, C. (2009) 'Tourism and victimization', in S.G. Shoham, P. Knepper and M. Kett (eds), *International Handbook of Victimology*, Boca Raton, FL: Taylor and Francis, pp. 319-345.

Mawby, R.l., Brunt, P. and Hambly, Z. (1999) 'Victimisation on holiday: a British survey', *International Review of Victimology*, **6**, 201–211.

McVeigh (2003) 'Faliraki: a Greek tragedy', *The Scotsman*, 23 August.

Moss, S., Ryan, C. and Moss, J. (2008) 'The life cycle of a terrorism crisis: impact on tourist travel', *Tourism Analysis*, **13** (1), 33–41.

Nelson, A. (1998) 'Security shutters: a double-edged sword', *International Journal of Risk, Security and Crime Prevention*, **3** (1), 11–19.

Peel, V. and Steen, A. (2007) 'Victims, hooligans and cash-cows: media representations of the international backpacker in Australia', *Tourism Management*, **28**, 1057–1067.

Pizam, A. (1999) 'A comprehensive approach to classifying acts of crime and violence at tourism destinations', *Journal of Travel Research*, **38** (1), 5–12.

Pizam, A. and Fleischer, A. (2002) 'Severity versus frequency of acts of terrorism: which has a larger impact on tourism demand?', *Journal of Travel Research*, **40** (1), 337–339.

Pizam, A. and Mansfeld, Y. (1996) *Tourism, Crime and International Security Issues*, Chichester: Wiley.

Pizam, A. and Smith, G. (2000) 'Tourism and terrorism: a quantitative analysis of major terrorist acts and their impact on tourist destinations', *Tourism Economics*, **6** (2), 123–138.

Povey, D., Coleman, K., Kaiza, P., Hoare, J. and Jansson, K. (2008) *Homicides, Firearm Offences and Intimate Violence 2006/2007*, London: Home Office (HOSB 03/08), at www.homeoffice.gov.uk, accessed 23 March 2009

Ritcher, L.K. and Waugh, W.L. (1986) 'Terrorism and tourism as logical companions', *Tourism Management*, **7** (4), 230–338.

Ryan, C. (1993a) 'Crime, violence, terrorism and tourism: an accidental or intrinsic relationship?', *Tourism Management*, **14** (3), 173–185.

Ryan, C. (1993b) *Tourism, terrorism and violence: the risks of wider world travel*. London : Research Institute for the Study of Conflict and Terrorism

Ryan, C. (1991) *Recreational Tourism: A Social Science Perspective*, London: Routledge.

Sonmez, S.F., Apostolopoulos, Y. and Tarlow, P. (1999) 'Tourism in crisis: managing the effects of terrorism', *Journal of Travel Research*, **38** (1), 13–18.

Tombs, S. (2007) '"Violence", safety crimes and criminology', *British Journal of Criminology*, **47** (4), 531–550.

Venditto, J. and Mouzos, J. (2006) 'The murder of overseas visitors in Australia', *Trends & Issues in Crime and Criminal Justice, no. 316*, at www.aic.gov.au/publications, accessed 12 November 2009

Wahab, S., (1996) 'Tourism and terrorism : synthesis of the problem with emphasis on Egypt', in A. Pizam and Y. Mansfeld (eds), *Tourism, Crime and International Security Issues*, Chichester: Wiley, pp. 174–186.

Walker, A., Flatley, J., Kershaw, C. and Moon, D. (2009) *Crime in England and Wales 2008/09*, London: Home Office (HOSB 11/09), at www.homeoffice.gov.uk, accessed 12 November 2009.

4 Vulnerable Victims

Paul Brunt

This chapter includes the following elements:

♦ A brief overview of the research evidence on the victimisation of tourists

♦ A discussion of the variations in risk of victimisation by tourist type

♦ A more detailed analysis of the tourist experience of gay holidaymakers, with particular reference to crime victimisation risks as well as experiences of harassment and discrimination more broadly.

Introduction

Being safe on holiday is an expected requirement. Places that develop an unsafe reputation can be substituted by alternative destinations that are perceived as safer for tourists. Beyond the obviously unsafe places in the world, where governments advise against travel, individuals must make up their own minds about where to go on holiday. One of the distinctive features of the tourism industry is that we cannot 'test-drive' a holiday beforehand. Judgements about where to travel are often made on the basis of imperfect knowledge and generalisation, and tourists learn about destinations from brochures, adverts and the media (Smith, 1989; Brunt, 1997). We typically think about what the destination has to offer in terms of accommodation, its environment and things to do (Crompton, 1979; Krippendorf, 1987) and many of us do not consider the issue of crime when we are planning the next holiday (Brunt *et al.*, 2000). Are we more at risk of crime as tourists than in our everyday lives? Most of us would probably prefer not to think about this, and certainly the tourism industry does not want us to think such things in case we decide to stay at home. Whilst it is true that only a minority of tourists suffer criminal victimisation while on holiday, it is important to explore variations in the crime experiences of different tourist types. Crime patterns vary according to factors such as the nature of tourism, its scale, the type of development, the season, as well as variations relating to the tourists themselves and issues associated with their behaviour. This latter issue is the focus of this chapter – what categories of tourist are particularly vulnerable to criminal victimisation?

Clearly when considering issues of tourist victimisation, a number of methodological issues are evident. Prominently there are the questions of how we measure crime, and how to quantify the extent of tourism, with many researchers relying on official statistics. However, recorded crime patterns depend to some extent on the discretionary behaviour of victims and police, individuals' willingness to report crimes and policing policy changes. All these factors can have a considerable impact on the official picture of crime independently of any variations in real rates of offending and victimisation. It is highly likely that tourists face different considerations compared with locals in deciding whether or not to report crimes, and that the police will also take into account whether or not the complainant is a tourist when they make decisions about recording marginal cases. Some tourist victims may be unwilling to report a crime for fear of 'secondary victimisation' (Campbell and Raja, 1999). This relates to further suffering of victims through prolonging or aggravating the victim's trauma by the attitudes or behaviour of unsympathetic or disbelieving law enforcement and other criminal justice authorities. Clearly some 'types' of victim are potentially more vulnerable to secondary victimisation than others and, as such, crimes against these kinds of people are likely to be under-reported.

Tourists as crime victims

There is a considerable body of research to demonstrate relatively high crime rates in tourist areas and this has been discussed in the previous two chapters. By 'high' what is often meant is the extent to which crime rates in 'tourist areas' differ from areas where tourism is less common, and hence comparisons between tourist and resident levels of victimisation are analysed.

An area of research that has received much less attention is the extent to which the *type* of tourist has an influence on tourist criminal victimisation. One study by Brunt and Shepherd (2004) was concerned with assessing the link between the type of tourist and the type of victimisation suffered and to examine the effect of the victimisation experience upon the tourist's future destination choice. The reports of 178 tourist visitors to Cornwall who were crime victims showed that vehicle and accommodation crimes occurred more frequently than violent crimes or other crimes against the person. In broad terms, younger people tended to be crime victims more frequently than the older tourists, especially for crimes against the person and of those relating to their accommodation. Middle-aged persons (35–54) were more prone to being victims of car crime, and males, in absolute terms, were generally more susceptible to crime than females. Females, though, were more prone than males to becoming victims of crimes against the person, especially theft. The number of hours spent out of the accommodation during the evening had a significant effect upon the type of crime suffered. Unsurprisingly, the more time spent out of the accommodation, the higher the incidence of crimes against the person and crimes related to the dwelling. To a large extent the study substantiated the contention that tourists, as victims of crime, appeared to be largely unaffected by their victimisation, in terms of future plans for destination choice. The majority stated that the experience would not alter their future plans as to whether or not to return to Cornwall. However, there were some tourist victims, small in number, who were deeply affected at the time and subsequently exhibited a varied range of responses, in terms of holiday decision-making post-victimisation.

Various other studies have also concluded that there may be a relationship between the type of tourist, their rate of victimisation and also the type of crime suffered. Age and gender may have a significant role to play in terms of both the levels and types of victimisation against tourists. In general terms, people experience higher rates of victimisation as tourists than they do while at home. One indication of this is evident from the *Holiday Which?* (1995, 1997) surveys of British tourists who holiday abroad. These asked respondents about their experiences of illness and (non crime-related) injuries as well as crime. While, as noted above, 0.5% said they had experienced a violent incident and 2% a theft, 15% had been ill while on holiday and 5% had suffered other injuries, falls alone accounting for far more injuries than violence *(Holiday Which?*, 1995). A subsequent survey revealed that 'One in 10 of our members surveyed said they had suffered some sort of illness while on holiday and one in 30 sustained an injury' *(Holiday Which?*, 1997: 132). A different approach was adopted by Brunt *et al.* (2000). Here holidaymakers were asked to look back on their experiences and identify what they would have changed about their holiday, 'something that wasn't as good as it might have been'. Despite the relatively high rate of victimisation cited by respondents, only 3% mentioned safety, 2% conflict with other holidaymakers, and 4% noise. These rated lower in tourists' list of priorities than the journey, weather, lack of things to do in the evenings and accommodation. Moreover, even among tourists who had experienced crime while away, only 8% cited safety as a factor they would have changed (see Mawby, 2000). It appears, then, that even if tourists are disproportionally at risk of victimisation, crime does not concern them as much as many other problems they experience.

Variations by tourist type

The fact that crime may not pose a problem for many tourists may suggest that it is only certain types of tourist who are at particular risk. In the tourism literature, Plog (1991) distinguished between tourist subgroups: at one extreme, 'allocentrics', who design their own, individually wrapped holidays, at the other the 'psychocentrics', who are the mass tourists choosing packaged holidays. Cohen (1972) draws a similar distinction between four subgroups: the organised mass tourist, the individual mass tourist, the explorer and the drifter. While Plog's typology has not been directly related to victimisation, in a later paper, Cohen (1987) adapted his typology and related it to crime, both committed by and against the tourist. He argued that the victimisation of tourists is closely related to lifestyle and could be explained through the distinction between institutionalised and non-institutionalised tourism. Cohen provides a number of examples of crimes committed against non-conventional tourists, and also argued that they often found themselves at the mercy of unsympathetic and sometimes corrupt law-enforcement agencies. However, he also accepted that additional variables might distort the picture. Thus the greater prosperity of conventional tourists made them a more attractive target and their naivety made them vulnerable to being cheated.

A key question here is the relationship between tourist typologies and more general lifestyle measures. There is extensive support in the victimology literature for theories that associate victimisation with lifestyle (Maxfield, 1987). However, while victimological research indicates that there is a positive relationship between general lifestyle variables and risk, there is no obvious relationship between them and tourist typologies. Thus the allocentric tourist may spend considerable time out in the daytime visiting areas 'off the beaten track', while the psychocentric tourist may laze by the hotel pool and venture into an 'English' bar and nightclub after sunset, but there is no logic or research evidence as to which lifestyle is the more risky. While Mawby et al. (1999) attempted to test the relationship between behaviour and victimisation, the homogeneity of their sample and the relatively small number of victims precluded any clear picture.

Victimologists accept that there is a close relationship between lifestyle and victimisation: how we behave – how often and when we go out, what we do when out and where we go – determines our risk of crime. In considering the relationship between tourists' behaviour and victimisation, we must therefore ask what it is that makes tourists in general at high risk, and why some tourists are more likely to be victimised than others. Four aspects of lifestyle may be particularly important:

♦ Relative affluence

♦ Awareness

♦ Precautionary behaviour

♦ Lack of sanctions.

All other things being equal, we might expect offenders to target affluent citizens rather than poorer people, at least for property offences. Thus in countries where tourists are affluent relative to the indigenous population, we might expect them to be especially at risk. This helps explain the high risk tourists face in post-communist societies. Equally, we might expect more prosperous tourists to suffer property crime to a greater extent than poorer tourists. There is little evidence to substantiate this, although the Mawby et al. (1999) finding of a high victimisation rates among their largely middle-class sample may be indicative of this. Second, we might expect tourists to be more at risk where they are unaware of the risks they face. More generally, though, where we are mindful of the notoriety of specific areas, so-called 'crime hot spots', we may avoid such areas. However, when on holiday we may be less aware of which areas to avoid. Gallivan (1994: 42), for example, interviewed a Miami police officer who claimed that much tourist-targeted crime was the result of new arrivals driving off the toll road and ending up in dangerous areas oblivious to their risk.

Even where tourists are aware of problem areas, however, they may disregard their knowledge. That is, a 'culture of carelessness' may pervade (Mawby *et al.*, 1999), where tourists behave in ways that suggest that they have left caution at home. As Ryan (1993: 181) notes: 'The intrinsic demand for relaxation engenders a situation where, by taking less care, and being more obvious, the tourist can more easily become a victim of crime.' Finally, and rather differently, tourists may be attractive targets because their temporary residence in the area makes it unlikely that they will be available to give evidence, should their case come to court (Inciardi, 1976).

As such, in tourist areas, we might expect crime rates to be higher in areas catering for mass tourism, and thus tourists in such areas would be more at risk. At a more local level, crime hot spots will include areas catering for night-time entertainment, and tourists frequenting them will also increase their chances of victimisation (Crotts, 1996). Equally, though, the relative prosperity of tourists and their careless behaviour may serve to attract more professional offenders into tourist areas where they deliberately target tourists.

It can be seen that there is a striking lack of research into the criminal victimisation of particular types of tourist. The criminology/victimology literature provides some assistance, such as the traditional view that women report a greater perceived risk and fear of crime than men (Lagrange and Ferraro, 1989) and that the elderly are least at risk of being victims of violent crime, while young men who drink heavily and spend several evenings out each week are most at risk (Hough and Mayhew, 1983). Taking these issues together, the question remains – what type of tourist is most at risk from victimisation? Past research suggests that typical tourist victims are male (and – to a less extent – female) drinkers, out in the evening, who are relaxed and off their guard in unfamiliar locations. Perhaps this is why the isolation of specific tourist types has been so difficult for researchers and why tourist victimisation rates generally exceed those of indigenous tourists and resident populations. Certainly it has been shown that 'lager louts' (typically groups of drunken British males on holiday in UK and Mediterranean seaside resorts) are often seen as being over-represented both as perpetrators and victims of crime (Brunt and Brophy, 2004; Agarwal and Brunt, 2006; Brunt and Davis, 2006; Brunt and Hooton, forthcoming). It is clear that a future research agenda could do more to explore the relationship between tourist type and crime victimisation.

Gay tourist victimisation: a special case?

There is a small body of literature related to the criminal victimisation of gay tourists. Much of this work is focused on destination avoidance as a result of the perceived risk of gay victimisation (Hughes, 2002a); the influence of behaviour on gay tourist victimisation (Pritchard et al., 2000) and the risk of victimisation associated with booking accommodation (Poria and Taylor, 2001). The problem faced by gay tourists as crime victims is, to some extent, more complex, as the risk is increased through the singling out of targets based on sexual orientation (Jones, 1996; Carr, 2000).

In many locations the gay (and lesbian) tourist segment is no longer considered the pariah market it once was in the 1950s and 1960s (Pitts, 1997: 31). Gay travel is increasing at, or above, the rate of mainstream travel (Wood, 1999). According to Wood (1999) and Hughes (2002a), the typical gay or lesbian traveller is a high spending, frequently travelling, brand-loyal client, who is more highly educated than the average, with few family commitments, more free time, more style consciousness, who is more individualistic and more likely to appreciate arts and culture. However, it is important to note that the 'gay tourist' is not a homogeneous category in terms of employment or income (Hughes, 1997). According to Tebje and Ozinsky (2004: 31), the global destinations which are most popular with gay tourists include: Amsterdam, Barcelona, Paris, Sydney, San Francisco, London, New Zealand, Cape Town, New York, Bahamas, Costa Rica, Canada, Thailand, Mexico, Hawaii, Key West and Brazil. Regarding holiday destination choices, it is well-documented that most gay tourists are likely to holiday in destinations that are known to be 'gay-friendly' and are brand loyal in supporting businesses and companies that have been proved to be 'gay friendly' (Hughes, 1997; Clift and Forrest, 1999; Wood, 1999; Tebje and Ozinsky, 2004).

Although tourist motivations are essentially the same whether gay or straight, with the range of holidays taken by gay travellers no different from that of the rest of the market (Russell, 2001), there is one important motivation that stands out as being different from those held by the general mainstream traveller. Clift and Forrest (2000) identify a strong presence of sexual reference and hedonistic party atmospheres within the holiday guides and brochures written by and produced specifically for the gay tourist market. This also provides a link with the youth tourist market, which is the only other tourist segment that holds sex, fun and hedonism as primary travel motivations. Tourists in these categories often attract trouble as a result, whether by indulging in deviant behaviour themselves or becoming the victim of crime as a result of the risks of associated with this behaviour.

According to Carr (2000), gay tourists are often subjected to social disapproval, prejudice and discrimination because of their sexuality. In a qualitative study into gay men's holiday destination choices involving both perceived risk and its avoidance, Hughes (2002b) raises some important issues. First, most informants have been subjected to some verbal and physical abuse whilst on holiday. Second, gay men face a 'greater physical risk' than other travellers given the possibility and fear of violent attacks, thefts and muggings. Third, the 'discomfort risk', whereby gay tourists fear the perceived risk of verbal abuse and threatening behaviour, tends to influence holiday behaviour, and consequently, avoiding destinations to minimise such risks is a particularly significant issue in the gay tourist's holiday choice process. Fourth, gay men tend to avoid destinations that are predominantly heterosexual, 'British-dominated' and that exhibit a 'lager-lout' culture as there is fear about the attitudes of such people against 'gays' and consequential victimisation whether verbal or physical. A further study by Pritchard *et al.* (2000) further adds to this by stating that gay tourists also tend to avoid some African and Islamic countries, where homosexuality is the subject of strong religious/cultural disapproval and may be criminalised, and anywhere else where hostile attitudes towards gay people are commonplace.

As was identified previously, many crimes against tourists may go unreported because the apprehension of offenders in tourist destinations takes longer than elsewhere, and also many victims fail to report offences due to the embarrassment of their own negligence, a reluctance to become involved in official proceedings whilst on holiday, especially considering the limited likelihood of apprehension of the perpetrator (Walmsley et al., 1983; Kelly, 1993). Moreover, in some countries that have become popular holiday destinations such as Jamaica, the Carribbean, and Malaysia, gay men who report attacks and incidents to the police are at best met with indifference and at worst face further secondary victimisation (Amnesty International, 2001). However, it is also worth considering that with gay tourist victimisation, there is a 'grey area' not experienced by straight counterparts. In some popular tourist destinations not perceived as risky to the general public, certain types of tourists are nevertheless subjected to consistent victimisation. This is not always explicitly 'criminal' victimisation, but rather amounts to a pattern of harassment and discriminatory behaviour which has extremely negative impacts on its victims. Although there are known destinations which would exhibit a high risk of 'gay victimisation' and are avoided as a result, (Muslim countries, Germany, Greece, Portugal, Jamaica, China and Turkey) quite often destinations that on the surface seem liberal and are popular holiday choices, do not welcome gay tourists (Pritchard et al., 1998; Hughes, 2002b). However, this may only be discovered after arrival.

Arguably the most frequently debated issue that fits into this 'grey area' of gay tourist victimisation is the problem faced by gay couples when booking a double hotel room. Wood (1999: 109) demonstrates that gay tourists can face sneers or open disapproval at their request for a double room. According to Poria and Taylor (2001: 130), lesbians and gay men are often reluctant to reveal their sexual orientations when booking hotel accommodation because of the harassment and discrimination they might be subjected to as a result. Ryan and Hall (2001: 106) note that destinations which are seen to be overtly unfriendly to gay tourists find that their tourism industry suffers, and they highlight the example of the State of Tasmania, Australia. In the UK, the Equality Act 2006 (and more specifically, the Equality Act [Sexual Orientation] Regulations 2007, make it unlawful for hoteliers to discriminate against guests on grounds of sexual orientation).

To summarise the limited body of literature, it can be said that there appears to be a strong link that can be made between the risk of victimisation, criminal and otherwise, and gay tourists (as opposed to other tourists); and that the motivations and inherent characteristics of gay tourists may also have an influence on the nature of the victimisation. These issues are summarised in Table 4.1.

Table 4.1: Gay holiday motivations and influence on victimisation

Gay tourist motivations	Influence on victimisation		Comment
	Yes	No	
Ability to lower barriers further and be more camp, outrageous, wear distinguishing clothes (Hughes, 1997; 2002b)	✓		Makes gay individual stand out from the crowd
Ability to enjoy comfort, relaxation and sunshine (Clift and Forrest, 1999)		✓	
Ability to escape pressure of being secretly gay in a hetero-sexual world – travel frees inhibition (Ryan and Kinder, 1996; Pritchard et al., 2000)	✓		Anonymity allows gay tourist to indulge in more risky or more outwardly gay behaviour than they would consider acceptable at home, increasing their visibility
Ability to go sightseeing and take in local culture (Clift and Forrest, 1999)		✓	
Opportunity to have casual and anonymous sex (Clift and Forrest, 1999, 2000; Hughes, 2000)	✓		Openly gay behaviour such as this could attract unwanted negative attention
Opportunity to indulge in hedonistic, 18–30 gay party lifestyle – gay clubs, pubs etc. (Clift and Forrest, 2000; Tebje and Ozinsky, 2004)	✓		Concentration of gay individuals in one known, gay-friendly area could provide potential offenders with the opportunity to victimise them (Pritchard et al., 2000)

Brunt and Brophy (2006) adopted an inductive approach in a qualitative study of victimisation of gay tourists (from the UK), which examined the perceptions, reactions and behavioural characteristics of gay tourists and the influence these may have on levels of victimisation while on holiday. In addition, the study attempted to establish an offender profile, reasons for attacks, and the most common forms of victimisation against gay tourists. All respondents interviewed in the Brunt and Brophy (2006) study indicated that they had either witnessed, been the victim of, or heard about crime victimisation through friends, and most could recount specific incidences, which echoed the findings of the previous study by Hughes (2002b). Nonetheless, all but one respondent stated that these incidences had not been reported with answers such as 'I didn't feel it was worth doing anything', 'I didn't want to talk to the police about something like that', 'he felt stupid' and 'he was too frightened to', being commonplace responses. This links to a study conducted by Amnesty International (2001) where in some countries that have become popular holiday destinations (e.g. Jamaica, the Caribbean and Malaysia), gay men who report attacks and incidences to the police have faced problems ranging from indifference to further victimisation.

Discrimination in the hotel setting has been seen as much a problem by gay tourists as crime victimisation. Almost half of all respondents in the Brunt and Brophy (2006) study felt that they had been discriminated against on holiday with most experiencing difficulty or discomfort in booking a double room in a hotel. However, whilst discrimination can arguably be acknowledged as a prominent problem, it was perceived by respondents that offenders often 'get away with it' for reasons such as 'it goes mainly unreported', it is 'more of an underhand way to target the gay individual' and it provides offenders with 'the opportunity be more covert'. Findings indicate that discrimination can be subtle and although it may have the potential to spoil the holiday of a gay tourist (Woods, 1999), it is often not illegal (Hughes, 2002b) and so is difficult to prevent and to avoid. Countries vary in the degree to which such discriminatory behaviour is lawful, and in any case, discrimination is notoriously difficult to prove in law. The nature of criminal victimisation of gay tourists is in some ways similar to the experiences of all tourists. Gay tourists in the Brunt and Brophy study defined 'crime' as physical abuse and illegal activity (i.e. opportunistic theft), whilst 'victimisation' was defined separately by respondents as verbal abuse, discrimination, homophobia and discomfort. Thus it could be suggested that while gay tourists may suffer similar crime and victimisation patterns to all tourists, it is extended by homophobic-related crimes and discrimination/victimisation where gay tourists are targeted specifically.

An important distinction, however, in the Brunt and Brophy study was that the majority of respondents felt that the level and type of gay victimisation was different from that of straight people. There was felt to be additional 'gay-specific' victimisation issues. It was argued that criminal acts against gay tourists were often more 'character-related' attacks rather than 'money-oriented' more typical of straight tourists. As such, gay people are being victimised explicitly because they are perceived as members of a particular group, in a manner similar to racially-motivated crime and domestic violence against women. Brunt and Brophy (2006) highlighted camp, visible, flamboyant, outrageous and overtly gay characteristics as those which would increase the risk of victimisation for a gay tourist. Yet these were noted by Hughes (1997, 2002b) as the key factors which gay men deemed important not to conceal whilst on holiday but instead to be able to exaggerate. Moreover, Pritchard et al. (2000: 279) argue that this is because a key motivation for gay tourists is to be able to behave in ways that would not be sanctioned or acceptable at home. This desire to behave in an exaggerated way on holiday arguably indicates that gay tourists are more likely to act in ways and operate in spaces that attract higher levels of crime, such as gay cruising and nightlife areas

(Hughes, 2002b) and so the likelihood of becoming a target for victimisation will increase. As stated by Pritchard et al. (2000) being conspicuously gay on holiday is perceived to increase the risk to safety.

Brunt and Brophy (2006) noted a variety of offenders described by gay respondents to include 'male youths', 'Brit tourists', 'lager louts', and resort staff. These findings are fairly consistent with the existing literature on the subject. The gay individuals who wrote in to a 'Critics Comments' web page for Kefalonia (www. kefhelm.tripod.com, 2004) described that the problems they experienced whilst on holiday there were attributed mainly to fellow British tourists, who were the most offensive. Furthermore, Hughes (2002b: 306) described the wish expressed by the majority of gay individuals studied to avoid any place which was associated with British holidaymakers, but also the desire to avoid places dominated by heterosexual 'lager-lout' types characterised by young, single people in groups. The perceived reasons for the victimisation of gay tourists include: homophobia/ ignorance, easy targets, religion and culture, aggressive behavioural characteristics of offending individuals, male bravado and alcohol. Hughes (2002b) highlights physical risk of attack and the discomfort risk of verbal abuse and threatening behaviour as major factors in the gay man's destination decision-making process.

The limited available research suggests that virtually all gay tourists have either witnessed, become the victim of, or heard, through friends, of incidents, yet most failed to report them, either being too frightened of secondary victimisation by the police or else too ashamed. Coupled with this, the fact that tourists generally choose not to report incidences on holiday because of the time and effort it takes to follow up, it would seem that homophobic crime on holiday is an extremely tough problem to monitor and would require a considerable effort from the resort's tourism industry and enforcement bodies to do so. Discrimination is also identified as an important issue for gay tourists with many choosing to hide their sexuality in situations such as booking hotel accommodation. However, this too seems to go unreported. The criminal victimisation experienced by gay tourists corresponds with that experienced by tourists in general, except that it seems the victimisation pattern experienced by the gay tourist is complicated by gay-specific discrimination and homophobic-related crimes that are character-related rather than money-motivated.

A further specific link may exist between the behavioural characteristics of gay tourists and the level of victimisation: gay tourists possess a set of motivations that involve actions and behaviours which can make individuals 'stand out from the crowd' and some indulge in casual sex and other deviant activities, congregate in overtly gay areas, and behave in an extrovert manner with overtly camp, or stereotypical characteristics. This, coupled with a determination not to let fear of victimisation influence destination choice (though avoidance of known 'risky' and intolerant destinations), puts gay males at much higher risk of victimisation than straight tourists (and gay females).

Conclusion

There are clear parallels between the victimisation experiences of gay tourists and the general level of victimisation experienced for all tourist types. Those who undertake what might be described as 'hedonistic' or 'deviant' activities on holiday are most at risk. While all tourists are at some risk, these enhance the chances of victimisation. In addition, gay tourists are more likely than their heterosexual counterparts to encounter victimisation that is directed against them as members of a specific group. Tourist places that serve the deviant are attractive to such tourists and criminals who are only too aware of their anonymity in the tourism zone and the lessened opportunities for arrest. Add to this the tourist behaviour traits of lack of awareness of the surrounding dangers and a culture of carelessness (possibly fuelled by alcohol) and a potent mix exists where criminal victimisation is a natural outcome for the unwitting or witless tourist.

References

Agarwal, S. and Brunt, P. (2006) 'Social exclusion and crime in English seaside resorts', *Journal of Tourism & Cultural Change*, **6** (1), 19–35.

Amnesty International (2001) *Crimes of Hate, Conspiracy of Silence: Torture and Ill-Treatment Based on Sexual Identity*, London: Amnesty International Publications

Brunt, P. (1997) *Market Research in Travel and Tourism*, Oxford: Butterworth-Heinemann.

Brunt, P. and Brophy, K. (2004) 'English seaside resorts and the deviant tourist', *Acta Touristica*, **16** (1), 3–30.

Brunt, P. and Brophy, K. (2006) 'Gay tourist victimisation', *International Review of Victimology*, **13**, 275–299.

Brunt, P. and Davis, C. (2006) 'The nature of British media reporting of hedonistic tourism', *Crime Prevention and Community Safety*, **8** (1), 30–50.

Brunt, P. and Hooton, N. (forthcoming) 'Community responses to tourism and crime', *Crime Prevention and Community Safety*.

Brunt, P. and Shepherd, D. (2004) 'The influence of crime on tourist decision-making: some empirical evidence', *Tourism*, **52** (4), 317–327.

Brunt, P., Mawby, R. and Hambly, Z. (2000) 'Tourist victimisation and the fear of crime on holiday', *Tourism Management*, **21**, 417–424.

Campbell, R. and Raja, S. (1999) 'Secondary victimisation of rape victims: insights from mental health professionals who treat survivors of violence', *Violence and Victims*, **14** (3), 261–275.

Carr, H. (2000) 'The gay market', *Travel Trade Gazette UK & Ireland*, August, 39–42.

Chesney-Lind, M. and Lind, I.Y. (1986) 'Visitors as victims: crimes against tourists in Hawaii', *Annals of Tourism Research*, **13**, 167–191.

Clift, S. and Forrest, S. (1999) 'Gay men and tourism: destinations and holiday motivations', *Tourism Management*, **20** (5), 615–625.

Clift, S. and Forrest, S. (2000) 'Tourism and the sexual ecology of gay men', in S.Clift and S.Carter (eds), *Tourism and Sex: Culture, Commerce and Coercion*, London: Pinter, Ch 11.

Cohen, E. (1972) 'Towards a sociology of international tourism', *Social Research*, 39(1), 164-84

Cohen, E. (1987) 'The tourist as victim and protégé of law enforcement agencies', *Leisure Studies*, **6** (2), 181–198.

Cohen, E. (1996) 'Touting tourists in Thailand: tourist oriented crime and social structure', in A. Pizam and Y. Mansfeld (eds), *Tourism, Crime and International Security Issues*, Chichester: Wiley, pp. 77–90

Cohen, E. (1997) 'Tourism-related crime: towards a sociology of crime and tourism', *Visions in Leisure and Business*, **16** (1), 2–14.

Critics Comments about Kefalonia (2004) The Way to go on Kefalonia, www.kefhelm.tripod.com/2ndSiteNewLayout/CriticsPages/Criticscoments.htm, accessed 11 March 2004.

Crompton, J.L. (1979) 'Motivations for pleasure vacation', *Annals of Tourism Research*, **6**, 408–424.

Crotts, J.C. (1996) 'Theoretical perspectives on tourist criminal victimisation', Journal of Tourism Studies, 7 (4), 2–9.

Gallivan, J. (1994) 'Looking for trouble with the Miami police department', *The Guardian*, 22 January, p. 42.

Holiday Which? (1995) 'Holiday hazards', *Holiday Which?*, May, 130–133.

Holiday Which? (1997) 'Staying healthy on holiday', *Holiday Which?*, Summer, 130–138.

Hough, M. and Mayhew, P. (1983) *British Crime Survey – First Report*, London: HMSO

Hughes, H. (1997) 'Holidays and homosexual identity', *Tourism Management*, **18** (4), 3–7.

Hughes, H. (2002a) 'Marketing gay tourism in Manchester: new market for urban tourism or destruction of "gay space"?', *Journal of Vacation Marketing*, **9** (2), 152–163.

Hughes, H. (2002b) 'Gay men's holiday destination choice: a case of risk and avoidance', *International Journal of Tourism Research*, **4** (4), 299–312.

Inciardi, J.A. (1976) 'The pickpocket and his victim', *Victimology*, **1** (3), 446–453.

Jones, D.A. (1996) 'Discrimination against same-sex couples in hotel reservation policies', *Journal of Homosexuality*, **31** (1), 153–159.

Kelly, I. (1993) 'Tourist destination crime rates: an examination of Cairns and the Gold Coast, Australia', *Journal of Tourism Studies*, **4** (2), 2–11.

Krippendorf, J. (1987) *The Holiday Makers: Understanding the Impact of Leisure and Travel*, Oxford: Butterworth-Heinemann.

Lagrange, R.L. and Ferraro, K.F. (1989) 'Assessing age and gender differences in perceived risk and fear of crime', *Criminology*, **27** (4), 697–719.

Mawby, R.I. (2000) 'Tourists' perceptions of security: the risk–fear paradox', *Tourism Economics*, **6** (2), 109–121.

Mawby, R.l., Brunt, P. and Hambly, Z. (1999) 'Victimisation on holiday: a British survey', *International Review of Victimology*, **6**, 201–211.

Maxfield, M.G. (1987) 'Household composition, routine activity and victimisation: a comparative analysis', *Journal of Quantitative Criminology*, **3** (4), 301–320.

Pitts, B.G. (1999) 'Sports tourism and niche markets: identification and analysis of the growing lesbian and gay sports tourism industry', *Journal of Vacation Marketing*, **5** (1), 31–50.

Plog, S.C. (1991) *Leisure Travel: Making it a Growth Market...Again!*, New York: Wiley.

Poria, Y. and Taylor, A. (2001) '"I am not afraid to be gay when I'm on the Net": minimising social risk for lesbian and gay consumers when using the Internet', *Journal of Travel & Tourism Marketing*, **11** (2/3), 127–142.

Pritchard, A., Morgan, N.J., Sedgely, D. and Jenkins, A. (1998) 'Reaching out to the gay tourist: opportunities and threats in an emerging market segment', *Tourism Management*, **19** (3), 273–282.

Pritchard, A., Morgan, N.J., Sedgley, D., Khan, E. and Jenkins, A. (2000) 'Sexuality and holiday choices: conversations with gay and lesbian tourists', *Leisure Studies*, **19** (4), 267–282.

Pritchard, A., Morgan, N.J. and Sedgley, D. (2002) 'In search of lesbian space? The experience of Manchester's gay village', *Leisure Studies*, **21** (2), 105–123.

Russell, P. (2001) 'The world gay travel market', Travel and Tourism Analyst, 2, 37–58.

Ryan, C. (1993) 'Crime, violence, terrorism and tourism: an accidental or intrinsic relationship?' *Tourism Management*, **14** (3), 173–183.

Ryan, C. and Hall, C.M. (2001) *Sex Tourism: Marginal People and Liminalities*, London: Routledge, Ch. 5.

Ryan, C. and Kinder, R. (1996). The deviant tourist and the crimogenic place – the case of the tourist and the New Zealand prostitute', in A. Pizam and Y. Mansfeld (eds), *Tourism, Crime and International Security Issues*, Chichester: Wiley.

Smith, S.L.J. (1989) *Tourism Analysis: A Handbook*, Harlow: Longman.

Tebje, M. and Ozinsky, S. (2004). 'The Pink Route – Cape Town, South Africa', *Insights*, January, 31–37.

Walmsley, D.J., Boskovic, R.M. and Pigram, J.J. (1983) 'Tourism and crime: an Australian perspective', *Journal of Leisure Research*, **15** (2), 136–155.

Wood, L. (1999) 'Think pink! – attracting the pink pound', *Insights*, January, 107–110.

Part II:

Tourists as Offenders

5 Child Sex Tourism: Is extra-territorial legislation the answer?

Heather Montgomery

In this chapter the following topics are considered:

♦ Child sex tourism
♦ Extra-territorial legislation
♦ Obstacles to enforcement
♦ The role of non-governmental organisations (NGOs) and the media
♦ Children's own accounts of child prostitution.

Introduction

If sex tourism is the dark, if debated, side of tourism, then child sex tourism represents the line in the sand that should never be crossed. While sex tourism involving adults provokes a variety of opinions and positions (Cohen, 1982; Oppermann, 1998; Kempadoo et al., 2005; O'Connell-Davidson and Sánchez Taylor, 2005; Sánchez Taylor, 2006; Day, 2007; Eades, 2009), child prostitution involving tourists is universally condemned and high-profile cases, such as the trial of Gary Glitter, point to the depths of public revulsion against such behaviour. The last 20 years have seen vocal campaigns against child sex tourism, resulting in changes in national legislation in many countries, statements and taskforces from the World Tourism Organization, the inauguration of World Congresses against the Commercial Sexual Exploitation of Children and a universal determination to stamp out a crime and a moral outrage.

Despite the public outcry and changes in legislation, however, child sex tourism continues and, in some ways, the moral indignation that the subject arouses obscures certain aspects of the situations in which children caught up in prostitution live and work. There is still a dearth of information about how children meet clients, what is expected of them and their paths in and out of prostitution (Montgomery, 2001a, 2001b). Their clients are even more unknown and there is very little research (as opposed to anecdotal) evidence that discusses their motivations, their modus operandi or their choices about which countries they will visit and where they can find opportunities for sexual activity with children (Ennew, 1986; Montgomery, 2008; for an excellent overview of the available evidence see O'Connell-Davidson, 2005). At both national and international levels, legislation to protect children, although much heralded, has proved inadequate, and left unanswered important questions about enforcement and practical help for the children affected. In this chapter, I examine the legislation in place to tackle the problem of child sex tourism, and contrast this with a case study from Thailand of a small community in which children worked as prostitutes in order to support their parents and themselves. In doing so, I am not arguing for any moral ambivalence or ambiguity in discussions of child sex tourism. Rather, I wish to point out the lacuna between those discussions and the lived realities of the children.

The legal and political situation in Thailand

Despite Thailand's reputation as a sexual paradise where 'anything' goes, all prostitution is illegal (Montgomery, 2001a). The laws against it are rarely enforced however, with police turning a blind eye and, in many cases, according to a recent US State Department's Human Rights Report, being actively involved (Bureau of Democracy, Human Rights, and Labor, 2008). The history of prostitution in Thailand is highly politicised and much debated with some commentators claiming that organised prostitution began only with the influx of Chinese migrants in the 1930s and was expanded by the American military in the 1960s. Others have argued that these influences simply mapped onto pre-existing social institutions and that prostitution was long regulated, taxed and implicitly condoned by the Thai authorities before becoming criminalised in 1960 as part of a wider plan to rid the country of 'undesirables' such as beggars and prostitutes (Landon, 1939; Fox, 1960; Hantrakul, 1983; Muecke, 1992; ten Brummelhuis, 1993; Boonchalaksi and Guest, 1994; Fordham, 2005). Undoubtedly, if rather uncomfortably, for many in Thailand, there is evidence of long-standing patterns of prostitution and varying degrees of exploitation. What is less clear is the exact extent of child prostitution before 1960 although it would be reasonable to believe that it was relatively common (Boonchalaksi and Guest, 1994). Based on the results of studies in the 1950s Maurice Fox (1960) claimed that 90% of prostitutes were between 15 and 20 and he found evidence of some as young as 13.

While the overwhelming majority of prostitutes were Thai women and girls with Thai clients, as early as the 1920s there was evidence of international involvement in the Thai sex industry and of both foreign women working in Thai brothels and of Thai women having foreign clients. In 1933, the League of Nations reported back on the organised brothels of Thailand claiming that Thai, Chinese, Annamese and even Russian women were selling sex in Thailand (League of Nations, 1933).

By the late 1940s, there is even evidence of an embryonic sex tourism industry in Thailand. In 1949, a book entitled *Dream Lover* was published, written by the pseudonymous author Black Shadow, which described to the foreigner where and how he could obtain the sexual services of Thai and Chinese women in Bangkok. Despite its florid and contorted language, Black Shadow makes no secret that the purpose of his book is to guide the uninitiated foreigner through the back street brothels of Bangkok.

> Now, my dear travellers, the time is reached to the aim of this book to guide you to roam the places of sweet romance – of Bangkok night rendezvous – to the rooms of those young showy Nightingales of the night. Every one keeps waiting and is ready, however, to be the best of your night companion – of your partner, to accompany you and guide you into and through the land of Aden – the place of bliss. By her your dream will become true. With sweet hours of her accompaniment, it will certainly be of the best to your disquieting sexuality. To men the women are sweet paradise.
>
> (Black Shadow, 1949: 1)

It is not known how many men availed themselves of Black Shadow's advice, what the print run was, or how popular the book became. Similarly, although the book hints that some women are 'very fresh, young and gay' (1949: 26), the number of children catering to foreign men was probably minuscule. Certainly, such a publication catered to a very niche market and it is safe to assume that before the 1960s the number of foreign men using local prostitutes in general was extremely small.

It was not until the influx of US servicemen on Rest and Recreation breaks from the Vietnam War, that prostitution for foreigners became a much larger and organised business with bars and brothels set up explicitly catering to them and it was during this period that Thailand became a byword for cheap, blatant, commercially available sex. After 1975, when most troops had gone, the government pursued tourism as a development strategy, promoting the sexuality of Thai women, and using the infrastructure of the sex industry left behind by the Americans, to appeal to Western tourists. Prostitution, although illegal, was not seen as immoral. Rather it was understood as part of the strategy to promote tourism in a poor country, with limited resources to modernise and industrialise. The Thai Deputy Prime Minister laid out this view of sex tourism quite explicitly in 1980 in an extraordinary statement to provincial governors:

> I ask all governors to consider the natural scenery in your provinces, together with some forms of entertainment that some of you might consider disgusting and shameful because they are forms of sexual entertainment that attract tourists . . . we must do this because we have to consider the jobs that will be created for the people.
>
> (quoted in Ennew, 1986: 99)

By the 1990s however, this policy of condoning sex tourism was coming under threat. Women's groups and anti-tourism groups began to campaign against the use of sex tourism as a way of promoting the tourist industry and began a series of high profile publicity stunts in which they attacked the image of 'brothel' Thailand. They picketed Bangkok airport and targeted flights from Taiwan and Japan, which were seen as the worst countries for sending sex tourists, with placards such as 'Thailand not Sexland' or 'Gonorrhoea Express' (Montgomery, 2008: 907). There was also mounting concern about the number of younger girls and boys who were working as prostitutes and whose clients were openly paying children for sex with no apparent fear of prosecution or even social opprobrium.

More than anything else it was the issue of child prostitution which galvanised public opinion nationally and internationally. Adult prostitution was illegal and was, increasingly, viewed as a vector for the spread of disease, particularly HIV and AIDS (Fordham, 2005) but there remained a debate about its morality and its necessity to the wider economy. Child prostitution was generally viewed as beyond the pale and the very lurid stories that came out around this time reinforced the notion that child prostitution was quite separate from adult prostitution and of a different magnitude of horror. At the forefront of these campaigns were ECPAT (End Child Prostitution in Asian Tourism, later End Child Prostitution, Child Pornography and Trafficking of Children for Sexual Purposes) and ECTWT (Ecumenical Council on Third World Tourism), both of which drew very explicit links between tourism, child prostitution and child trafficking (ECTWT, 1990; ECPAT, 1993; Montgomery, 2001a). Their campaigns often relied on heartbreaking accounts of individual children's lives that had been ruined by abuse and HIV infection due to the selfishness of Western men. These stories tended to follow a reliable pattern involving a young Thai girl tricked into leaving home, or sold by impoverished parents into a brothel, where they were repeatedly raped and terrorised into servicing many foreign clients a night, before being rescued by a charitable organisation, only to be discovered to be suffering from HIV (Montgomery, 2001a). One story which gained particular prominence was that of Rosario Baluyot, an 11 or 12-year-old girl living on the streets of Olangapo in the Philippines, whose story has since been retold a number of times, often as an example of the typical fate of a child prostitute with foreign clients (O'Grady, 1992; Axelsson, 1997; Kane, 1998). Although not Thai, her story had great resonance for the Bangkok-based ECPAT and was widely publicised as typical both of the misery and squalor suffered by young prostitutes and also of the corruption and lack of interest in prosecuting the perpetrators.

Rosario was a young street child who sold sex to a variety of men, including those from the nearby American base, and to an Austrian doctor, Heinrich Ritter, who in 1986 took her to a hotel room and abused her with a vibrator. He did not remove it and it became infected, causing septicaemia. This, in conjunction with liver failure caused by glue sniffing, led to Rosario's death in 1987. Those who had cared for Rosario in her last few days campaigned against police indifference and forced the police to investigate her death. Several months later they arrested Ritter. He responded by offering $800 to Rosario's grandmother if she did not press charges and he was granted bail. The case however had generated huge publicity thanks to the efforts of social workers, women's groups and various Catholic organisations. They petitioned the public prosecutor to reinvestigate the case and Ritter was subsequently re-arrested and charged with Rosario's rape and murder. In 1989 he became the first foreigner to be convicted of child sexual abuse in the Philippines.

Rather than being seen as uniquely horrific, this case was viewed as the tip of the iceberg. In 1989 Norwegian Save the Children (Redd Barna) published a report on what was known of the nature and extent of child prostitution (Narvesen, 1989) in developing countries, which suggested that although figures and research were scant, the sexual exploitation of children by tourists was a serious and previously ignored problem, particularly in south-east Asia. Fired up by successful, hard-hitting campaigning by ECPAT, stories began to emerge of Westerners in Thailand not only being arrested for molesting children but also of then jumping bail or being let off on technicalities. In 1992, a Swedish man, Bengt Bolin, was caught with a naked boy in his bed, but claimed that he had been led to believe that the boy was over 15 and therefore of legal age. Before he could be prosecuted, he applied for a new Swedish passport and left the country. The following year an Australian, Bradley Pendragon, was arrested in Chiang Mai after trying to develop photographs clearly depicting the sexual abuse of a young girl. Pendragon was sentenced to 30 years in prison but released in 1996. In 2008 he pleaded guilty to downloading child pornography at an Internet cafe in Perth, Australia and was sentenced to 12 months in an Australian prison. Thai newspapers ran a steady stream of articles about child prostitution, documenting many cases of child abuse by foreigners (for example: 'German couple recruiting kids for sex photos', *Pattaya Mail*, 4 January 1993; 'German engineer arrested on perverted sex charge', *Nation*, 3 March 1994; 'Swiss caught with small boy', *Pattaya Mail*, 23 March 1994; 'Child molester flees Thailand', *Bangkok Post*, 31 January 1995). The fact that many of these men did manage to leave the country or bribe police to drop charges created justifiable outrage, and groups such as ECPAT bravely campaigned against these abuses and also against the corruption and incompetence that allowed these men to escape punishment.

Chid prostitution: ethnographic evidence

With these stories being reported in great detail in the Thai and international media (see Montgomery, 2001a or Fordham, 2005 for a discussion of how the newspapers reported tales of child prostitution), I went to Thailand to undertake ethnographic fieldwork with child prostitutes. I was based in a small slum community, situated on the edge of a larger tourist resort in Thailand, which we shall call Baan Nua. It was a poor community that survived through the prostitution of some of its children. The children's clients were exclusively Western and their parents were well aware of, and even encouraged, what they did. There were 65 children in Baan Nua, around 35 of whom worked regularly or occasionally as prostitutes; this number included both boys and girls aged between 6 and 14. I spent 15 months doing this research, interviewing the children, gathering life histories and acting as a participant observer in their lives (for a full discussion of methods and ethical dilemmas see Montgomery, 2007).

As I have argued elsewhere (Montgomery, 2001a), children in Baan Nua turned to prostitution only after they had tried a variety of other ways to make a living such as scavenging, working in sweat shops or begging. Prostitution paid them considerably more than these activities and they perceived it as less physically demanding. Begging, for instance, while potentially lucrative in the high tourist season could bring in nothing during the rainy season, when there were fewer tourists. Furthermore, the children did not like to beg because there was a risk of being arrested by the police or having their money stolen by older street children. They also did not like to scavenge because of fears that they would hurt themselves on broken glass or metal on the dump and because of their terror of rats. While they never claimed to like prostitution, they often described it to me as better and easier than other jobs they had tried and, although they seemed wilfully ignorant of the threat of pregnancy or sexually transmitted diseases, they argued that prostitution gave them access to benefits such as staying in good hotels or apartments, eating well and being given large, occasional payments.

More importantly they used prostitution as a way of fulfilling what they understood to be their filial duties. The children felt that by earning money for their parents and keeping the family together they were acting in socially sanctioned roles as dutiful daughters and sons and that prostituting themselves with the 'right' intentions meant that there was no moral opprobrium on what they did. Prostitution with foreign clients was not entirely about poverty, although that played a part, nor was it about abuse, although again that was also evident (in my eyes). In the children's own analysis of what they did, and why they did it, selling sex was about social relationships and fulfilling their filial obligations to their families (Montgomery, 2007). In all the conversations I had with the children about what they did and their feelings about it, it was to this point that they kept referring. Prostitution was an unpleasant thing but done with the very best of intentions: as one twelve-year-old informant put it, 'it's only my body but this is my family' (Montgomery, 2001a: 84).

The children also had very strong views about their clients, who they consistently refused to see as abusers and saw instead as friends and even protectors. Although the Western men who visited the children in Baan Nua had superior financial and structural power, the children were able to manipulate these men to some extent and, in certain cases, make them enter into reciprocal arrangement with the community. The mother of one 14-year-old girl frequently sent requests to one man for money, and the fact that he always responded enabled her to see him as a friend. He played a similar role in another family's life whereby their 12-year-old daughter had sex with him and found him other child sex partners and in return he gave them regular money. These two families were very protective of him, and the children very loyal and would hear no criticism of him. During the Christmas period I watched them making Christmas cards for their friends and families. Several children asked me how to write 'Thank you' and 'We love you' in English on their cards, in order to give a card to this man.

Another client was protected and defended in a similar way. He was a British businessman who had lived in Thailand for many years and paid for sex with a number of the children. Recounting an incident a few years before I did fieldwork, the children in my study told me that a girl from another slum in the city had told her parents that this man had propositioned her and tried to pay her for sex. This child's parents went to the police and reported him and also gave the police the name of several children in Baan Nua. However when the police investigated they were met with flat denials of his involvement and instead the people in Baan Nua gave him a character reference, saying what a good man he was, how much he had helped them, and how he had given some of the children scholarships to put them through school. (I found no evidence the children had ever been to school.) With no witnesses and such firm denials, the police were helpless and could not press charges. The man was released without charge and continued to live in the city, paying for sex with the children. When I was doing fieldwork, he still lived and worked there and had become such a regular client that nobody referred to the fact that he bought sex from the children. He was always euphemistically referred to as a friend by the adults or, by the children themselves, as a boyfriend.

I am in no way suggesting that because these children did not feel they had not been abused then they were not. I believe that when older, Western men, with their obvious financial, social, structural and physical power have sex with children, abuse is inevitable, and whatever the children said, they did not, and could not know, the wider political and economic forces under which they made their decisions. However the children were adamant that prostitution should be understood in terms of filial duty not abuse and, in the absence of other help available to them, saw their clients as sources of help, not exploitation. As I will go on to argue, this attitude is one of the many factors that makes bringing such men to justice problematic.

Extra-territoriality

Given the apparent invulnerability of such men, the appalling nature of the crimes being committed, and the public outcry about them, in the mid-1990s pressure began to mount on sending countries to pass extra-territorial legislation which would enable men to be prosecuted in their home countries for offences committed against children on foreign soil. In some cases men who had escaped justice in

Thailand were untouchable in their home countries. Sweden, for instance, does not extradite its citizens to non-Nordic countries while the UK insisted that crimes committed abroad must remain in the jurisdiction of the country in which they were committed (Hirst, 2003: 268). In 1994, Australia became the first country to introduce extra-territorial legislation, passing the Crimes (Child Sex Tourism) Amendment Act which brought in penalties of up to 17 years imprisonment for those convicted of sexual crimes against children overseas (Hall, 1998). Norway, Germany, France, Belgium, New Zealand and Sweden all passed similar laws and successful prosecutions were quickly obtained in 1996 in Australia and in 1997 in France (Hodgson, 1995; National Center for Missing and Exploited Children, 1999; Hoose et al., 2000; Seabrook, 2000; Montgomery, 2008; for a summary of the laws in each country see WTO, n.d). Interestingly the first case to be success-fully brought before the Swedish courts was that Bengt Bolin, mentioned above, who was sentenced to three months' imprisonment in 1995 for his crime of having sex with a teenage boy in Thailand. It was his case more than any other that pur-ported to show the value of extra-territorial legislation. Here was a man who had escaped justice in Thailand and yet found no hiding place in his home country.

After its initial reluctance, and in response to public and NGO pressure, the UK government passed The Sex Offenders Act in March 1997, which empowered the courts to prosecute people who committed sex offences against children abroad if what they had done constituted a crime in both countries. In 2003 the law was changed again, making it compulsory for those with a conviction for a sex offence against a child to inform the police if they planned to travel abroad for more than three days (Sexual Offences Act 2003). This law also allowed the courts to issue Foreign Travel Orders, which could be used to ban convicted paedophiles from travelling to countries where there was a risk of them abusing children (Beddoe, 2008). In 2008 the government amended further the laws on sexual offences. The Criminal Justice and Immigration Act 2008 (Section 72) withdrew the 'dual crimi-nality' clause, meaning that men could now be prosecuted for offences abroad, even if the offence, such as 'grooming', was not a crime in the country where it took place.

Despite these legal initiatives, the UK's record on enforcing such laws has not been good. There have been a limited number of prosecutions and these have not always been straightforward. One of the first cases to be brought under this legislation, for example, was not a sex-tourism case but involved the rape of a 15-year-old girl by her mother's boyfriend during a holiday to Barbados. Although the man was convicted, this conviction was later quashed on the grounds that the offence had taken place before the Act was in force (Hirst, 2003: 271). There have been only five convictions in the UK since 1997 compared with over 65 in the USA and 28 in Australia. Similarly Foreign Travel Orders have only been issued to three men convicted of child sex abuse, compared to over 3000 issued to football hooligans (Beddoe, 2008: 18).

Although there have been only a few convictions, these stories have received wide-spread publicity and the idea that having sex with children abroad is now a risk-free venture is slowly changing. In 2001, Mark Towner received an eight-year sentence for hiring two seven-year-old girls in Cambodia, having sex with them and filming himself doing so. In 2008, Alexander Kilpatrick was given six years for 17 assorted sex offences against boys under 13 in Ghana. He was also banned from travelling to Africa, Thailand, Cambodia, Goa or Costa Rica. In April 2009, Dean Hardy was also sentenced to six years in prison in the UK for indecent assault and taking and possessing indecent photographs of young girls in Thailand.

The push for changes in international legislation has come alongside a greater will-ingness for tourist receiving countries to prosecute British nationals. Despite the paucity of convictions in the UK, there is evidence of more men being arrested and convicted abroad, not only in countries such as Thailand and Cambodia but also in places such as Kenya, Albania and India. In response to international pressure and the shame of developing a reputation as a paedophiles' playground, Thailand introduced new laws in 1996 designed to protect children. Amongst other things, these allowed for the prosecution of parents, procurers and the customers of child prostitutes so that anyone who had sex with a child under 15 could be sent to jail for between two and six years and could be imprisoned for up to three years if the child was between 15 and 18 years old. ECPAT started to monitor the arrests of British men throughout the world and claims to have data on over 120 British nationals arrested or convicted for sexual abuse of children since the early 1990s (Beddoe, 2008). Perhaps the most notorious of these cases is that of Gary Glitter, whose arrest for sexual offences against young girls in Vietnam caused a media storm in the UK, but also showed up very clearly how, despite the legislation in place and the good intentions to find and punish those responsible for sexual offences against children, there were still major loopholes in the system.

The 1970s glam-rock star Gary Glitter (the stage name of Paul Gadd) was first identified as a child abuser in 1997 when he took his computer into a branch of PC World in Bristol to be repaired. On it, a technician found images of child pornography, including ones involving the sexual torture of very young children. Glitter was arrested and sentenced to four months' imprisonment in the UK in 1999. The case generated sensational headlines and at the end of his sentence the press were determined to watch him closely and follow his next moves. First Glitter moved to Cuba but the media frenzy led to the Cuban authorities demanding that he left. He then travelled on to Cambodia where he lived before the government in Phnom Penh began to investigate his past and, worried that the country might become seen as a safe haven for paedophiles, asked him to leave voluntarily in May 2002. When he returned later that year, he was arrested for alleged sexual assaults against young boys and deported to Thailand with an order banning him from travelling to Cambodia again. He moved from Thailand to Vietnam and it was there, in 2005, that the Vietnamese and British press announced that he was wanted by the Vietnamese authorities for sexual crimes against children, including rape. On 19 November 2005 he was arrested at Ho Chi Minh airport trying to board a plane to Thailand.

When his case came to trial, it quickly became a media circus, fuelled not only by Glitter's celebrity status but also because the charge of child rape in Vietnam carries the possibility of death by firing squad. Glitter was originally charged with rape and sexual misconduct against a 10 and an 11-year-old girl, although the rape charge was dropped due to insufficient evidence. Glitter reportedly gave money to the girls' families and they petitioned the court for clemency on his behalf. Nevertheless, Glitter was convicted and sentenced to three years in prison (he could have been sentenced to up to seven). In August 2008 he was released and this time the media furore turned into a farce. Glitter was supposed to leave Vietnam for the UK where he was due to arrive just as the Home Secretary, Jacqui Smith, planned to announce new legislation to prevent sex tourism abroad (Drummond, 2008). Glitter however boarded a flight to Thailand and because he had no convictions in Thailand, and because the Thai authorities had not been informed that he was arriving, or that he had been deported from Vietnam having been convicted of sexual offences against children, he was free to enter the country. It was only the international media storm that alerted them and led to a 48-hour standoff at Bangkok airport during which Glitter claimed to be ill, shouted abuse at consular officials and refused to leave the immigration area. Eventually he was put on a plane to Hong Kong with instructions to Hong Kong officials to return him to Thailand with their own deportation paperwork so that they could send him back to London (for a full account of these 48 hours see Drummond, 2008).

Not surprisingly there was little sympathy for Glitter but his trip back to the UK exposed some serious flaws in the international child protection system. Glitter had been caught, not by the coordinated efforts of international police forces but by the media. While there was undoubtedly something distasteful about the way Glitter was hounded before and after his trial and the obvious disappointment in some quarters that he would not face a firing squad, it was also clear that he was only denied entry to Thailand and returned to the UK thanks to the efforts of particular journalists. The Thai authorities claimed to have no knowledge of Glitter's crimes in the UK or his deportation from Vietnam. The Child Exploitation and Online Protection Unit (CEOP), set up by Scotland Yard in 2006 with the remit of 'tracking and bringing offenders to account either directly or in partnership with local and international forces' (CEOP, 2009) claimed to have told the Thai authorities about Glitter's crimes but the warnings had not been passed on. A CEOP officer in Bangkok did not have an official, written record of Glitter's convictions from the UK and had to try and persuade him to leave Thailand but had no authority to force him (Drummond, 2008).

Glitter might have been one of the highest profile abusers abroad but even so there was no coordinated effort to make sure that he was deported and, more importantly, that he was in no position to abuse children again. For less well-known abusers, there is even less pressure to track them and protect other children. Bangkok-based journalist Andrew Drummond points out that in 2009 there has not been a Police Liaison officer at the British Embassy for two years and that reports of child sex abuse made to the Serious Organised Crime Agency (SOCA) based in Bangkok are usually referred back to a London press office. CEOP's website has a report form for members of the public to report their concerns about possible child abuse but it is not possible to report suspicious activity from Thailand or Cambodia, only Australia, Canada, Italy and the United States. There seems to be no way of reporting fears about British men behaving inappropriately in the very countries that have the most serious problems.

Discussion and conclusions

All these new laws have come too late for the children of Baan Nua. In 1998 the first confirmed AIDS-related deaths occurred in Baan Nua (there had been deaths before from tuberculosis, which I assume, but cannot prove, were HIV-related). These had shocked an already vulnerable community and it quickly disbanded, with some families travelling to Bangkok, others going back to rural communities and a few others staying on in the city in which I encountered them, continuing to sell sex to foreigners while they still could. The laws of extra-territoriality would have had little impact on their lives, compared to sympathetic interventions which enabled parents and children to stay together. Their case is interesting however because it suggests the messy complexities of children's lived experiences and, even a brief description of these children's lives and their relationships with their clients, shows the difficulties of formulating legislation that would protect them. For a start, the children and their families had no interest in seeing their clients prosecuted, or even stopped from entering Baan Nua. In the absence of any social support or any form of welfare, these men were the only form of protection they had, no matter how damaging that might seem to outsiders. Obtaining a conviction, in either Thailand or the UK, would be close to impossible. Second, the men who used these children were, on the whole, long-term residents of Thailand. They did not come on holiday as part of any sort of tourist package or as part of any organised paedophile organisation. The extent to which they were tourists was highly debatable. They were already breaking the law but there seemed limited interest in prosecuting them and they lived quite openly in Thailand. Third, the change of law in Thailand meant that parents could now be prosecuted if they allowed or encouraged their children to work as prostitutes. Given the emphasis the children placed on family relationships and filial obligations, such laws would make it extremely difficult for the children to ask for help, even if they recognised they needed it. Keeping the family together was their primary justification for what they did, the prosecution and imprisonment of their parents their worst fear.

Trying and condemning individual men has a neatness to it which is appealing: it unites Western NGOs and governments with their Thai counterparts, and it makes a symbolic gesture that this problem is also the West's responsibility. It makes the accused paedophiles confront the seriousness of their abuse and, one would hope, makes other men reflect before they travel to buy sex from children. Yet it is questionable whose needs are fulfilled by these prosecutions. For NGOs and governments there are tangible benefits to prosecution; proof that something palpable is being done, in spite of the legal and constitutional difficulties. For the child prostitutes however, the picture is less clear; compensation may be offered or they may feel a certain satisfaction in seeing their abusers go to prison. Set against this is their risk of exposure, of the trauma of being made to give evidence and the issue of what happens to them on their return home. Will their parents be prosecuted? Will they be placed in care, given counselling and alternatives to prostitution? Will they be stigmatised in the eyes of the government and their communities? Or will they simply be forgotten? Reflection is needed on all these areas.

It is hard to know what effect the publicity about paedophiles being prosecuted abroad or in the UK has had on other men who may be tempted to travel overseas to have sex with children or who might decide to do so once they are there. Internationally, the media emphasis has shifted from Thailand to Vietnam and Cambodia which might suggest that Thailand is no longer seen as the safe haven it once was for child sexual abusers. However while the arrests of British and other foreign men in Thailand no longer make international news, a trawl through the Pattaya Daily News (Pattaya being one of the main destinations for sex tourism) shows the problem is as rife as ever. In May 2008, a headline read 'British man arrested in Pattaya for luring underage boy for sexual purposes' while in December the paper sounded positively weary: 'Yet another foreign gay arrested in Pattaya with underage boys'. The following May, it announced, '2 Swedish, 1 British paedophiles arrested in Pattaya'. Clearly in some parts of the Thailand the message has still not got through and it is safe to assume that while a handful of men have been arrested, there are plenty others who have not and who continue to buy sex from children. Andrew Drummond, on his website, continues to report the Western men who are arrested, as well as those alleged offenders who evade justice, and continues to comment on the inadequacy of CEOP14. He discusses a number of incidents, including a recent case from July 2009 in which a number of men from outside Thailand were arrested for sexual offences against children as part of Operation Naga, led by the CEOP in collaboration with the Royal Thai Police. Once the CEOP officers left the country, the legal case collapsed, largely due to the disappearance from protective custody of a key witness (Drummond, 2009).

In this instance it may well be unfair to criticise CEOP. They cannot, and should not, have authority over the Royal Thai Police and it was clearly the latter's responsibility to secure convictions and jail sentences for these men if found guilty. Nevertheless, once again, such cases show the gaps in the system which many men are still using to exploit children and which show no signs of being closed, despite the best of intentions. Again the issue of enforcement is crucial. The many changes in the law have not, as ECPAT have acknowledged, proved a great deterrent (Beddoe, 2008: 7), although it is impossible to know if they have altered some men's behaviour. There still remains a belief that it is possible to get away with the sexual abuse of children overseas in a way that it is not in the UK or other tourist sending countries. It is also true that the poverty of several South East Asian countries results in some families allowing their sons and daughters to work as prostitutes and that for many, a rich, white foreigner still represents a good source of income. Compared with the low wages and brutal conditions of many local brothels (DaGrossa, 1989; Fordham, 2005), selling sex to foreigners is by no means the worst form of sexual abuse. While it may sound deeply crass to come up with a hierarchy of abuse, the children that I knew in Baan Nua were very clear on this point. Prostitution was not something they liked doing but with foreign men they had the chance to eat well, go to places they could not afford, such as amusement arcades or theme parks and, paradoxically, enjoy some aspects of a childhood otherwise denied to them. Compared with being debt-bonded in a brothel, working in a sweatshop or scavenging for rubbish, this was an easier option.

Yet because of the emphasis on extra-territorial legislation, and the pursuit of individual men, the problem of child sex tourism has become cast as a straightforward moral issue concerned with the moral depravity of the tourists in contrast to the betrayed innocence of the children. In the case of Thailand, questions about sex tourism as an overall strategy for development have been sidestepped, as have issues of police corruption and lack of enforcement. The focus of anti-child abuse campaigns has been on the despicable abusers and other issues such as rehabilitating the children affected, or indeed, changing government policy have been given less importance than pursuing and punishing the wrongdoer.

It is also the case that it is the media that continues to pursue paedophiles most enthusiastically and who are bringing paedophiles to justice by collecting evidence, informing the authorities and even shaming national governments in action. As Drummond (2008) concludes:

> A British child sexual abuser in Thailand is much more likely to be identified by a member of the British public. And the public are much more inclined to call a British tabloid newspaper than Thai police, or even CEOP.

While much of this reporting is responsible, informative and campaigning, it also remains the case that stories about paedophiles sell newspapers and much of the reporting of their crimes remains prurient and sensationalist. Serious questions need to be asked about the delegation of justice, and punishment, to the media. This may be condoned as an effective, if rough sort of justice, especially if no other form seems to be available but it is also a dangerous strategy, not least because it does little to help the child victims or indeed, to prevent the abuse of other children.

References

Axelsson, M. (1997) *Rosario is Dead*, Manila: Anvil Publishing.

Beddoe, C. (2008) *Return to Sender. British Child Sex Offenders Abroad – Why More Must Be Done*, London: ECPAT UK.

Black Shadow (1949) *Dream Lover: The Book for Men Only*, Bangkok: Vitayakorn.

Boonchalaksi, W. and Guest, P. (1994) *Prostitution in Thailand*, Mahidol University, Bangkok: Institute for Population and Social Research.

Bureau of Democracy, Human Rights, and Labor (2008) Human Rights Report: Thailand, Washington: 2008 Country Reports on Human Rights Practices, http://www.state.gov/g/drl/rls/hrrpt/2008/eap/119058.htm, accessed 25 November 2009.

CEOP (Child Exploitation and Online Protection) 'About us', http://www.ceop.gov.uk/, accessed 27 November 2009.

Cohen, E. (1982) 'Thai girls and Farang men – the edge of ambiguity', *Annals of Tourism Research*, 9 (3), 403–442.

DaGrossa, P. (1989) 'Kamphaeng Din: a study of prostitution in the All–Thai brothels of Chiang Mai City', *Crossroads*, 4 (2), 1–7.

Day, S. (2007) *On the Game: Women and Sex Work*, Pluto Press: London.

Drummond, A. (2008) 'Gary Glitter – where they went wrong', http://www.andrew-drummond.com/2008/11/20/gary-glitter-where-they-went-wrong/, accessed 25 November 2009.

Drummond, A. (2009) 'Briton arrested for third time on child sex charges – Thailand', http://www.andrew-drummond.com/2009/07/22/briton-arrested-for-third-time-on-child-sex-charges-thailand/, accessed 25 November 2009.

ECPAT (1993) *Report on International Consultation*, ECPAT: Bangkok.

ECTWT (1990) *Caught in Modern Slavery: Tourism and Child Prostitution in Asia*, ECTWT: Bangkok.

Eades, J.S. (2009) 'Moving bodies: the intersections of sex, work, and tourism', in D. Wood (ed.), *Economic Development, Integration, and Morality in Asia and the Americas*, Bingley: Emerald Publishing Group, pp. 225-253.

Ennew, J. (1986) *The Sexual Exploitation of Children*, Cambridge: Polity Press.

Fordham, G. (2005) *A New Look at Thai AIDS: Perspectives from the Margin*, Oxford: Berghahn.

Fox, M. (1960) Problems of Prostitution in Thailand, Bangkok: Department of Public Welfare.

Hall, C.M. (1998) 'The legal and political dimensions of sex tourism: the case of Australia's child sex tourism legislation', in M. Oppermann (ed.), *Sex Tourism and Prostitution: Aspects of Leisure, Recreation, and Work*, New York: Cognizant Communication.pp. 87-96.

Hantrakul, S. (1983) 'Prostitution in Thailand', paper presented to the Women in Asia Workshop, Monash University.

Hirst, M. (2003) *Jurisdiction and the Ambit of the Criminal Law*, Oxford: Oxford University Press.

Hodgson, D. (1995) 'Combating the organized sexual exploitation of Asian children: recent developments and prospects', *International Journal of Family and the Law*, **9** (1), 23–53.

Hoose, J., Clift, S. and Carter, S. (2000) 'Combating tourist exploitation of children', in S. Clift and S. Carter (eds), *Tourism and Sex: Culture, Commerce and Coercion*, London: Pinter. pp. 74-90.

Kane, J. (1998) *Sold for Sex*, Aldershot: Ashgate.

Kempadoo, K., Sanghera, J. and Pattanaik, B. (2005) *Trafficking and Prostitution Reconsidered: New Perspectives on Migration, Sex Work, and Human Rights*, Boulder, CO: Paradigm.

Landon, K. (1939) *Siam in Transition: A Brief Survey of Cultural Trends in the Five Years since the Revolution of 1932*, Oxford: Oxford University Press.

League of Nations (1933) *Report of the Council by the Commission into theTraffic in Women and Children in the East*, Geneva: League of Nations.

Montgomery, H. (2001a) *Modern Babylon? Prostituting Children in Thailand*, Oxford: Berghahn.

Montgomery, H. (2001b) 'Child sex tourists: myths and realities', in D. Harrison (ed.), *Tourism and the Less Developed World. Issues and Case Studies*, 2nd edn, Wallingford, CABI. pp. 191-202.

Montgomery, H. (2007) 'Working with child prostitutes in Thailand: problems of practice and interpretation', *Childhood*, **14** (4), 415–430.

Montgomery, H. (2008) 'Buying innocence: child sex tourists in Thailand', *Third World Quarterly*, **29** (5), 903–917.

Muecke, M.A. (1992) 'Mother sold food, daughter sells her body – the cultural continuity of prostitution', *Social Science and Medicine*, **35** (7), 891–901.

Murray, A. (1998) 'Debt-bondage and trafficking: don't believe the hype', in K.Kempadoo and J. Doezema (eds), *Global Sex Workers: Rights, Resistance, and Redefinition*, Routledge: New York. pp. 51-64.

Narvesen, O. (1989) *The Sexual Exploitation of Children in Developing Countries*, Oslo: Redd Barna.

National Center for Missing and Exploited Children (1999) *Prostitution of Children and Child-Sex Tourism: An Analysis of Domestic and International Responses*, Virginia: National Center for Missing and Exploited Children.

O'Connell Davidson, J. (2005) *Children in the Global Sex Trade*, Polity Press: Cambridge.

O'Connell-Davidson, J. and Sánchez Taylor, J. (2005) 'Travel and taboo: heterosexual sex tourism to the Caribbean', in E. Bernstein and L. Schaffner (eds), *Regulating Sex: The Politics of Intimacy and Identity*, New York: Routledge, pp. 83-100

O'Grady, R. (1992) *The Child and the Tourist*, Bangkok: ECPAT.

Oppermann, M. (1998) 'Who exploits whom and who benefits', in M. Oppermann (ed.), *Sex Tourism and Prostitution: Aspects of Leisure, Recreation, and Work*, New York: Cognizant Communication. pp. 153-160.

Sánchez Taylor, J. (2006) 'Female sex tourism: a contradiction in terms', *Feminist Review*, 83 (1), 42–59.

Seabrook, J. (2000) *No Hiding Place: Child Sex Tourism and the Role of Extraterritorial Legislation*, London: Zed Books.

ten Brummelhuis, H. (1993) 'Do we need a Thai theory of prostitution?', paper presented at the Fifth International Conference on Thai Studies, SOAS, London 1993.

World Tourism Organisation (n.d) 'Protection of children in tourism – legislation', http://www.unwto.org/protect_children/campaign/en/legislation.php?op=1&subop=7, accessed 25 November 2009.

6 Flying without Wings: drug tourism and the political economy of pleasure

Michael Shiner

This chapter includes a discussion of the following themes:

◆ Drug tourism and the legal prohibition of drugs
◆ The social meaning of drug tourism
◆ Drug use at home and away
◆ Drug use and social change.

Drug use offers a potentially fertile meeting ground for criminology and tourism studies. One of the most obvious intersections between these two fields of study occurs when tourism involves criminal behaviour, which is generally the case with drug tourism. There are, moreover, notable conceptual links as drug use raises a series of themes, including the pursuit of pleasure, excitement and escape that are relevant to the study of both crime and tourism. Despite several potential points of contact, criminology and tourism studies have tended to develop their interest in drug use in isolation from one another (but see Belhassen et al., 2007). The aim here is to promote dialogue between them. To this end, the following discussion is divided into three parts: the first considers political and ideological dimensions of drug tourism, paying particular attention to the role of prohibition and reform; the second is more conceptual in its focus and highlights some striking parallels between the way in which criminology and tourism studies have sought to understand drug use, with both fields of study having linked this behaviour to broader existential concerns such as the search for meaning and fulfilment in 'late industrial' or 'post modern' societies. The third part seeks to locate drug tourism within broader debates about social change. The unifying theme, linking the different parts of the chapter together, is provided by the claim that criminology and tourism studies offer ways of looking at drug use that are simultaneously different yet complementary, creating opportunities for synthesis and exchange.

Before starting the analysis, some preliminary comments are required about exactly what it is that constitutes drug tourism. This is a matter of some debate, with definitions varying in terms of the range of behaviours they cover. According to

Valdez and Sifaneck (1997: 880) drug tourism refers to 'the phenomenon by which persons become attracted to a particular location because of the accessibility of licit or illicit drugs and related services'. Such a definition applies only to those for whom drug use provides the main motivation for travel and excludes various other manifestations of drug use in the context of tourism. A broader, and arguably more satisfactory, definition is provided by Uriely and Belhassen (2005: 239), which includes tourists for whom drug taking appears to be more spontaneous:

Accordingly, tourists who are aware of the accessibility of illegal or illegitimate drugs in a particular location and consume these drugs during their stay in these locations are defined here as drug tourists. This definition refers to both tourists who are attracted to a specific destination because of their previous knowledge about the accessibility of drugs at this site and tourists who become aware of the accessibility of drugs only during their stay in a particular location. Moreover, drug consumption might not necessarily function as the major travel motivation for these tourists but only as a by product of their tourist experience.

Drug tourism and the politics of control

Drug tourism is sometimes attributed to liberal drug regimes that are said to act as a 'magnet' to drug tourists. While international conventions aim to restrict the use of controlled substances to 'legitimate' medical, industrial and scientific purposes, the specifics of implementation are left to individual states, with the result that there are marked variations between jurisdictions (Elvins, 2003). Some states have adopted significantly less punitive and restrictive forms of drug control than others, but, even so, the suggestion that liberal policies are responsible for drug tourism is difficult to sustain. Such claims fail to appreciate that liberal regimes only act as a magnet to drug tourists in the context of prohibition: that is to say, it is inconsistencies between jurisdictions, rather than liberal regimes per se, that promote drug tourism and channel it in certain directions. More fundamentally, liberal regimes are neither a necessary nor sufficient condition for drug tourism. It is not just that drug tourism is evident in places where such behaviour is criminalised, but that there are also cases where the introduction of more liberal policies has not generated the expected upsurge in drug tourism. In illustrating these points particular attention will be paid to the Netherlands, Mexico and Portugal.

The Dutch policy of *Gedogen*

The Netherlands has adopted one of the most explicitly tolerant approaches to drug control of all Western industrial nations and, in so doing, has highlighted some important, albeit fairly subtle, legal and practical distinctions (MacCoun and Reuter, 2001). Consistent with the broader policy of gedogen (condoning), whereby small wrongdoings are tolerated in order to prevent more serious offences, the Dutch have sought to separate the market for cannabis from that for more harmful substances, so that young people, in particular, may experiment with cannabis without being exposed to more harmful substances at the same time. What this means in practice is that cannabis can be bought openly from 'coffee shops' in several towns and cities and, though possession remains formally illegal, penalties are not imposed for small amounts. Neither legalisation nor decriminalisation accurately describe this system, which is, perhaps, best understood in terms of de-penalisation and commercialisation or 'de facto legalisation' (MacCoun and Reuter, 2001).[1] In 1976 the authorities adopted a formal written policy of non-enforcement for violations involving the possession or sale of up to 30 grams of cannabis and, during the 10 years that followed, guidelines were formulated which paved the way for a form of regulated supply or quasi-legal commercial availability. According to these guidelines coffee-shop owners could avoid prosecution by complying with the rules of: (1) no advertising; (2) no 'hard' drug sales on the premises; (3) no sales to minors; and (4) no public disturbances. Under these guidelines, depenalisation evolved into de facto legalisation in the form of an expanding network of coffee shops engaging in increasingly overt forms of promotion: from a handful of establishments in the early 1980s, the number of coffee shops increased to something like 1200 to 1500 by 1995, with approximately 350 to 450 in Amsterdam alone (MacCoun and Reuter, 2001). It remains something of an oddity that, while the retail sale of cannabis has been commercialised, the wholesale end of the operation remains unregulated, with the result that coffee-shop owners have to break the law on the trade and/or growth of cannabis (Pakes, 2004).

The Dutch policy of isolating the cannabis market, alongside an explicit commitment to harm reduction, has been credited with a range of positive outcomes including a low number of heroin addicts, relatively few drug-related deaths and low rates of HIV infection among addicts (Pakes, 2004; see also MacCoun and Reuter, 2001). Contrary to the predictions that were made in some quarters, moreover, these outcomes have not been gained at the expense of particularly high rates of cannabis use: the initial phase of de-penalisation had no discernable effect on the prevalence of cannabis use domestically and, though commercialisation has created a very visible drug presence, it is one that gives an exaggerated impression of the 'true magnitude of Dutch drug problems' (MacCoun and Reuter, 2001: 239). Cannabis use did increase sharply with the growth of the coffee shops, though there is some debate about the extent to which this trend can be attributed directly to commercialisation, with some commentators pointing to broadly similar increases in other states (Korf, 2002). Even allowing for the possible effects

1 Decriminalisation refers to the removal of drug offences from the realm of the criminal law. Prohibition remains the rule, but only non-criminal sanctions, such as fines or treatment requirements, are imposed. Depenalisation represents a less radical alternative based on the reduction or removal of penal sanctions provided for by law. Applied to drugs, depenalisation often refers to the elimination of custodial penalties, though other criminal sanctions, such as fines, police records, probation, remain available. Under fully blown legalisation, the law imposes no prohibitions of any kind on the manufacture, sale, possession, or use of drugs (see Greenwald, 2009).

of commercialisation, levels of cannabis use in the Netherlands remain someway below those that are evident in other jurisdictions, including some such as the United States and United Kingdom that have continued to pursue punitive policies (Police Foundation, 2000; MacCoun and Reuter, 2001). While domestic levels of cannabis use remain unexceptional, there is no doubt that Dutch coffee shops attract a large tourist trade. According to one, admittedly dated, estimate, foreign visitors buy cannabis worth $180 million a year directly from such establishments, whilst spending considerably more on hotels, restaurants and visiting other tourist sites, so that 'narco-tourism' accounts for as much as 25 per cent of the country's total tourist income (Morais, 1996). More recent research conducted in four border towns on behalf of the Justice Department reported a quadrupling of cannabis sales from 1993 to 2001 and identified approximately 2000 drug tourists in Maastricht alone, who were said to spend an estimated €87,000 on an average weekend day: figures that the local association of coffee shops used to estimate the annual turnover from cannabis sales to be €36,000,000, claiming that revenue from cannabis outstripped that from conventional tourism (see Lemmens, 2002).

Although positively regarded in some quarters, the position of the Dutch coffee-shop system remains precarious. The coffee shops continue to operate in a legal grey area and have faced something of a political backlash in recent years, which has led to tighter regulation. Whilst the introduction of a more restrictive approach has been part of a broader realignment of Dutch crime control strategy (Pakes, 2004), it also reflects specific anxieties about foreign drug tourists and border control. With the prospect of the free movement of people and goods, European unification brought unwanted attention to Dutch policy, with one French legislator branding the Netherlands a 'narco-state' and another French official describing it as: 'An airport surrounded by coffee-shops' (cited in MacCoun and Reuter, 2001: 248). In 1992, the President of the United Nation's International Narcotics Control Board warned the Dutch authorities that the policy of tolerating cannabis sales was in violation of the 1961 Single Convention and, as such, constituted a breach of international law. The Dutch authorities responded by implementing something of a crackdown, introducing a licensing system, lowering the 30-gram limit on sales to 5 grams and threatening to close up to half of all coffee shops. In the event, the number of coffee shops declined by slightly more than a third, from around 1200 in 1997 to slightly less than 750 in 2004 (*Deutsche Welle*, 2007). More recently, the Ministry of Foreign Affairs has expressed particular concerns about the 'frequent' trouble caused by coffee shops along the German border, while conservative politicians, such as Cisca Joldersma, have resisted further liberalisation on the grounds that it 'would only mean more drugs tourists and encourage the criminals' (cited in Donkin, 2006). Calling for 'one strong European policy, which the Netherlands has to adopt', Joldersma has proposed that most coffee shops be closed and identity cards be issued to Dutch users, so that foreign visitors can be kept out of those that remain.

Despite these pressures, the Dutch authorities have refused to abandon the coffee-shop system altogether and the backlash has not gone unchallenged, with some commentators arguing that the situation requires greater liberalisation, not less. In a short film, *Smoking without Borders: Drug Tourism in the Netherlands*, the Hungarian Civil Liberties Union (2009) concluded that the problem of drug tourism is not caused by the coffee shops so much as by the restrictive policies pursued in neighbouring countries. The limitations of prohibition have also been highlighted by Gerd Leers, Mayor of Maastricht, which lies close to the Belgian and German borders. Drawing attention to a series of problems related to the current system, ranging from harassment and pubic order offences by drug tourists to the activities of international crime gangs that operate drug supply lines, Leers called for a common 'pragmatic approach' to 'soft' drugs throughout Europe, including the creation of 'cannabis boulevards' in border areas to ease problems associated with drug tourism and the extension of the current licensing system on the grounds that this would promote more effective regulation and allow coffee-shop owners to grow their own cannabis, cutting ties with 'the criminals' (Farrington, 2005; Donkin, 2006).

What has actually transpired is much closer to the 'strong' system advocated by Joldersma. In May 2009 Mayor Lees announced that the province of Limburg would start issuing membership cards, effectively turning the region's 30 or so coffee shops into 'private members' clubs' in an attempt to exclude foreign drug tourists (The Age, 2009; Kievit, 2009). While Leers has maintained that closing the coffee shops is not viable because it risks 'chasing clients into illegality', the introduction of membership cards represents an unambiguous departure from the relatively liberal tradition of Dutch cannabis control. This move has the backing of national government and is being seen as a pilot project for possible expansion to other areas. According to the Home Affairs Minister, Guusje ter Horst, the introduction of the membership system is the first step in a 'harder approach to illegality' by law enforcement, while the Dutch Council of State has asked the European Court of Justice to weigh the legality of limiting access to coffee shops to Dutch citizens.

The 'war on drugs' in Mexico

Drug tourism takes on particular significance in Mexico because of its proximity to the United States, which represents one of the world's largest illicit drug markets while simultaneously providing the main driving force behind global prohibition. Since the early 1970s, US authorities have pursued an aggressively interventionist policy throughout Latin America under the banner of the 'war on drugs', applying intense political pressure to countries that are closely involved in the production and/or transit of illicit substances and promoting greater use of the military and chemical defoliants. What this has meant for Mexico is 'an absolute dependency referred to in the euphemistic language of diplomacy as bilateral cooperation'

(Astorga, 2001: 428). Initially, at least, Mexico was fairly isolated from the negative consequences of the drugs trade – heroin and cocaine were not widely used, drug production and trafficking were not considered major issues and there was no great popular or political support for the war on drugs – but these circumstances changed dramatically during the course of the 1980s. As US authorities disrupted established trafficking routes through the Caribbean (Mares, 2003), Colombian drug cartels required alternative routes into north America and began trafficking large amounts of cocaine and heroin though Mexico, drawing local gangs into the operation and creating massive problems of addiction, corruption and violence (Carlsen, 2007; The Economist, 2009). These problems have, in turn, been used by US authorities to support further intervention and investment in militarisation, albeit expressed through the language of cooperation and partnership. Retired US army general and former 'drugs tsar', Barry McCaffrey (2008), declared that Mexico could become a 'narco-state' in the next decade, claiming that its 'dangerous and worsening problems... fundamentally threaten U.S. national security', while President George Bush introduced a three-year $1.4 billion programme of security aid for Mexico and Central America, known as the Merida Initiative. As a result, the Mexican government under Felipe Calderón has agreed to unprecedented levels of cooperation with US authorities, extending to the extradition of drug traffickers and talk of joint military operations (Daniel, 2007; The Guardian, 2009). Further militarisation has, nonetheless, been accompanied by an escalation of violence and a sharp increase in the murder rate, with more than 5000 deaths attributed to drug-related violence in 2008 alone and growing fears of kidnap and extortion amid claims that the drug gangs are winning the war for Mexico (Carpenter, 2009).

Although Mexican drug policy has been greatly influenced by the USA, inconsistencies and tensions remain, giving rise to ongoing anxieties about border control and drug tourism. Drawing parallels with the position of cannabis in the Netherlands, Valdez and Sifaneck (1997) note how differences in the availability of prescription drugs have created a specific form of cross-border drug tourism. This phenomenon, they note, is 'driven by the inexpensive costs of these substances, legal access to drugs whose distribution is loosely controlled in Mexico, and the close physical proximity of Mexico to the United States' (1997: 880). Because of the relatively loose controls that operate in Mexico, US visitors can legally purchase prescription drugs for recreational purposes, before exploiting a loophole in US customs law to take them back across the border under a Mexican prescription. Despite the concerns that US authorities have raised about the quality of the products obtained in this manner, including the risks posed by 'mishandled' or 'counterfeit' drugs, the practice continues and there are numerous pharmacies located near the main crossing points in most Mexican border towns which actively target customers from the north (Timothy, 2005; Melville, 2009).

The control of illegal drugs has been a source of strain between the two countries. Such matters came to a head when President Calderón's predecessor, Vicente Fox, sought to distance his administration from the 'war on drugs'. Towards the end of his term in office, having previously proposed, but not implemented, the demilitarisation of domestic drugs policy, President Fox sought to liberalise the law on drugs possession, arguing that this would enable the authorities to concentrate on supply-side activities (McKinley and Broder, 2006). A bill de-penalising possession of small amounts of marijuana, ecstasy, cocaine, heroin and other illicit substances was passed by Congress, awakening fears in the USA that holiday destinations, such as Cancún and Acapulco, which are popular among American college students, would become a magnet for drug tourism and that border towns, such as Tijuana and Ciudad Juárez would become the Mexican equivalent of Amsterdam (Hider and Reid, 2006; McKinley and Broder, 2006). Under intense diplomatic pressure from the USA, Fox vetoed the bill, which he returned to Congress, calling for changes to be made in order 'to make it absolutely clear that in our country the possession of drugs and their consumption are and continue to be crimes' (cited in McKinley and Broder, 2006). Very similar proposals were approved by the legislature in 2009, which President Calderón is expected to authorise and which are not being publicly opposed by the newly installed US administration under President Obama (Transform, 2009; Tuckman, 2009).

Decriminalisation in Portugal

The notion that liberal regimes are responsible for drug tourism rests on the 'common-sense' assumption that punitive regimes provide an effective deterrent. This assumption does not stand up well to scrutiny, particularly given recent evidence that countries with stringent regimes do not have lower rates of drug use than those with liberal regimes (Degenhardt *et al.*, 2008). There are, moreover, numerous examples of drug tourism operating in the context of prohibition and of drug tourists readily assuming the risks associated with the violation of national and international drug law (Uriely and Belhassen, 2005). To a large extent, therefore, drug tourism may be considered to be the result of cultural practices that exist despite, rather than because of, any state-sponsored policy.

While liberal policies are not necessary for drug tourism to take place, nor are they sufficient to create it. That liberalisation does not inevitably lead to mass drug tourism is evident from recent experience in Portugal, which remains the only European Union member state to pursue an explicit policy of 'decriminalisation' (Greenwald, 2009). A national law, introduced in July 2001, removed possession of all illegal drugs for personal use from the criminal realm, deeming such offences to be administrative infractions. This reform was introduced with the aim of reducing drug use, drug abuse and related harms, but, in contrast to the situation in the Netherlands, has not involved any move towards commercial availability: 'drug trafficking' remains a criminal offence defined by the possession of more than the 'average' dose for ten days of use. Despite dire predictions from some quarters, the Portuguese approach has been largely successful: drug use has declined in many key categories, drug-related harms have been contained much more successfully than previously and fears about drug tourism have not materialised (Greenwald, 2009). With the introduction of the new law, Paulo Portas, leader of the conservative Popular Party, declared: 'There will be planeloads of students heading for [Portugal] to smoke marijuana and take a lot worse, knowing we won't put them in jail. We promise sun, beaches and any drug you like' (cited in Greenwald, 2009: 6). Such concerns have proved 'completely unfounded', with Portuguese nationals still making up the vast majority of those cited for drug offences (close to 95 per cent) and almost none being citizens of other EU states (Greenwald, 2009: 6). When considered alongside Dutch coffee shops and Mexican pharmacies, this suggests that, in so far as official policy has an impact, it is commercialisation rather than decriminalisation or de-penalisation that encourages drug tourism.

The meaning of drug tourism

The social meaning of drug tourism has received relatively little attention. In so far as tourism studies has considered deviant or marginal behaviour it has concentrated on sex tourism and the few studies that have focused on drug use have, until recently, been largely descriptive. Consequently, 'the phenomenon of drug consumption while travelling needs to be further examined in light of both existing theories and other seminal issues in tourism studies' (Uriely and Belhassen, 2005: 238).

The sacred and the profane

In an attempt to move beyond description, Uriely and Belhassen (2005) drew on Erik Cohen's (1979) phenomenological typology of tourist experiences. Influenced by Eliade's (1971) work on religious cosmology, Cohen conceptualised tourism in terms of movement between 'spiritual centres', which he defined as the centre – be it religious or cultural – that symbolises ultimate meanings for the individual. From a structural functionalist perspective, he noted tourism represents a 'temporary reversal of everyday activities – it is a no-work, no-care, no-thrift situation', that is, in itself, devoid of 'deeper meaning' (Cohen, 1979: 181). Challenging this 'simplistic' conception, Cohen contends that many 'moderns' are alienated from their society and may seek meaning in the centre of other societies, arguing that modern mass tourism is predicated upon 'the gradual abandonment of the traditional, sacred image of the cosmos, and the awakening of interest in the culture, social life and natural environment of others... Hence, it leads to a movement away from the spiritual, cultural or even religious centre of one's 'world', into its periphery, toward the centres of other cultures and societies' (ibid: 182–183).

At the heart of his analysis, Cohen identified five modes of tourist experience that are said to represent points on a continuum, ranging from the conception of space that is characteristic of modern tourism at one end to that of the pilgrimage at the other. Accordingly, these modes are ranked to span 'the range of motivations between the desire for mere pleasure characteristic of the sphere of "leisure" and the quest for meaning and authenticity, characteristic of the sphere of "religion"' (ibid.: 193). Each mode is defined by tourists' attitudes to their own culture and routine living, as well as the motivations and meanings they assign to engaging in the culture of the visited destination. The first and second modes, which were labelled recreational and diversionary respectively, are essentially palliative, resting on entertaining, but 'shallow' activities that do not involve any attempt to access the centre of the 'other'. Consequently, the 'intent and meaning' of the 'religious voyage' is 'secularized', losing its 'deeper, spiritual content' (ibid.: 184). What separates these modes from one another is the orientation they involve to the culture of origin: tourists in the recreational mode are committed to the centre of their own society, so that tourism serves as a 'pressure valve', refreshing and enabling them to return to the wear and tear of 'serious living'; whereas those in the diversionary mode are alienated from the goals and values of their everyday existence, so that travel loses its recreational significance and becomes purely diversionary: 'a mere escape from the boredom and meaninglessness of routine, everyday existence, into the forgetfulness of a vacation, which may heal the body and sooth the spirit, but does not "recreate" – i.e. it does not re-establish adherence to a meaningful centre, but only makes alienation endurable' (ibid.: 186). Noting that recreational and diversionary modes have been savagely criticised for lacking authenticity, Cohen suggests that the former, like other forms of mass-entertainment, appears from the perspective of 'high' culture to be 'shallow', 'superficial', 'trivial' and often 'frivolous', and that individuals travelling in this mode often appear 'gullible' and easily taken in by blatantly contrived, commercialised displays of culture. Whilst noting that recreation-seeking tourists may well thrive on 'pseudo-events', Cohen maintains that the contempt in which they are held on this account by intellectuals and 'serious' travellers is misplaced: these tourists get what they really want – the pleasure of entertainment, for which authenticity is largely irrelevant – and, as such, are quite eager to accept the make-believe without questioning its authenticity.

The remaining modes all involve a search for meaning in the centre of other cultures, each representing a different level of meaning. 'What', asks Cohen (1979: 186) 'happens when the disenchanted or alienated individuals become growingly aware of their state of alienation, and the meaninglessness and fatuity of their daily life, as many younger members of the middle classes in the "postmodern society" have become?'. One possibility, he notes, is that they attempt to transform their own society through revolution, while another, less radical, alternative is to look for meaning in the life of others through tourism. The third, experiential, mode of tourist experience is based on a quest for authenticity and is deemed an essentially religious quest involving observation of the 'authentic life' of others, albeit without any attempt to be converted or even engaged in their life. For tourists in this mode the main problem is telling for sure if the experience is authentic or not; a problem which is intensified by the deceptive machinations of the tourist establishment which 'stages authenticity' in an attempt to mislead tourists into believing they have succeeded in breaking through the contrived 'front' of the inauthentic into the authentic 'back' regions of the host society. The experiential mode is followed by 'still more profound modes of touristic experiences', which lead to the eventual closure of the gap separating the mode of experience of the modern mass tourist from that of the traditional pilgrim (Cohen, 1979: 188). Immediately after the experiential mode, comes the experimental mode, which extends beyond observation and includes attempts to participate in the authentic life of others without committing to any of the cultures that are encountered. Finally, the existential mode refers to travellers who are committed to an 'elective centre' that is culturally and geographically external to their own society. The acceptance of such a centre is said to come phenomenologically closest to a religious conversion, with travel to remote centres enabling individuals to actualise and sustain their spiritual existence.

The parallels between drug use and tourism were not lost on Cohen. Recognising that the quest for meaning may take forms other than travel, he suggested that mysticism and drug use may serve as alternative paths to the same goal and noted that Eliade (1971) considered internal and external quests for the centre to be homologous. Previously, Cohen (1973), followed by Westerhausen (2002), had considered drug use in the context of the drifter subculture, but did not do so in relation to tourism more broadly. Drawing on Cohen's (1979) work, Uriely and Belhassen (2005) sought to establish whether drug-related tourist experiences should be understood as a shallow sort of relaxation involving the pursuit of 'mere pleasure' or as a meaningful quest for uniquely profound experiences. In seeking answers to these questions, they also sought to establish how drug use while travelling relates to tourists' estrangement from their routine of everyday life and the pursuit of meaningful experiences in other cultures. Based primarily on depth interviews with 30 'homecoming' drug tourists, Uriely and Belhassen found a diversity of experience, validating previous indications that drug taking in the context of tourism might be associated with both a quest for 'meaningful experience' (see also, de Rios, 1994) and the 'pursuit of mere pleasure' (see also, Bellis et al., 2000; Sellars, 1998). More specifically, 20 interviewees were considered to comply with Cohen's two modes of pleasure-oriented experiences, 13 of whom conformed to the recreational mode and seven of whom conformed to the diversionary mode. The remaining interviewees were said to comply with the three modes that Cohen identified as being concerned with the quest for meaning, plus another – the humanist mode – that was added subsequently to refer to those who might look for meaning in other centres without being alienated from their own culture (Uriely et al., 2002). One interviewee was deemed to comply with the existential mode, four with the experimental mode, one with the experiential mode, and four with the humanistic mode.

Uriely and Belhassen (2005) identified three different types of cultural centre that provided the focus for the quest for meaning through drug tourism – local cultures, drug subcultures and alternative subcultures. Local cultures are place bound and include the goals and values that drug tourists identify as authentic aspects of the culture they are visiting. In this context, drug use acts a marker of the local culture and forms part of an attempt to experience aspects of that culture illustrating a particular version of the common quest for authenticity in tourism. The remaining centres are less territorialised. Drug subcultures are said to emerge around particular drugs, such as cannabis or peyote, users of which may share certain goals, values, practices and lifestyles. Unlike the first type of centre, where the drug serves as a marker of the local culture, in this type of centre the destination serves as a marker of the drug-related subculture: coffee shops in Amsterdam and peyote-related gatherings in Latin America provide examples of such cultural centres. Alternative subcultures, including rave and New Age, involve extensive use of various drugs alongside other practices and, like drug subcultures, are not place-bound, emerging within and across national boundaries.

The notion that tourism involves movement between cultural centres raises important questions about the relationship between tourists' behaviour in the visited destination and that in their place of origin. As far as drug use is concerned, Uriely and Belhassen (2005, 2006) found that this relationship varies with individuals' motivations. Many of those searching for 'deep meanings' first used drugs while on holiday, whereas most of the pleasure-seekers had already engaged in such behaviour as part of their ordinary leisure activities, suggesting that their drug-related tourist experiences are an intensified extension of their everyday leisure activities (see also Sellars, 1998; Bellis *et al.*, 2000). While this pattern of intensification is consistent with the idea that tourism offers a time and space where people feel less restrained and more able to undertake adventure, the notion of the risk-taking tourist as an unrestrained action seeker has been challenged. Uriely and Belhassen (2006) report little evidence that such influences form part of the motivation to use drugs while travelling and found that drug tourists continue to restrain their behaviour in line with their perceptions of the associated risks. These authors also cast into doubt the underlying assumption that drug tourism represents an attempt to escape the boredom of routine life or involves estrangement from the mainstream culture of the home society (Uriely and Belhassen, 2005: 245). Less than half their interviewees complied with modes of experience that involve a quest for escape, while neither those seeking meaningful experiences nor those who were pleasure oriented were necessarily estranged from their own culture. As such, it was argued that hedonistic tourist behaviour is closely related to residual cultures that shape leisure behaviour in the home environment rather than being triggered by a discrete tourist culture. Or, put another way, there is an 'underlying commonality' between pleasure-oriented tourism and leisure (Carr, 2002: 981).

Subterranean play and leisure

Criminological studies of drug use typically focus on domestic settings and, illustrating the potential for cross-fertilisation, help to explain the commonality between drug tourism and leisure. Something like a distinct sociology of drug use began to emerge under the umbrella of the 'new' deviancy theories almost half a century ago, with notable contributions being made by Howard Becker (1963), Edwin Schur (1963, 1965), Troy Duster (1970) and Jock Young (1971). Building on that which came before, Young's work proved particularly significant, marking the culmination of the initial phase in the sociology of drug use and helping to stretch the 'new' radical conception of deviance to its 'absolute limit' (Sumner, 1994: 262).

Addressing the themes of pleasure, meaning and alienation in 'late' or 'post' industrial societies, Young (1971) argued that drug use represents a form of 'subterranean play'. This concept was borrowed from Matza and Sykes (1957), who claimed that the values behind much juvenile delinquency are far less deviant than is commonly supposed. The assumption that delinquency is rooted in deviant values, they noted, rests on a gross oversimplification of the dominant value system that glosses over some inherent contradictions and ambiguities. While the search for adventure is generally held in abeyance, Matza and Sykes observed that this does not mean it is completely rejected by society as a whole or never appears in the motivational structure of the law-abiding. Rather, the realisation of such desires is compartmentalised and allowed to take precedence at certain prescribed times in the form of sports, recreation and holidays. Put another way (Matza and Sykes, 1957: 716):

The search for adventure, excitement, and thrills, then, is a subterranean value that now often exists side by side with the values of security, routinization, and the rest. It is not a deviant value, in any full sense, but it must be held in abeyance until the proper moment and circumstances for its expression arrive.

Rather than reflecting a deep-seated commitment to an oppositional morality, therefore, much juvenile delinquency is said to result from an exaggerated adherence to subterranean values.

What was distinctive about Young's (1971) analysis was the way it linked subterranean values to the political economy of 'late industrial' societies. Such values are held to be identical to the customary definition of play and are contrasted with formal values, which are said to be consistent with the structure of modern industry in that they serve to maintain diligent, repetitive work. Rather than forming isolated moral regions, subterranean values and formal values are considered to be mutually dependent upon one another: 'the money earned by work is spent in one's leisure time' and individuals 'must produce in order to consume, and consume in order to produce' (1971: 128). Within 'late industrial' societies, moreover, Young maintained that subterranean values are largely subsumed under the dominant ethos of productivity, with the result that they can only be expressed legitimately if, and when, the individual has earned the right to do so by working hard and being productive. Alcohol and other 'psychotropic' drugs are said to play a key role in this regard, providing a *'vehicle* which enhances the ease of transition from the world of formal values to the world of subterranean values' (1971: 135).

The notion of subterranean play, as developed by Young, helps to explain the underlying commonality between drug tourism and leisure in the home society. Rather like the assumption that juvenile delinquency is based on deviant values, the notion that drug tourism involves escape and alienation from one's own society rests on a gross oversimplification of life in late industrial societies. Such societies routinely provide spaces and opportunities for escape from the drudgery of the work-a-day world and, for young people in particular, illicit drug use features prominently in these spaces, forming an important part of the weekend ritual based on pubbing, clubbing and intoxication (Shiner, 2009). While such spaces and opportunities tend to be fairly tightly compartmentalised, being fitted around work or study, holidays offer an extended opportunity for a more intense realisation of the subterranean goals of adventure, freedom and hedonistic pleasure. So it is that the drug-related experiences of pleasure-seeking drug tourists can be seen as an extension of their leisure activities at home.

Pleasure, meaning and authenticity

Applied to drug tourism, Young's (1971) analysis raises very different possibilities to those suggested by Uriely and Belhassen (2005). Rather than viewing the pursuit of pleasure as 'shallow' and 'superficial', Young considers it fundamental to the human condition, providing the basis of man's natural state. Drawing on Freud's theory of personality, he notes that the socialisation of a child involves a transition from the pleasure principle to the reality principle, from a world of free expression and hedonism to one of deferred gratification and productivity. As a result: 'Every man having tasted the paradise of play in his own childhood holds in his mind as an implicit utopia a world where economic necessity does not hold sway and where he is capable of free expression of his desires' (1971: 131). This implicit utopia, argues Young, provides the psychological basis of subterranean values and it is in one's leisure time that a watered-down expression of 'free time' and play holds sway. While the ethos of productivity seeks to incorporate and legitimise the world of subterranean values, there are cracks and strains in this moral code which mean people doubt both the sanity of alienated work and the validity of their leisure: 'socialisation for work inhibits their leisure and their utopias of leisure belittle their work' (1971: 129). Among groups that exist outside the ethos of productivity, bohemian youth – or 'hippies' – were said to have discovered that, as largely middle-class young people, they can disdain work, which they regarded as being inherently alienating, and criticise 'leisure' as an outpost of work or 'a mere consumption game which satisfies no one' (1971: 151). Rather, they demanded that authentic 'play', the free expression of subterranean values, be the major focus of human existence, elevating drug use to a paramount position. For Young (1971) and Davis (1970) these demands represented a common response to the incipient problems of work, leisure and identity that arose in an age of 'overproduction', 'staggering material abundance' and unprecedented opportunities for 'creative leisure'. Thus, they suggested, the hippies might be rehearsing possible cultural solutions to the central life problems of the future.

Whilst paying little attention to the details of earlier work, recent criminological studies have continued to argue that the social meaning of drug use is tightly bound up with the pursuit of pleasure. According to Parker *et al.* (1998: 119–120) young people make decisions about drug use based on cost–benefit assessments, whereby the likelihood of bad experiences, health risks and the impact of 'getting caught' are 'weighed against the pleasure and enjoyment of particular drugs and their ability either to blank out stress and distress or most often help deliver cost effective, deserved "time out" through relaxation and enjoyment from the grind of ordinary, everyday life'. Some criminological accounts have pointed to a lack of authenticity in youthful pleasure-seeking behaviour, claiming that night-time leisure seems 'nothing more than the cynical marketing of spectacular hedonism aimed at persuading young people to consume and accept their vicarious existences in themed, simulated realities' (Winlow and Hall, 2006: 187). Nonetheless, the suggestion that the social meaning of drug use lies in the pursuit of pleasure challenges one of the organising assumptions of Cohen's (1979) and, by extension, Uriely and Belhassen's (2005) analysis. If pleasure is meaningful then it makes little sense to view the 'desire for mere pleasure' as the antithesis of the 'quest for meaning and authenticity'. Rather it suggests that these themes are better conceived as discrete dimensions rather than opposite ends of a single continuum. Cohen's original formulation is further complicated by the way in which drug tourists find meaning in non-territorial, as well as territorial, centres (see Uriely and Belhassen, 2005).

The complications of pleasure, meaning and non-territorial centres are well illustrated by what is variously described as dance or rave culture. Based on the fusion of music, dance and drug use this is an inescapably pleasure-oriented culture, which has been interpreted by some as a gesture of avoidance signifying a shirking of adult responsibility in favour of a universe of pleasure and play (Osgerby, 1998). While fleetingly threatening the vested interests of the mainstream leisure industry, rave culture, like many previous youth styles, was facilitated by, and ultimately incorporated into, the world of corporate youth entertainment. What started out as an 'underground' of unlicensed outdoor events and warehouse parties was quickly co-opted and repackaged by established commercial interests, with the result that distinctions between pubs and bars, night clubs and dance clubs, raves and festivals became blurred (Collin with Godfrey, 1997; Measham et al., 2001). As part of this process, global aspects of rave culture have been absorbed into the traditional holiday business, gaining corporate sponsorship from the likes of Pepsi, Sony and Silk Cut, and attracting 'the new drug tourist [who] travels the neo-hippie trail where the aim is to experience the rave event rather than the local culture' (Blackman, 2004: 176). Although the focus is not on the local culture, rave-events are not devoid of meaning and authenticity for as, Uriely and Belhassen (2005) note, they attract drug tourists of all kinds, including pleasure-seekers and those searching for meaningful experiences. Nor can pleasure seeking be readily separated from meaningful experiences in the context of rave:

for some participants hedonistic excess is an integral part of the broader search for meaning, taking on a religious or spiritual dimension (St John, 2004; Sylvan, 2005). So it is, that D'Andrea (2004: 251) points to an affinity between Techno and New Age, which, he says, embody powerful 'living fields' of problematisation for Western life that help 'alternative subjects' or 'global nomads' in their efforts to escape 'the alienation and routine of modern life' and 'rearticulate labor, leisure and spirituality in an exquisitely meaningful way'.

Just as distinctions between pleasure-seeking and meaning are not clear cut, so there is a blurring between consumerism and authenticity. This is, perhaps, particularly the case as producer countries become increasingly aware of the commercial possibilities associated with drug tourism. With the growth of cocaine-tourism in Colombia, for example, treks include visits to 'cocaine factories' (Baker, 2008) and tours have been set up based on the life of Pablo Escobar, former head of the Medellin Cartel who was, on his death, said to control 80 per cent of the global cocaine market (see http://www.pabloescobartours.com/). That the quest for authenticity carries the potential for exploitation is evident from de Rios' (1994: 6) claims that what purport to be 'religious ceremonies' involving the use of *ayahuasca* in various remote locations in the Amazon are actually 'farces' staged for foreign tourists by phoney 'traditional healers' and 'common drug dealers'. Even in the absence of deliberate deception, encounters with indigenous practices depend upon, and are sustained by, mainstream commercial tourist services, whether this be in the form of flights, hotels, tour guides or some other such provision. As with the counter-culture more generally, the search for authenticity through tourism represents an alternative form of consumerism rather than an alternative to consumerism (see Heath and Potter, 2005).

Drug tourism and social change

The influence of globalisation and commercialisation demand that drug tourism be located within broader debates about drug use and social change. To this end, we must look beyond the specific literature on drug tourism, which has little to say on the matter, and consider more general developments in tourism theory. Claiming to offer a 'new approach', Franklin (2003: 280) argues that 21st century tourism, or what he might have called 'post-modern' tourism, 'belongs to a mobile, liquid modernity in which the older certainties that informed earlier tourism theory have vanished'. In developing this claim, Franklin casts doubt over the wisdom and continued relevance of earlier perspectives, such as those developed by MacCannell (1976) and Urry (1990), which, he argues, were formulated at a time 'when the world and the tourism that took place in it were different' (2003: 266) and 'were overly embedded in the social thought and anxieties of their day or...were too anchored in a past that no longer applies' (2003: 279). At the heart of his analysis, Franklin distinguishes between two periodisations of mobility that were said to have had a profound effect on tourism. Mobilities I began with the establishment of dense networks of railways and stretched up to the beginnings of mass car ownership and the establishment of commercial airlines in the 1950s – a period of approximately 150 years in many parts of the Western world. Mobilities II followed, with the arrival of cheap air transport, multi-car families and the advent of superhighways.

According to Franklin, Mobilities I was structured around fairly stable forms of capitalist production. Both capital and labour were comparatively immobile during this period, producing dense local networks of families and friendships and taste cultures that were largely homogenous. Under these circumstances, tourism was characterised by a one-week annual holiday, often taken collectively at the nearest seaside, and a few public holidays. Mobilities II, which can also be thought of as 'globalisation' and is said to have 'radically transformed the world' (Franklin, 2003: 79), was driven by a combination of technological developments and the needs of more mobile forms of capitalism. Cheaper and more efficient forms of travel meant shortening travel times and shrinking geography, with the result that taste in tourism changed, becoming both more frequent and more adventurous: '...by the 1980s there were few places that people could not and did not travel to' (2003: 79). This greater mobility, it is suggested, reconfigured taste structures more generally, blurring the boundaries between what is familiar and unfamiliar. Noting that objects, as well as people, have flown more freely and further in Mobilities II, Franklin suggests that food has moved quite impressively through the media of tourism. New tastes, he argues, that were established first of all by tourism (or migrants) have been routinised and entrenched in modern taste formation. This leads to one of Franklin's main criticisms of established perspectives on tourism: namely, the claim that the world of tourism is separable from the everyday, providing a world in which the new and unusual form the focus for depthless experiences of pleasure. According to Franklin (2003), the difference between the everyday and spaces of tourism has blurred, if not collapsed: globalisation means we find the exotic other on our doorstep and reminders of ourselves and the western everyday when we travel abroad. Almost everywhere, he argues, has become mantled with touristic properties and our stance to the world, whether we are at home or away, has become increasingly touristic.

Franklin's analysis has some obvious applications to drug use. As one of the central pillars of 21st century tourism, what he describes as Mobilities II may be considered a precondition of contemporary forms of drug tourism. His emphasis on the blurring between the familiar and unfamiliar, moreover, helps to make sense of the underlying continuity between drug use in the context of tourism and leisure. Drawing, as it does on postmodern theory, Franklin's analysis also sits comfortably with recent developments in the sociology of drug use and related strands of criminological thought, though it may also be said to share some of their weaknesses. Most notably, perhaps, claims that the 'normalisation' of recreational drug use is a feature of post-modernity, requiring a new explanatory framework (Parker et al., 1998, 2002; Measham, 2004), have been challenged on the grounds that they exaggerate the extent and pace of change, disregard key elements of continuity and encourage a form of 'chronocentricism' (Rock, 2005), whereby the insights of past work are forgotten, reinvented and proclaimed as new (Shiner, 2009). Similar criticisms have been levelled at the 'distinctly overblown' claims made on behalf of the 'new cultural criminology', which, it has been suggested, 'is not, in fundamental respects, all that new' (Downes, 2005: 320).

Although Franklin's analysis includes an historical dimension, it remains susceptible to such criticisms. Life under Mobilities I was, perhaps, never quite as unbearably dull and predictable, nor taste structures quite as unchanging and bland as the contrast with Mobilities II suggests. This was, after all, a period of rapid industrialisation and urbanisation, of colonial administration and burgeoning overseas trade. Certainly, what Courtwright (2002: 2) refers to as the 'psychoactive revolution' was, by his own account, the result of a protracted process that combined the discoveries and innovations of the early modern period with new techniques of industrial production and distribution aimed at refining and mass marketing 'an impressive array of psychoactive pleasures', including alcohol, caffeine, cannabis, coca, cocaine, opium, morphine and tobacco; so that, by the early 20th century, 'millions of ordinary people throughout the world could lead, in neurochemical terms, a life-style unimaginable for even the wealthiest five hundred years earlier'. For all his criticism of previous work, moreover, Franklin offers some familiar arguments, suggesting that 'tourists are doing more than being pleasured by the new and unusual', and, 'in a great many cases', are 'seeking some sense of personal change, growth or transition', noting that individual anticipation and performance 'is a common feature of tourism and, in this sense, it is more like pilgrimage than carnivalesque' (2003: 269). The desire to get away, he acknowledges, remains a feature of present-day tourism, albeit expressed in a 'new' pattern, whereby people caught up in the contemporary fast-time world are seeking respite, shelter, relief, rest or the 'ritualised space of the present'. Finally, Franklin (2003: 280) maintains, travel and tourism are worth the hassles and the risks involved because of the multiple benefits they potentially provide: 'At the very least we can say that tourism is very often assumed to deliver some kind of catharsis, a ritual act of purification and deliverance'.

The emphasis on personal growth, the allusion to pilgrimage and the suggestion of catharsis draws us back into the realm of what Cohen (1979) was writing about some 30 years ago and brings this chapter to an appropriate end. That the insights of Cohen (1979) and Young (1971) continue to illuminate contemporary patterns of drug use, whether in the context of tourism or leisure, suggests a continuity of motive and meaning that is all too often disregarded. In thinking about such phenomena, we should not be so preoccupied with change that we lose sight of that which is familiar and enduring or of what I have referred to elsewhere as continuity within change (Shiner, 2009).

Conclusion

My aim in this chapter has been to show that drug use provides a potentially fertile meeting ground for criminology and tourism studies. As well as identifying several points of contact, which raise the possibility of dialogue and exchange, I have argued that these fields of study offer distinct yet complementary perspectives on drug use. Almost inevitably, the field of tourism studies involves a comparative dimension, which highlights some notable fault lines in global drugs control. Some states have adopted less punitive and restrictive systems of control than others and such inconsistencies have been heavily implicated in the creation of particular forms of drug tourism, including those described above in the Netherlands and Mexico. While these examples confirm that commercialisation can channel drug tourism in certain directions, it remains something of a leap to claim, as some have, that liberal policies are somehow responsible for drug tourism. Such claims rest on the assumption that punitive regimes provide an effective deterrent, which does not stand up well to empirical scrutiny. People are prepared to flout national and international drug laws in large numbers, whether at home or whilst travelling, and explaining why this is so provides an important focus for both criminology and tourism studies. Criminology has much to offer in this regard, having extensively chronicled the limitations and failings of prohibition (see Shiner, 2006), while recent developments in both fields have noted the limited impact of legal deterrents alongside the importance of other sources of self-regulation (cf. Shiner, 2003 and Uriely and Belhassen, 2005).

Drug use cannot simply be understood as the result of a failure of legal deterrents, but also requires consideration of the motives and meanings involved. In addressing such matters criminology and tourism studies have explored some common themes, including the role of pleasure and the nature of meaning, authenticity and alienation in late industrial or post-modern societies. Recent developments in tourism studies provide a rich typology of the motives and meanings involved in drug use whilst travelling, which turns on the proposed contrast between 'mere pleasure' and 'authentic meaning'. The prominence of pleasure-seeking motives points to an underlying commonality between tourism and leisure, providing a potentially fertile meeting ground for different fields of study. From the perspective of tourism studies, such commonality casts doubt over claims that drug tourism provides escape from the boredom of routine life in the home society and alienation from its mainstream culture. Broader developments within tourism theory also highlight the influence of globalisation or increased mobility, which is said to have blurred the boundaries between home and away and between that which is familiar and unfamiliar (though the suggestion of post-modern transformation should be tempered by an awareness of the historical dimensions of the processes involved). Criminology further clarifies the relationship between tourism and leisure by showing that life at home routinely provides spaces and opportunities for escape through, among other things, participation in the night-time economy and associated forms of consumption such as illicit drug use. As well as helping to flesh out the link between leisure and tourism, dialogue between criminology and tourism studies offers the possibility of conceptual clarification and opens up new lines of enquiry. Criminological studies suggest that the pursuit of pleasure and the desire for meaning and authenticity are better thought of as distinct dimensions rather than opposite ends of a single spectrum, while tourism studies alerts us to the diversity of motives involved in drug use and the importance of looking beyond pleasure to the role that spiritual dimensions and the quest for authenticity may play in regard to drug use at home.

References

The Age (2009) 'Dutch cannabis cafes to become private members' clubs', 13 May, http://www.theage.com.au/travel/travel-news, accessed 12 December 2009.

Astorga, L. (2001) 'The limits of anti-drug policy in Mexico', *International Social Science Journal*, **53** (169), 427–434.

Baker, V. (2008) 'The rise of the cocaine tourist', *The Guardian*, 1 April, http://www.guardian.co.uk/travel/, accessed 14 June 2009.

Becker, H.S. (1963) *Outsiders: Studies in the Sociology of Deviance*, London: Macmillan.

Belhassen, Y., Almeida Santos, C. and Uriely, N. (2007) 'Cannabis usage in tourism: a sociological perspective', *Leisure Studies*, **23** (3), 303–319.

Bellis, M.A., Hale, G., Bennett, A., Chaudry, M. and Kilfoyle, M. (2000) 'Ibiza uncovered: changes in substance use and sexual behaviour amongst young people visiting an international night-life resort', *International Journal of Drug Policy*, **11**, 235–244.

Blackman, S. (2004) *Chilling Out: The Cultural Politics of Substance Consumption, Youth and Drug Policy*, Maidenhead: Open University Press.

Carlsen, L. (2007) 'Militarizing Mexico: the new war on drugs', Foreign Policy in Focus, 12 July, http://www.fpif.org/, accessed 15 June 2009.

Carpenter, T. (2009) Drug Gangs Winning the War for Mexico, Washington, DC: CATO Institute, 7 February, http://www.cato.org, accessed 15 June 2009.

Carr, N. (2002) 'The tourism–leisure behavioural continuum', *Annals of Tourism Research*, **29** (4), 972–986.

Cohen, E. (1973). 'Nomads from affluence: Notes on the phenomenon of drifter tourism'. *International Journal of Comparative Sociology*, 14(1-2): 89-103

Cohen, E. (1979) 'A phenomenology of tourist experiences', *Sociology*, **13** (2), 179–201.

Collin, M., with Godfrey, J. (1997) *Altered State: The Story of Ecstasy Culture and Acid House*, London: Serpent's Tail.

Courtwright, D. (2002) *Forces of Habit: Drugs and the Making of the Modern World*, Cambridge, Ma.: Harvard University Press

D'Andrea, A. (2004) 'Global nomads: techno and New Age as transnational countercultures in Ibiza and Goa', in G. St John (ed.), *Rave Culture and Religion*, London and New York: Routledge. pp. 236-255.

Daniel, F. (2007) 'Mexico extradites drug cartel bosses to U.S', Reuters, 20 January, http://www.reuters.com.Accessed 20 June 2009

Davis, F. (1970) 'Focus on the flower children: why all of us may be hippies someday' in J.D. Douglas (ed.), *Observation of Deviance*, London: Random House. pp. 327-340.

de Rios, M.D. (1994) 'Drug tourism in the Amazon: why Westerners are desperate to find the vanishing primitive', *Omni*, 16 (4), 6.

Degenhardt, L. *et al.* (2008) 'Toward a global view of alcohol, tobacco, cannabis, and cocaine use: findings from the WHO world mental health surveys', *PLoS Medicine*, 5 (4), 1053–1067.

Deutsche Welle (2007) 'Dutch Coffee Shops Close as Authorities Weed out Drug Tourists', 29 April, http://www.dw-world.del, accessed 9 June 2009.

Donkin, M. (2006) 'Dutch Cannabis Policy Changed', 9 January, http://news.bbc.co.uk, accessed 9 June 2009.

Downes, D. (2005) 'Reviews – City Limits: Crime, Consumer Culture and the Urban Experience, by K. Hayward', *Criminal Justice*, 5 (3), 319–321.

Duster, T. (1970) *The Legalisation of Morality*, New York: Free Press.

The Economist (2009) 'Briefing – dealing with drugs: on the trail of the traffickers', 7–13 March 2007, 28–31.

Eliade, M. (1971) *The Myth of Eternal Return*, Princeton, NJ: Princeton University Press.

Elvins, M. (2003) *Anti-Drugs Policies of The European Union: Transnational Decision-Making and the Politics of Expertise*, Basingstoke: Palgrave MacMillan.

Farrington, M. (2005) Drug Tourists Go Dutch, 27 May, http://www.alternet.org/drugreporter/, accessed 8 June 2009.

Franklin, A. (2003) *Tourism: An Introduction*, London: Sage.

Greenwald, G. (2009) *Drug Decriminalization in Portugal: Lessons for Creating Fair and Successful Drug Policies*, Washington, DC: CATO Institute.

The Guardian (2009) 'Drug Violence Along Mexican Border May Prompt Increased US Role', 29 January, http://www.guardian.co.uk/world/, accessed 14 June 2009.

Heath, J. and Potter, A. (2005) *The Rebel Sell: How the Counterculture Became Consumer Culture*, Chichester: Capstone Publishing.

Hider, J. and Reid, T. (2006) 'Drug tourism fears as Mexico lifts ban on pot, heroin and cocaine', *The Times*, 4 May, http://www.timesonline.co.uk, accessed 12 June 2009.

Hungarian Civil Liberties Union (2009) *Smoking without Borders: Drug Tourism in the Netherlands*, 12 January, http://www.youtube.com, accessed 10 June 2009.

Kievit, R. (2009) 'Pass system will restrict cannabis sales', Radio Netherlands Worldwide, 14 May: http://www.rnw.nl (accessed 12 December 2009.

Korf, D.J (2002) 'Dutch coffee shops and trends in cannabis use', *Addictive Behaviors*, **27** (6), 851–866.

Lemmens, P. (2002) 'Dutch cannabis policy evaluated', *Addiction*, **97** (1), 119–120.

MacCannell, D. (1976) *The Tourist: A New Theory of the Leisure Class*, New York: Schocken.

MacCoun, R.J. and Reuter, P. (2001) *Drug War Heresies: Learning from Other Vices, Times and Places*, New York: Cambridge University Press.

Mares, D. (2003) 'U.S drug policy and Mexican civil–military relations: a challenge for the mutually desirable democratization process', *Crime, Law and Social Change*, **40**, 61–75.

Matza, D. and Sykes, G.M. (1957) 'Techniques of neutralization', *American Sociological Review*, **22**, 664–670.

McCaffrey, B. (2008) *Narco-Violence in Mexico: A Growing Threat to U.S Security*, Chapel Hill, NC: American Diplomacy Publishers, www.unc.edu/depts/diplomat, accessed 12 June 2009.

McKinley, J.C and Broder, J. (2006) 'Under U.S pressure, Mexico President seeks review of drug law', *New York Times*, 4 May, www.nytimes.com, accessed 12 June 2009.

Measham, F. (2004) 'Drugs and alcohol research: the case for cultural criminology', in J. Ferrell, K. Hayward, W. Morrison and M. Presdee (eds), *Cultural Criminology Unleashed*, London: GlassHouse. pp. 207-218.

Measham, F., Aldridge, J. and Parker, H. (2001) *Dancing on Drugs: Risk, Health, Hedonism in the British Club Scene*, London: Free Association Books.

Melville, N.A. (2009) 'Are over-the-border prescriptions worth it?', *Road and Travel Magazine*, http://www.roadandtravel.com, accessed 22 July 2009.

Morais, P. (1996) 'Just say maybe', *Forbes*, 17 June, 114–120.

Osgerby, B. (1998) *Youth in Britain Since 1945*, Oxford: Blackwell.

Pakes, F.J. (2004) 'The politics of discontent: the emergence of a new criminal justice discourse in the Netherlands', *Howard Journal of Criminal Justice*, **43** (3), 284–298.

Parker, H., Aldridge, J. and Measham, F. (1998). *Illicit Leisure: The Normalization of Adolescent Recreational Drug Use*, London: Routledge.

Parker, H., Williams, L. and Aldridge, J. (2002) 'The normalization of sensible recreational drug use: further evidence from the North West England Longitudinal Study', *Sociology*, **36** (4), 941–964.

Police Foundation (2000) *Drugs and the Law: Report of the Independent Inquiry into the Misuse of Drugs Act 1971*, London: Police Foundation.

Rock, P. (2005) 'Chronocentricism and British criminology', *British Journal of Sociology*, **56** (3), 473–491.

Schur, E. (1963) *Narcotic Addiction in Britain and America*, London: Tavistock.

Schur, E. (1965) *Crimes Without Victims*, Englewood Cliffs, NJ: Prentice Hall.

Sellars, A. (1998) 'The influence of dance music on the UK youth tourism market', *Tourism Management*, **19** (6), 611–615.

Shiner, M. (2003) 'Out of harm's way? illicit drug use, medicalisation and the law', *British Journal of Criminology*, **43** (4), 772–796.

Shiner, M. (2006) 'Drugs, law and the regulation of harm', in R. Hughes, R. Lart and P. Higate (eds), *Drugs: Policy and Politics*, Maidenhead: Open University Press. pp. 59-74.

Shiner, M. (2009) *Drug Use and Social Change: The Distortion of History*, Basingstoke: Palgrave Macmillan.

St John, G. (2004) *Rave Culture and Religion*, London and New York: Routledge.

Sumner, C. (1994) *The Sociology of Deviance: An Obituary*, Buckingham: Open University Press.

Sylvan, R. (2005) *Trance Formation: The Spiritual and Religious Dimensions of Global Rave Culture*, London and New York: Routledge.

Timothy, D.J. (2005) *Shopping Tourism, Retailing and Leisure*, Bristol: Channel View Publications.

Transform (2009) Mexico to Decriminalise Possession of Drugs, 6 May, http:// transform-drugs.blogspot.com, accessed 13 June 2009.

Tuckman, J. (2009) 'Hilary Clinton admits US role in Mexico drug wars', *The Guardian*, 26 March, http://www.guardian.co.uk, accessed 13 June 2009.

Uriely, N. and Belhassen, Y. (2005) 'Drugs and tourists' experiences', *Journal of Travel Research*, 43 (3), 238–246.

Uriely, N. and Belhassen, Y. (2006) 'Drugs and risk-taking in tourism', *Annals of Tourism Research*, 33 (2), 339–359.

Uriely, N., Yonay, Y. and Simchai, D. (2002) 'Backpacking experiences: a type and form analysis', *Annals of Tourism Research*, 29 (4), 520–538.

Urry, J. (1990) *The Tourist Gaze*, London: Sage.

Valdez, A. and Sifaneck, S.J. (1997) 'Drug tourists and drug policy on the U.S–Mexican Border: an ethnographic investigation of the acquisition of prescription drugs', *Journal of Drug Issues*, **27** (4), 879–897.

Westerhausen, K. (2002) *Beyond the Beach: An Ethnography of Modern Travellers in Asia*, Bangkok: White Lotus.

Winlow, S. and Hall, S. (2006) *Violent Night: Urban Leisure and Contemporary Culture*, Oxford: Berg.

Young, J. (1971) *The Drugtakers: The Social Meaning of Drug Use*, London: MacGibbon and Kee.

7 Blagging Leads and Other Hustles:
British street workers in Tenerife's timeshare industry

Esther Bott

This chapter includes a discussion of the following topics:

♦ Timeshare industry and crime
♦ Street canvassing and its freedoms/risks
♦ Identity, status and deviance
♦ Freelance employment relations
♦ 'Personality market'.

Timeshare in Tenerife is a growing and predominantly British-run industry, whose operations and profitability depend largely on young[1] British migrants working as street canvassers whose job it is to entice tourists to a sales presentation by sales teams on company premises. This chapter is an exploration into the deployment of various 'persuasion' tactics and tricks used by these British street workers, and the illegal activities surrounding selling timeshare by British migrants in Tenerife. It raises questions about employment relations that occur within such a framework and explores how the status quo is maintained by employers by way of their exploitation of the perceived meanings of risk, individualism and sometimes crime/deviance to these particular workers.

Specific attention is paid to the ways in which the unregulated, freelance employment relation characteristic of timeshare canvassing work allows employers to capitalise on the emotional labour, and its subjective aspects, involved in this form of 'extreme' selling. It points to the risks and costs carried by workers who canvass for timeshare companies, showing, in short, that timeshare sales work is risky, exploitative, insecure, stressful and potentially hazardous to health and

---

1 'Youth', is a category that presents definitional problems. It is used here to mean people in their late teens to early thirties. The research concentrates on casual/informal work and 'hedonistic' consumption practices which typically attract 'young' people, but which, in Tenerife, are also attracting people into their mid- or even late-thirties.

well being. And yet this is not how it is perceived by the workers. Rather, the subjects of this study imagine their work as having extraordinary qualities that set it apart from 'regular' employment. Their work is often intimately connected to their practices as drug dealers and /or users, as 'hustlers' and survivors, which in turn are connected to their wider migration/mobility narratives. This is a form of migrant labour in which, partly because of its criminal and deviant associations, it is possible to reject a negatively evaluated, mundane 'working class' or even 'under-class' identity, and assert, affirm and express a positively self-evaluated white British individualism.

The timeshare industry

Timeshare is a form of holiday home ownership. Those who buy timeshare, or join a 'holiday club' pay a one-off sum plus yearly maintenance fees in exchange for the right to spend a set amount of time per year in self-catering apartments or villas in popular holiday resorts. The two most popular forms of timeshare are 'fixed week' and 'floating system'. Fixed week timeshare means that a certain week is 'owned', usually in fixed accommodation, although accommodation and dates may be swapped with other timeshare owners of similar properties throughout the world. The floating system means that a week (or longer) must be booked in advance and must be within a seasonal time band.

The industry began in the early 1960s when a German property developer invented the concept as a result of purchasing an apartment in a ski resort in the French Alps with a group of friends. The group realised that if they pooled their money and shared the apartment the purchase would become affordable. Thus the use of the property was shared between the buyers in weekly intervals, the number of weeks assigned being relative to each member's financial contribution. The time-share concept lay relatively dormant until the mid-1980s; apparently the victim of 'boiler-room tactics' applied by some 'unscrupulous developers' (Woods, 2001: 71–73). However, a market eventually developed and the high-pressure sales and management methods of the timeshare operators soon earned the industry a bad reputation. In the USA, where timeshare has expanded rapidly in the last three decades, the 'high-pressure sales tactics caught the attention of state legislators, and promoting timeshares as an investment is illegal in most states today' (Woods, 2001: 71–72). In 2003, the European Consumer Centre (ECC) has produced several reports on complaints received in connection with European timeshare and reports that 'Tourists from throughout Europe… are recruited by industry sales reps by means of wholly misleading and deceptive techniques' (ECC, 2003: 3).

Since the early 1980s, European timeshare has also expanded rapidly and in 2001 generated a yearly revenue of €2.4 billion (OTE report, 2003). Europe has the second largest timeshare market in the world after the United States. The dominant market within Europe for timeshare ownership has traditionally been the

UK, though other significant markets are emerging. Perhaps unsurprisingly, tourist resorts most popular with the British and other Northern Europeans are where the majority of timeshare properties are purchased. The Canary Islands, mainland Spain, the Balearics and Portugal are among the most popular destinations. Haylock notes that Spain saw 'phenomenal growth in timeshare ownership from 1990–93, with the number of domestic owners growing from 3000 families in 1990 to 36,000 by the end of 1993' (1994: 334). In 2007, 1.45 million families in Europe owned timeshare weeks and the industry currently contributes more than €10 million to tourism in Europe every year (OTE, 2007).

Timeshare in Tenerife relies almost entirely on British marketers and salespersons and is heavily associated with fraud and other criminal activities. In 1999, Spain introduced new laws to protect timeshare consumers from fraudulent sales techniques, but these laws applied only to timeshare deals lasting three or more years, and some companies responded by adapting the traditional timeshare package to a short-term (less than three years) 'holiday club' membership in order to circumnavigate the new laws and enable them to charge large, non-returnable deposits and offer no cooling-off period to buyers. In 1990 the Office of Fair Trading (OFT) produced a report which identified problems for consumers including: 'misleading mail shots offering prizes; the aggressive and deceptive behaviour of canvassers; sales staff trained in high pressure selling techniques which seek to control buyers' behaviour and suppress rational decision making; and incomplete, misleading and untrue statements by sales staff' (Marks, 2003: 8).

In 2007/08, the Organization for Timeshare in Europe (OTE) launched a €130,000 project to expose timeshare fraud in Spain, primarily in Tenerife where fraud is most prevalent, leading to the closure of 10 fraudulent holiday clubs and 23 fake property re-sale companies. The OFT, who work closely with the OTE, estimate that 400,000 Britons each year are defrauded of £1.2 billion (gotimeshare, 2009).

Timeshare companies employ street touts or 'On-sight Personal Contacts' (OPCs – also known as 'Off-premises Contacts') who work in sales teams that pitch to passers-by on the streets and promenades of Europe's busiest holiday resorts. The Timeshare Consumers Association (TCA) estimates that during the time of data collection (2003/04) there were approximately 40 to 50 timeshare outfits operating in Tenerife, 80% of which were British owned and run, although British companies may be registered abroad for tax or other reasons (www.ote-info.com). Each of these companies employs a number of OPC teams. Because OPCs are employed on an informal basis, official head-counts of OPC team members are very difficult to obtain. In the 1990s and early part of this century local authorities tolerated timeshare street canvassing in Tenerife and other parts of Spain. Towards the middle of this decade, however, at around the time of data collection, some local authorities were beginning to clamp down on OPCs – Tenerife, Fuengirola on Spain's Costa del Sol and Malta being the most prominent of these authorities – imposing a licensing system to limit the number of OPCs operating in any given area of a town. The purpose of these police clampdowns was to reduce the intimidation and harassment of holidaymakers by OPCs.

OPC teams are reputedly 'looked after' (controlled) by protection rackets, contracted by timeshare companies, although interviewees were very reluctant to talk about this directly. There have been numerous arrests and convictions over recent years of racketeers involved in money laundering, drug dealing and arms dealing in, or in connection with, Tenerife timeshare. In July 2003, the Tenerife penitentiary was holding eight Britons on Mafiosi (protection racketeering) pre-trial allegations. Fraud is also prevalent. Timeshare boss John Palmer was sentenced to serve eight years in prison in 2001 for defrauding an estimated 16,500 timeshare consumers in Tenerife. In 2006, two of Palmer's friends and business associates, Billy and Flo Robinson were brutally mutilated and murdered on the island. More recently, seven fraudulent re-sale brokers were arrested in Tenerife in 2009 for taking €30,000 in taxes and fees from individual timeshare owners for bogus sales of their ownership packages. In July 2007, 29 British nationals were charged for fraud in Tenerife. Their crimes included posing, either by telephone or on the street, as lawyers and charging fees for assisting customers who had already been conned by timeshare fraudsters.

The research

The chapter is based on both qualitative and quantitative data gathered during the course of a three-year, Economic and Social Research Council funded project which involved ethnographic research on the informal tourism economy (and its intersections with the domestic and sex work markets) in Tenerife. This entailed three periods of data collection using a variety of participant observation techniques. My first field trip in spring 2003 lasted five weeks and a second visit spanned July and August 2003. A third four-week field trip was made in December 2003/ January 2004. During these periods I made contact with nearly 200 young British migrants to Tenerife (YBMTs). Thirty-six depth, semi-structured interviews with young, white British people working in a variety of tourism-related areas were conducted. Interviewees included people between the ages of 16 and 37 who were living in Tenerife at that time and working, amongst other things, as timeshare salespersons, bar/restaurant/club staff or street promoters (PRs), cooks, bartenders, waiters, lap dancers and DJs. The research especially focused in on exploring the working lifestyles of men and women working in the timeshare industry and women lap dancers. All interviewees were from the United Kingdom and all but one self-identified as white.

This chapter stems specifically from 16 semi-structured interviews with timeshare sellers. Interviews lasted for approximately one hour and were recorded, where possible, on paper in note form. As I was collecting detailed life-span biographies from interviewees, the interviews were of necessity flexible and open-ended, allowing interviewees to narrate their life-stories in their own terms.

Researching into street selling of timeshare raised difficult methodological issues, the most notable of which were around access, researcher safety, researcher subjectivity and reflexivity in the field. The timeshare selling environment can be a particularly hostile one. As noted above, the industry has been heavily associated with serious criminal activity, including racketeering, fraud and drug dealing. There is a widespread culture of cocaine use among salespersons, and an overall atmosphere of mania resulting in part from drug use but also from the relentless demands of high pressure sales work. OPCs are extremely busy, often very excitable and can be enormously unsympathetic to outsiders. Approaching teams during working hours usually meant that they were too busy or hyped-up to give a meaningful interview, but approaching them after work risked finding them intoxicated. On several occasions I experienced open hostility directed at me in relation to my being a woman, an academic and being perceived as privileged, 'leftie' or 'posh'. I was subjected to numerous verbal affronts, often fuelled by cocaine, beer and the 'buzz' of high-pressure sales work. One-to-one interviews were often invaded by other OPCs, and sometimes I found myself fighting off (albeit mostly playful) abuse from several men at once. I was searched, followed, and repeatedly propositioned. Interviews frequently became heated, especially around the subject of immigration to the UK which emerged as a dominant motive for migration from Britain (Bott, 2004).

Extreme selling and commission payments

The majority of timeshare is sold using a two-tier system of, first, face-to-face street touting by OPCs, followed up by a 'harder sell' by higher level salespersons on company premises, often involving a tour of timeshare properties and enticement with 'gifts' (e.g. a case of wine or a food hamper). OPCs do not receive a basic wage or benefits. Instead they are paid a commission (known as an 'up') for every 'couple'[2] they manage to persuade to attend a sales presentation. OPCs can earn €100 per 'up'. They can earn further commission if the couple then buys timeshare as a result of attending the sales presentation, though this is of secondary importance to OPCs as this commission is of a relatively low value (approximately €40) and can take several months to materialise. As Korczynski (2002: 106) points out, commission systems encourage a 'more instrumental orientation' from the salesperson, and the customer becomes little more than a means to an end (the commission payment). The way timeshare selling is organised, however, means that the actual sale itself becomes marginalised, because the OPC receives commission solely on the potential customer entering the firm's premises for a presentation, irrespective of whether or not the sale actually materialises. Because the importance of the sale itself is minimal to the OPCs, and their interest in

---

2 OPCs have strict so-called 'qualifications' or criteria for targeting potential customers. Among other things, 'ups' must be heterosexual couples, preferably married or living together for a set period of time, homeowners, employed and so on. If couples that turn up for the presentation do not meet these criteria, the OPC does not receive the commission.

the customer terminates once they have been escorted by the OPC to company premises, their investment in the customer and even the sale is especially hollow and passing. On several occasions I even observed OPCs explaining the payment system to tourists and offering to split the commission with them if they agreed to attend a sales presentation.

Commission-only payment systems generate a strong pressure to sell. Further, the alienation of the OPC from the actual sale engenders an 'anything goes' atmosphere and consequently, as noted above, OPCs are renowned for using ethically and legally dubious sales tactics, ranging from staging fake scratch-card winnings and outright lying, to bribery, intimidation and harassment.

Front-line timeshare selling involves an ideology which Barry Ley, veteran OPC and author of the best-selling book *Blaggers* captures when he describes timeshare as an industry where '...the only guidelines worth noting were to earn money in any way possible and spend it equally quickly on hard living' (2001: 12). Clearly confident in the effectiveness of their two-tier, commission-based sales system, timeshare bosses need not concern themselves with the manipulation techniques of their OPC teams. Employing on a commission-based system limits the firm's corporate and legal responsibility for their OPCs and this has a number of benefits for the industry.

Other benefits of this employment relation

Limiting their responsibility for, and connection to, OPC team members allows employers to cut down on some of the many risks associated with this form of extreme sales. It is level one, the street-level contact with tourists that implies the greater risk for companies. An obvious reason for this is that street canvassing is being increasingly policed in Spain and penalties can be serious if enforced. Yet even before the police clamp-downs, timeshare companies were not using directly employed salespersons as the returns on time and effort invested in street-level sales are uncertain. Level two operations (where the OPCs has already escorted the potential buyer to a building for a sales presentation) are less risky as the sale is more likely once the 'up' actually enters the office, making returns on salespersons' time and labour more predictable and of higher value. Demand is directly stimulated by OPCs, whose work consists of persuading a completely cold audience that they are interested in attending a timeshare sales presentation. There is little or no sense that the customer has been 'pre-sold' (Glazer, 1993) the idea of timeshare (by media advertising for example) previous to the initial interaction between the salesperson and her/his target. On the contrary, the poor reputation of the timeshare industry precedes the interaction between OPCs and their wary targets. Therefore the work done by OPCs is very labour-intensive, competitive and time-consuming, with few opportunities for efficiency gains and great potential for the constant rejection associated with cold selling.

If timeshare companies were to employ OPCs directly, giving a contract, salary, package of employment rights and benefits and so on, they would effectively be investing a set amount of capital for an extremely variable, unreliable return. Moreover, they would face extensive problems of control and supervision over large and sprawling sales teams, again greatly increasing costs. Paying commission only to freelance employees means that issues of labour control, even the quality and reliability of workers, and retention of skilled, effective labour become less problematic.

OPC teams, usually consisting of approximately five or six British migrants, are headed by a team leader. The team leader is responsible for overseeing team members, liaising between bosses and workers and ensuring that sales targets are met. Team leaders receive commission payments on their team members' 'ups' as well as their own and this serves as an incentive for team leaders to encourage dubious and unfair sales techniques. Team leaders also work informally (without contracts, etc.) so they too effectively work as freelancers. These freelance 'supervisors' provide a minimalist, cheap layer of 'control' over workers whilst significantly boosting profitability themselves. Such individualised, commission/freelance systems create what Korczynski terms a 'managerial vacuum' (2002: 106). Again, this means that the supervisor carries risks that would more normally be carried by the employer, and also that they assume certain functions that would, with direct labour, be undertaken by management (proper supervision, labour discipline, planning of work schedules, etc.), something that is of great financial benefit to employers. So, for example, sales targets are not only set by bosses in timeshare. Rather, the pressures of the commission system impose targets upon salespersons, as Joe, aged 24, who works for Tenerife's largest timeshare company, explains:

> You have to really get two or three 'ups' a day... not that they [employers] care how well you do, it's just that you need the money... you get into a certain lifestyle and it's a horrible job if you're not winning. If you can't get the ups, it's only you who suffers. They let you carry on until you're sick of earning nothing ... Most people know whether they can hack it within a week.

Because of the commission system and its 'managerial vacuum', very little financial investment is made in recruiting or training OPCs. This means that firms can afford to have large teams of OPCs and remain relatively unaffected when individual workers perform poorly, and when new recruits fail to achieve and fall by the wayside. By sheer force of numbers of OPCs, the presence or absence of individual enterprise is, to some extent, irrelevant to the overall accumulation process.

Unlike in wider corporate culture, which, as Du Gay explains, normally 'reconciles the autonomous aspirations of the self-steering individual employee with the collective entrepreneurship of the flexible corporation' (1996: 63), timeshare companies prefer to separate themselves from the worker's entrepreneurship, creating a more individualistic working atmosphere. Timeshare bosses rely on the idea that because they are not earning a basic wage, employees will either succeed, in which case they will generate profit for the company as well as earnings for themselves, or they will fail to make sales and be forced to quit. Hence there is little pressure to meet sales targets on OPCs from 'above'. Rather the pressures are faced individually, often being eased by drug usage and trading.

As well as workers assuming responsibility for their own 'training', work schedule, effort levels and earnings, timeshare employers also pass the risks involved in illegal street selling directly to the freelance OPCs. It is the OPC who must keep a wary eye out for the police and deal with irate, often aggressive tourists and so, effectively, protect the company from the consequences of its illegal and/or unpopular trading practices. Nor does the employer protect OPCs from other hazards associated with their employment. The prime time for winning 'ups' is between 11am and 3pm, the hottest part of the day, and OPCs routinely spend six hours a day in the sun. Yet timeshare companies do not issue workers with sunscreen, hats, sunglasses or advice on protecting themselves from sunburn. Consequently, many OPCs allow themselves to burn and several interviewees had serious facial blistering and scarring resulting from over-exposure to the sun.

Meanwhile, the work itself is extremely stressful, not least because it involves facing continual rejection. OPCs must approach members of the public, the vast majority of whom have no interest whatsoever in buying timeshare (and who are in fact often wary of and sometimes hostile towards timeshare 'touts'); they must somehow interrupt passers-by and persuade them to listen to a sales pitch. More often than not, these passers-by will have already been approached by a number of OPCs from different teams on the same street, so there is an ever-increasing demand for OPCs to devise creative methods for attracting listeners. Successful OPCs learn to trade on their own personality and charm (and, as discussed below, for female OPCs, often their physical appearance) to win people's interest and confidence. In this sense, their work involves what Gorz terms, regarding the freelance relation, the 'sale of self':

> All who give wholly of their persons in the service of activities which are gratifying in themselves, but by way of which they become the…eager instruments of an alien will: in which they sell themselves. For what they get paid for is not an objectivized product which could be detached from their persons, but the deployment of their 'talents' for purposes dictated by their employer or client. Sovereignly free within limits imposed by someone else.
>
> (1999: 42–43, original emphasis)

The handing over of one's person – that is 'one's body, one's intelligence, one's talent or any other resource which is *not detachable* from the subject deploying it…' (1999: 43) always, according to Gorz, places one's integrity at risk, because it turns working people into 'working commodities'. Within freelancing, labour power and the self are especially inseparable because:

The ideology which makes 'knowing how to sell oneself' the greatest virtue plays a decisive role... and contributes to the development of [the] 'personality market'... Henceforth the personality is an integral part of labour power.

(Gorz, 1999: 43)

The personality of OPCs is absolutely key to productivity – their knowing how to sell themselves through various 'blagging' techniques. The negative public perception of timeshare has to be surmounted and OPCs do this by not only promoting the product, but also, more importantly, by exploiting their own creative skills (the ability to 'blag' an 'up'). Employers also exploit this ability because it increases productivity, and are therefore willing to accept the flouting of formally stated 'rules' around lying to or harassing clients, drinking alcohol or taking/buying/ selling drugs. The widespread use of cocaine is tolerated, or even encouraged, by employers because of its positive affects on productivity.

The Playa de Las Americas dream

As I have argued elsewhere, for many young British people, moving to Tenerife, whether seasonally, semi-permanently or permanently, can represent a significant, self-initiated step towards a greatly improved lifestyle (Bott, 2004, 2006). All but two of the OPCs that I interviewed had come from disadvantaged backgrounds. They had failed at school, often had unemployed parents, were unqualified and unskilled, and for the main part painted a grim picture of Britain, describing it as cold, depressing and lacking in opportunity. Tenerife, on the other hand, was imagined as a land of opportunity, glamour and hope.

Like its neighbouring Canary Islands, Tenerife has a thriving tourism sector with ample job opportunities (especially for English speakers) and EU agreements mean that Britons are able to migrate and work there relatively freely. Budget air fares between Britain and the Canary Islands also facilitate travel and migration, and because Tenerife has warm winters and attracts visitors year-round, job opportunities are not seasonal as they are in the Balearics or mainland Spain. This means that timeshare salespersons and other tourist industry workers can remain employed for the whole year without needing to return to the UK. Many stay in the same job for several years and forge lucrative careers in the timeshare industry. Some successful OPCs that I interviewed claimed to earn a 'tax-free' income of up to €2000 a week.

Timeshare therefore offers the potential for extremely highly paid work to unqualified Britons who often said that similar opportunities are not available to them in Britain. When I asked Graham, a 30-year-old OPC from Scotland, why he sells timeshare in Tenerife, he replied:

> I heard there was a lot of money to be made here, well, a damn sight more than in Scotland anyway... I chose Tenerife because it had a good reputation for timeshare opportunities...

> The worst thing about Britain is the lack of opportunities for people who aren't born with a silver spoon and all that. I would have to be a drug dealer or a criminal to be earning what I earn here in Britain. I am extremely well paid [*laughs*].

Graham chose to live in Tenerife and specifically to work in timeshare because of a belief in his ability to succeed in the timeshare business. He feels that a British person of his social and economic background has few lucrative career options besides crime, and so decided to widen his options by leaving the UK. Graham later revealed that he was indeed selling cocaine alongside timeshare, using his position on the street and contact with tourists as vehicles for dealing. His primary clientele, however, were other British migrants whose custom provided a regular supplement to his earnings from timeshare. Graham's ironic and ambiguous claim that a person of his background would need to be a criminal in the UK in order to enjoy the sort of lifestyle he enjoys in Tenerife, followed by the disclosure that he is in fact engaging in criminal activity in Tenerife, suggests a different set of meanings are being attached to crime carried out in Britain and crime committed in Tenerife. 'Home' represents a harsh, grim reality and Tenerife very much the opposite: a paradisiacal fantasy island where processes of leisure and tourism intersect, in this example, with everyday life; work, consumption, social interaction and so on. Tourism has been explored as the search for places that are set apart from the ordinary and mundane (MacCannell, 1999; Urry, 2002), and is associated with the search for 'authentic' experiences and sensations to counteract the corrosive and alienating conditions of modernity (Cohen, 1988; MacCannell, 1999). Modernity, writes Meethan, 'is dystopia and tourism the search for utopia (2001: 91). Places themselves are fragmented and partly reconstructed for tourists (Watt, 1992; Urry, 2002) in order for them to fulfil the expectations and romanticisations of the 'tourist gaze' (Urry, 2003).

The consumption of tourism places (and their people) that have been historically idealised and thus imagined as paradisiacal has been well explored in relation to the Caribbean, for example, perhaps most importantly by theorists with a focus on the powerfully racialised 'tropical tourist gaze' and the dangerous sense of 'abandon' experienced by visitors with cash to spend (Enloe, 1989; Sánchez-Taylor, 2001; Sheller, 2003). Consumption and other behaviour undertaken away from home, in a state of 'fantasy' carry different symbolic meanings. For example, consumer 'goods' become imbued with the stereotypical, often mythical (mis)understandings of that place. Mimi Sheller's analysis of how the Caribbean is consumed discusses how the representations of it as a collection of imaginary geographies reinforce it as a site in which to fulfil fantasies, e.g. the hedonistic consumption of sex, illicit substances, etc. which might not necessarily be undertaken at home (Sheller, 2003:

165). Places can therefore be understood as 'assemblages' through which complex mobilities are produced, embodied and performed. Graham discusses crime at home as an inevitable symptom of class immobility, whereas in Tenerife, on the other hand, his symbolic connections with cocaine – the 'champagne drug' – and its associated glamour enables an altogether different set of meanings of mobility to be attached to crime, mediated locally through timeshare cultural discourse.

Other interviewees expressed their anger and resentment towards their upbringings and social class backgrounds in stronger terms, also spelling out self-conscious notions of mobility:

> You don't want to know about where I grew up. The place is a fucking shit hole...no jobs, houses boarded up, burned out cars everywhere, syringes on the floor, you name it...fucking filthy shit hole, Britain.

> It's not a life that... life sentence more like. No, I ain't gonna bring my kids up like that. Out here, they'll go to a decent school; they can play in the pool...play in the pool for God's sake! I'm out here selling timeshare, making a fortune. I'm never going back...I really couldn't go back there.
>
> (Kevin)

Money and owning luxury consumer goods emerged as important themes in interviews, specifically manifested in the belief that wealth equals success, and OPCs tend to self-reflect in these terms. In so doing, they set up a dichotomy of success versus failure within their migration to Tenerife from Britain and entry into the timeshare business, as opposed to other less well paid forms of work (Bott, 2006). For example, Karen, aged 27, who has worked as an OPC in Tenerife for several years explains:

> Back home I mostly worked in shops around Liverpool. I hate shop work though – it's crap money, it's depressing; you see the same people every day, mates from school who've got kids, all the single parents... I just can't imagine going back to that now, you know, I earn between... about €200 and €300 a day, sometimes more than that... for less than five hours' work, and I get to stand in the sun all day long talking to people. People I know back home would kill for my job. They're all having nervous breakdowns because they're in so much debt. That's why I love Tenerife...nobody's depressed.

The data revealed that OPC work is widely considered a considerably more favourable labour option to other 'unskilled' jobs, especially those on offer in the UK. Karen associates Britain with poorly paid, unrewarding retail work and worn down, depressed, unfortunate people. She idealises her new life and especially her job, preferring to concentrate on its financial and status-related benefits rather than its potential costs. For Karen, timeshare represents a form of social and economic mobility; a means of escape from working-class Liverpool and a vehicle for earning well in an apparently desirable work environment. However, Karen had been drinking on several occasions during normal working hours on the days that I spoke with her, and insisted on drinking heavily during our second interview, which was conducted immediately after her shift on the street (for ethical reasons, I have not transcribed or analysed this data). Karen was extremely agitated during the first part of the interview because she had had 'a terrible day' and had failed to make any commission. She was also seriously sunburnt.

As I argue above, the work of the OPC can be extremely stressful, not least because the commission system generally causes OPCs to work in a state of intense and often anxious arousal in order to reach personal sales targets. Inevitably the high earning potential of timeshare selling, as with other forms of extreme sales, is not always reached and this makes OPCs permanently financially vulnerable. The interview data have highlighted the pressure of these burdens, as well as outline some of the coping strategies adopted by OPCs. One important way in which OPCs deal with the demands of their work is to use alcohol and other mood stimulants at, and after, work. Many OPCs described the need to stay 'hyper' and 'wound up' in order to be able to 'blag' successfully for hours at a time. Many use cocaine and alcohol in order to stay 'up' enough to perform, and cannabis and/or alcohol to wind down in the evening and during days off. This helps to feed the cycle of OPCs' dependency on success, as these consumables can of course become costly.

Hochschild discusses drug use in terms of its potential for 'displacing emotional labour'. She argues that in some cases, the labour required to withstand stress and boredom on the job can be performed by the drugs rather than by the worker (1983: 54). This idea is also applicable to substance abuse in timeshare sales; it is arguably often the coke and booze 'blagging' the 'up', as much as the OPC. Whilst it would be difficult to prove that timeshare bosses actually sponsor substance abuse at work as Hochschild (1983: 54 – citing Howard, 1981) comments on in relation to certain telecommunications firms in the USA, they are certainly guilty of failing to discourage or prevent it.

But besides the costs and risks, arguably more interesting and revealing are the symbolic, subjective and experiential dimensions of drug and alcohol use in time-share selling. Further to the financial incentives to drink and do drugs at work, timeshare sales work encourages the celebration of 'maverick' behaviour, and this too incentivises OPCs to maintain drink and drug habits. Keith, a 29-year-old OPC, explains the prevalence of drug and alcohol use amongst his colleagues:

> It feels too much like an extended holiday out here, which is bad for you. Being on holiday and working is hard to juggle and loads of people lose their jobs because they're partying too much and can't get up early enough. You're always knackered 'cos you've been up all night, so then you need a few lines to get you buzzin' again. Everyone's coked up...not everyone, but most of us are. It's everywhere, it's like it's expected of you if you're in timeshare.

Keith also explained how, although officially it is prohibited, alcohol and drug consumption at work is almost always overlooked by supervisors and managers because it can have a positive effect on productivity. Indeed, team-leaders, who are in theory responsible for preventing the use of drink and drugs at work, seem to be amongst the heaviest users and dealers. Keith explained how a blind eye is also turned to OPCs who supplement their income by dealing cocaine and other drugs to co-workers and tourists. Thus drinking and drug-taking in the workplace appear to serve two purposes. First, they help OPCs to gain confidence, become less inhibited and maintain the 'buzz' needed to sell effectively. Second, drug taking and drinking as forms of crime/deviance underpin the perceived and celebrated 'maverick' quality of timeshare culture.

It is the idea that drinking and drug-taking are 'expected of you if you're in time-share' which points to what it means to 'be' to those who sell timeshare. It points to one's subjectivity and identity as a certain type of worker, one whose behaviour can have maverick qualities and whose work is definitely *not* routine. 'Deviance' and maverick behaviour in the workplace help to set timeshare apart from 'regular' work and OPCs often construct timeshare selling as not really proper work at all. This idea is upheld by Jason's take on drug use:

> I do do coke at work. A fair bit I suppose... it's because I have to nowadays, because the day can seem really flat without it... it's not just that though, I mean its everywhere, it's a part of a normal day.

> You know, like, I wish it wasn't cos it's no good for you in the long run, but let's face it, timeshare's mad. It's a mad job; that's why we love it and that's why I'd find an office job impossible now. What other job lets you get shit-faced every day without getting sacked?

Timeshare selling allows for a degree of freedom in the workplace (itself a shifting and non-restrictive outdoor 'patch') and this is an important factor to OPCs. The potential to partake in deviant behaviour helps OPCs to construct their work in direct contrast to the kind of 'mundane' jobs ordinarily on offer, whilst satisfying a longing for freedom characteristic of timeshare rhetoric (and central to wider migration imperatives for young British people living in Tenerife, see Bott, 2004).

OPCs also perceive the organisation of timeshare selling as being advantageous, particularly in terms of the 'freelance' employment relation. Rather than viewing the freelance/commission system as a risky form of exploitation, the status of freelancer actually appeals to many OPCs. They read it as a form of independence from authority, and this is valued highly:

> I'm quite independent really and I hate to be controlled, especially when I'm at work. The good thing about this job is the freedom it gives you...I can be my own boss and there's no-one breathing down my neck all the time...it's risky, yeah, because you never know how much money you're gonna make in a week, but that's what keeps you going...knowing you've got to make

your rent... the police come down now and again on their motorbikes but they're easy enough to avoid...

I'm good at this job, it's the first job I've ever stuck to...it's not a normal job, which is why I like it. I'm just not a 9–5 girl.

(Sam)

The idea of following a 'legitimate' career path does not connect to the individualised discourse of timeshare culture. OPCs do not wish to return to 'a normal job' and go back to low salaries, long hours and mundane work. Direct employment is recognised as entailing hierarchical power relations, whereas the non-standard employment relation of OPC work is imagined as implying autonomy for the worker. The elements of criminality, risk and independence in timeshare sales are crucial to this construction of OPC work as different from 'normal' work.

Patricia Adler, in her ethnography of upper-level drug dealing in the USA, notes that the value of deviant occupations lies in their direct contrast to the 'bureaucratisation and rationalisation' of conventional forms of work. Drug dealing and smuggling, she writes, are:

[F]lexible, creative, exciting and personal enterprises...uninhibited by the constraints of bureaucratic rules...[whose] relationships were imbued with individuality, feeling and meaning...[t]his made character attributes a very important part of the business.

(1993: 148 – emphasis added)

Despite the fact that timeshare is heavily associated with drug-dealing itself, these appeals of drug-dealing as a deviant career can also apply to timeshare selling. Interviewees talked of the benefits of working outdoors on the streets and at a distance from their bosses, about enjoying creative freedom in their sales tactics, and the excitement and individuality of the job. Relative autonomy and the freedom to work to more or less self-determined sales targets and methods means that OPCs have a high level of control over the details of their job and, in that sense, as with Adler's dealers and traffickers, have a low degree of alienation from it.

Work/play

Timeshare's deviant elements, its tourist setting and 'party' atmosphere, together with its anti-bureaucratic organisation, help OPCs to construct it as something extraordinary; something *other* than work. The distinctions and divisions between what constitutes work and non-work, and, more specifically, between work and leisure are becoming increasingly blurred in Western post-industrial (increasingly leisure-based) societies (Grint, 1991; Gershuny, 2000). Stanley Parker has discussed extensively the subjective meanings of the relationship between work and leisure, and argued (albeit in 1971) that whilst most people regard their jobs merely as a means to an end and not as a source of positive satisfaction, this does not mean that work can be set up in direct opposition to leisure. According to Parker, work extends into leisure, and vice versa, and this flow occurs on an individual level. But Parker also pointed out that this process (individuals choosing to bring work into leisure and leisure into work) can only occur when it is structurally facilitated (by a society that does not keep 'places of work free from the influences of leisure and places of leisure free from the taint of work') (1971: 102).

The OPC subjects of this study regard their jobs as a source of satisfaction, and actually more like leisure than work (many discussed how the job involves periods of time when they are free to do as they please, as well as 'artistic' freedoms, and their perception of the workplace as resembling 'paradise'). The timeshare market is itself located in the leisure industry and employers actively encourage practices more normally associated with leisure than with work. They allow OPCs to bring leisure into work and work into leisure because they are well aware of the financial benefits this will bring. Employers allow their OPCs to play (to consume recreational drugs and alcohol, to have access to a degree of freedom and autonomy, to partake in 'horseplay' and so on) during working hours because they know these things are integral to most OPCs' sales techniques and will therefore ultimately generate profit.

Sex sells: women in timeshare

Although the timeshare workforce is male-dominated (around 80% of OPCs are male) and reproductive of 'laddish' masculinity, there are nonetheless significant numbers of women OPCs working in Tenerife. Like Karen (quoted earlier), timeshare work often gives women the opportunity to leave an unfulfilling career in retail, for example, for better paid, more exciting and enjoyable work. There also seems to be an equal tendency for women to consume cocaine and alcohol at work as men (although women are not reputed to be dealers).

Blagging techniques, for women, tend to rely on their own sexuality. Female OPCs generally prefer to aim their pitch at 'husbands' – 'English geezers, on holiday with their wives' – and whilst male OPCs attract the attention of other male clients through imagined shared masculine or 'geezer' affiliation and then go on to 'charm wives' in order to win an 'up', women OPCs use their sexuality to attract 'husbands' and follow up by playing on imagined feminine bonds with 'wives'. As Tammy, aged 24, explains:

> You've got to look nice, wear sexy clothes, 'cause it helps attract attention. You go for the bloke, flirt with him a bit, 'cause he's the one with the money, and it definitely helps if he thinks you're attractive… men only think about one thing don't they? Then, because you don't want the wife to get funny, you ask her about the hotel, or tell her she's nice and brown.

Within the overall hyper atmosphere of selling, there is the persistent need for women OPCs to behave flirtatiously in order to make 'ups'. The drama of blagging requires, especially of women, a sexualised performance. Indeed, it could be described as allowing oneself to be sexually harassed in order to make an 'up', as Stacey, aged 21, explains:

> Let's face it, girls only do well in this game if they're fit-looking, or if they know how to really work blokes…I know that if I come to work in a low-cut top and a miniskirt, I'm gonna do far better than if I was wearing a jumper. That's why we don't like the crap weather… blokes like to see a bit of skin…they don't mind talking to you if they can get a bit of an eyeful or you let them get away with being a bit cheeky…they love the attention… if you've picked a good couple, the wife won't give a shit.

Tammy and Stacey, as well as the three other women OPCs interviewed use cocaine and alcohol before, during and after work.

Conclusions

This chapter has discussed how the organisation of timeshare sustains an almost entirely unprotected, self-sufficient street-sales workforce. Rather than having to invest in shop premises, salaries, benefits and other outgoings, timeshare employers send their vendors onto the streets to recruit custom, only paying out when they are reasonably certain that OPCs' endeavours will translate into a sale. Almost all risk is passed onto the OPC and employers gain extremely good returns on relatively low, safe investments. Market forces are being capitalised upon by employers within timeshare, who rely on their workforce's dependence on commission as their only form of payment, and are thus able to exercise a level of control over work rate and intensity without the need for direct (costly) supervision.

But, as has been seen, timeshare employers are also dependent on the so-called 'personality market' and the importance of 'non-work' (consumption and play). Within the culture of timeshare, where work is constructed and enjoyed as being not 'real' work, OPCs' self-exploitation is constructed as a form of 'play'. Besides the physical and emotional health risks involved in using alcohol and drugs as performance enhancers, for women OPCs, the working day may also entail capitalising on their own sexual exploitation.[3] Under the freelance system, without the safety net of a basic wage or any assurance of employment continuity, there is little doubt that OPCs need trade on their personalities through processes involving consumption, deviance and play. It is necessary to consider the relevance of these concepts to the OPC consciousness – and how they work within the market

---

3 Gendered, as well as racialised, aged, sexualised and nationalised identities all play a considerably more important role to OPC work than this chapter has the capacity to discuss.

relation set up by employers – in order to understand both the mechanics of time-share employers' control over workers and the subjective dynamics of this kind of employment relation.

A number of scholars have commented on how the development of the service industry (especially 'interactive' service work, which includes leisure jobs) as an increasingly consumption-related sphere has led to a blurring of the boundaries between work and non-work and production and consumption (Du Gay 1993, 1996; Crompton, 2003). The data suggest that young Britons move into timeshare in Tenerife in order to partake in a working lifestyle characterised by consumption; of sunshine, drugs, alcohol, and sex. They consume Tenerife as a form of revolt from their original communities (see Douglas, 2003), which often signified class inequality: poverty, disenfranchisement, lack of opportunity. New identities are forged through consumption and often pedalling of illicit substances, and OPC work is heavily underpinned by identity reproduction because as a job it supports a culture of consumption as revolt. Importantly, status is displayed and reproduced via conspicuous consumption (Veblen, [1899] 1994), allowing OPCs a sense of control over their social identities – instead of being the 'loser' living on a 'sink estate', struggling to make ends meet at the bottom of a classed pecking order, they now have the wherewithal to engage in consumption practices that visibly mark their success.

The individualised nature of timeshare presents certain rewards to OPCs, because although in reality they are, as freelancers, arguably selling themselves as 'instruments of an alien will' (Gorz, 1999), they nonetheless self-identify as independent, autonomous, free-market actors and not as normal 'workers', answerable to and controlled by an employer or other authority figure. Employers, in exercising the commission/freelance system, uphold this myth by constructing OPCs as equal players and the wage–labour exchange as the meeting of buyers and sellers across a non-hierarchical market. Practically speaking, the freelance system is also straight-forward and non-bureaucratic, which benefits not only employers supporting an often illegally marketed trade, but also pleases workers with their individualistic, non-conformist, anti-bureaucratic, maverick ideals.

Timeshare work does, therefore, simultaneously engender and reflect the 'individualistic, rather than collectivist sentiments' that Crompton believes the service industry increasingly generates (2003: 161). But at the same time, this form of labour can be understood as being connected to a type of class-consciousness, manifest in the widespread resentment amongst OPCs toward their class backgrounds. They experience their work as a vehicle for mobility – social, cultural and economic, as well as physical.

Timeshare employers, through their manipulation of employment relations, are in a position to exploit these young people's 'revolt' against their own position within, and attachment to, the class structure. That is to say, in their exploitation of the 'attendant risks' of individualised labour market fate (Beck, 1992: 92), timeshare employers are able to take advantage of the resentment provoked by the consciousness and meaning of class inequality entrenched elsewhere.

Selling timeshare is 'extreme' on many levels. The way it is organised places enormous and relentless pressure on OPCs whose psychological and emotional investments are significantly high. There is little or no support available to OPCs who shoulder many of the financial and legal risks associated with the industry. Emotional labour is performed using a range of 'acting' techniques such as clowning and flirting, and these are often aided by the use of alcohol and other 'social lubricants'.

The harmful consequences of performing this emotional labour are indisputable in the sense that it can bring various occupational hazards: drug and alcohol dependency, arrests, exhaustion, stress, sunstroke and black eyes were all recorded in my field diary. Less determinable though is the likelihood of OPCs becoming alienated or 'detached' from an 'aspect of self – either the body or the margins of the soul – that is *used* to do the work' (Hochschild, 1983: 7), although Korczynski (2002) holds that claims about the inevitability of this risk are meaningful only when we neglect to consider the subjective and socially embedded aspects of emotional labour.

The positively held subjective dimensions of selling timeshare are so pronounced within the interview data that they are impossible to neglect. Many aspects of this work are empowering: the *hope* of earning decent wages; the *honour* in individual endeavour; freedom of action; autonomy and independence from authority, standardisation, routinisation and (explicit) control. Timeshare selling and the lifestyle closely attached to it facilitate the reproduction of positively self-evaluated classed, gendered and racialised identities and the circulation of (upward) mobility narratives. Timeshare allows these people to 'be'.

Male and female OPCs invest emotions in order to 'blag' but it is they who sharpen the basic rules set by the market. They allow themselves to be exploited as a means to an end but the extent of that exploitation is not corporately monitored or controlled in the manner that led Hochschild to worry for the integrity of human dignity. OPCs are well aware that their character attributes are essential to productivity, and allow them to be exploited as a means to these complex sets of ends.

References

Adler, P.A. (1993) *Wheeling and Dealing: An Ethnography of an Upper-Level Drug Dealing and Smuggling Community*, New York, Columbia University Press.

Beck, U. (1992) *Risk Society: Towards a New Modernity*, London: Sage.

Bott, E. (2004) 'Working a working-class utopia: marking young Britons in Tenerife on the new map of European migration', *Journal of Contemporary European Studies*, **12** (1), 57–70.

Bott, E. (2006) 'Pole-position: Migrant British women producing "selves" through lap dancing work', *Feminist Review*, 83 (1), 23–41.

Cohen, E. (1988) 'Authenticity and commoditization in tourism', *Annals of Tourism Research*, 15 (3), 371–386.

Crompton, R. (2003) 'Consumption and class analysis', in D. Clarke, M. Doel and K. Housiaux (eds), *The Consumption Reader*, London: Routledge, pp. 157–62.

Douglas, M. (2003) 'The consumer's revolt', in D. Clarke, M. Doel and K. Housiaux (eds), *The Consumption Reader*, London: Routledge. pp. 144-50.

Du Gay, P. (1993) 'Numbers and souls: retailing and the de-differentiation of economy and culture', *British Journal of Sociology*, 44, 563–587.

Du Gay, P. (1996) *Consumption and Identity at Work*, London: Sage.

ECC Report (2003) http://ec.europa.eu/consumers/redress/ecc_network/timeshare_europe2003.pdf, accessed 10 May 2009.

Enloe, C. (1989) *Bananas, Beaches and Bases: Making Feminist Sense of International Politics*, London: Pandora.

Gershuny, J. (2000) *Changing Times: Work and Leisure in Postindustrial Society*, Oxford: Oxford University Press.

Glazer, (1993) *Women's Paid and Unpaid Labor*, Philadelphia: Temple University Press.

gotimeshare (2009) http://www.gotimeshare.org/consumer-alerts/0053-ote-targets-timeshare-scams, accessed 8 July 2009.

Gorz, A. (1999) *Reclaiming Work: Beyond the Wage-Based Society*, Cambridge: Polity Press.

Grint, K. (1991) *The Sociology of Work: an Introduction*. Cambridge: Polity Press.

Haylock, R. (1994) 'The European timeshare market: the growth, development, regulation and economic benefits of one of tourism's most successful sectors', *Tourism Management*, 15 (5), 333–341.

Hochschild, A. (1983) *The Managed Heart*, Berkeley: University of California Press.

Korczynski, M. (2002) *Human Resource Management in Service Work*, Basingstoke and New York: Palgrave.

Ley, B. (2001) *Blaggers: Adventures Inside the Sun-kissed but Murky World of Holiday Timeshare*, Edinburgh: Mainstream Publishing Company.

MacCannell, D. (1999) *The Tourist: A New Theory of the Leisure Class*, Berkeley and Los Angeles: University of California Press.

Marks, S. (2003) *Paradise Lost: CAB Clients' Experience of Timeshare and Timesharelike Products*, Citizens' Advice Bureau Report.

Meethan, K. (2001) *Tourism in Global Society: Place, Culture, Consumption*, London: Palgrave.

OTR (2003) http://www.ote-info.com/ (15 February 2003) accessed 7 July 2009.

OTE (2007) Response to the OFT consultation 28 February 2007:http://www.oft.gov.uk/shared_oft/about_oft/349517/OTEresponse.pdf, accessed 7 July 2009.

Parker, S. (1971) *The Future of Work and Leisure*, London: Paladin.

Sánchez-Taylor, J. (2001) 'Dollars are a girl's best friend? Female tourists' sexual behaviour in the Caribbean', *Sociology*, 35, 749–764.

Sheller, M. (2003) *Consuming the Caribbean: From Arawaks to Zombies*, London: Routledge.

TRI Hospitality Consulting (2001) *The European Timeshare Industry in 2001*, London: Organisation for Timeshare in Europe.

Urry, J. (2002) *The Tourist Gaze*, 2nd edn, London: Sage.

Urry, J. (2003) 'Death in Venice', in Sheller, M. and J. Urry (eds), *Tourism Mobilities: Places to Play, Places in Play*, London: Routledge.pp. 205-216.

Veblen, T. ([1899] 1994) *The Theory of the Leisure Class*, New York: Dover.

Watts, M. (1992) 'Spaces for everything (a commentary)', *Cultural Anthropology*, 7, 115–129.

Woods, R.H. (2001) 'Important issues for a growing timeshare industry', *Cornell Hotel and Restaurant Administration Quarterly*, 42, 71–82.

Part III:

Responses to Tourist-related Crime

8 Cross-border Cooperation in Criminal Investigations

Toine Spapens

This chapter:

♦ Confirms that police and judicial cooperation in criminal matters still depends largely on a system of assistance upon request.

♦ Reviews how, over the years, an extensive legal and organisational framework has been developed for the exchange of requests for mutual legal assistance.

♦ Concludes that substantial police and judicial cooperation with regard to crimes involving tourists is seldom necessary. In most cases, the authorities of the country where the crime was committed are able to conduct the investigation and prosecution.

♦ Considers exceptional cases where the tourist was the perpetrator but was able to return home before being apprehended or identified.

♦ Provides an example of a recent promising development: the institution of joint operations with regard to public order policing of tourist areas and the reining in of drug tourism.

Introduction

Whilst on holiday abroad, tourists may become the victims of crime or commit crimes themselves. The police and the judicial authorities of the country where the offence occurs will usually conduct the investigation and prosecution. In some cases, however, concluding the case will require information from the authorities in the tourists' country of origin or further investigation on the part of these authorities.

This chapter concerns cross-border police and judicial cooperation in cases involving tourists, the term 'tourist' being taken in a broad sense. My definition includes not only tourists travelling abroad for a number of days but also those who do not stay overnight while visiting another country for purposes of recreation. With regard to police and judicial cooperation, this contribution will focus largely on mutual legal assistance. The topic of extradition I shall consider only briefly.

Throughout history, authorities of sovereign states or independent jurisdictions have always cooperated on an *ad hoc* basis in specific cases of cross-border crime. From the end of the 1950s onwards, the United Nations (UN), the Commonwealth of Nations, the Council of Europe, and the European Union (EU) developed an extensive legal framework for mutual legal assistance. This framework consists of a patchwork of conventions. I first address the most significant conventions adopted within Europe, and then focus on the legal framework for mutual legal assistance outside Europe. Both sections will be limited to multilateral arrangements. Countries may also have adopted bilateral treaties, but space restrictions mean that they cannot be discussed in the present chapter. Police and judicial cooperation still depends largely on a system of assistance upon request, the usual practice being that the police and judicial authorities exchange written requests for legal assistance within an established organisational framework. At the international level, Interpol, which operates a worldwide network of national bureaus for exchanging information between the police of different countries, is the best-known organisation. Other provisions are police liaison services and, particularly within the EU, Europol, the European Judicial Network (EJN) and Eurojust.

The next section of the chapter describes the organisational framework for law enforcement cooperation. The subsequent three sections address practical police and judicial cooperation with regard to tourism. They first give some examples of law enforcement cooperation with regard to criminal investigation involving tourists, and then address cooperation with regard to public order policing in places frequented by tourists and, lastly, police cooperation with regard to controlling drugs tourism in the Dutch border areas. Finally, some general conclusions are offered.

The legal framework for police and judicial cooperation within Europe

Over the years, both the Council of Europe and the EU have developed a number of treaties, Council, Acts, and Council Framework Decisions in order to enhance police and judicial cooperation.[1] This section presents the most important multilateral conventions:

♦ the European Convention on Mutual Assistance in Criminal Matters (1959)

♦ the European Convention on the Transfer of Proceedings in Criminal Matters (1972)

♦ the Schengen Implementation Convention (1990)

---

1 The Council of Europe is not to be confused with the European Council, the principal decision-making organ of the European Union. The Council of Europe was founded in 1949 with the aim of furthering European integration. It currently comprises 48 countries.

- the Convention on Mutual Assistance in Criminal Matters between the Member States of the European Union (2000)
- the European Arrest Warrant (2002)
- the Treaty on stepping up of cross-border cooperation, particularly in combating terrorism, cross-border crime and illegal migration (Treaty of Prüm) and its incorporation into the legal framework of the EU (2005/2008)
- the Council Framework Decision 2006/960/Justice and Home Affairs (JHA) on information exchange (2006).

The 'European Convention on Mutual Assistance in Criminal Matters' of 1959 was the first important multilateral treaty concerning police and judicial cooperation in Europe[2]. Drawn up by the Council of Europe, it provides for the exchange of letters rogatory, which are formal requests for mutual legal assistance exchanged by the prosecution services of different countries. A letter rogatory describes the offence(s) under investigation and, if known, the identities of the suspects involved as well as the assistance required. The party whose assistance is sought after can only comply with a request if the offence is also punishable under its own domestic penal law. Therefore, the sending authorities will usually attach the relevant paragraphs of its penal code to the rogatory letter. This Convention also includes specific provisions for interrogating suspects, interviewing witnesses, searching premises, and exchanging information from criminal and judicial records. A party may also request another to institute proceedings in its own territory (Article 21).

The Council of Europe also established the 'European Convention on the Transfer of Proceedings in Criminal Matters'. This convention extended Article 21 of the European Convention of 1959 by permitting the transfer of proceedings between contracting states when the requesting state appears to be in a better position to bring those proceedings to a successful conclusion (McClean, 2002: 193). This can be of particular use in crimes involving tourists from the same country. If, for example, two Dutch nationals on holiday in Turkey become involved in a fight, the prosecution may be transferred to the Netherlands. Application of this Convention, however, is somewhat limited because it has been implemented in only 25 of the member states of the Council of Europe, not including the United Kingdom, France, Italy, Germany and others[3].

The third important treaty, the 'Convention implementing the Schengen Agreement of 14 June 1985 between the Governments of the States of the Benelux Economic Union, the Federal Republic of Germany and the French Republic on the gradual abolition of checks at their common borders', was signed in 1990. The treaty, more commonly known as the Schengen Implementation Convention, considerably enhanced the legal framework for police cooperation. In 1988,

---

2 The Convention is available at the website of the Council of Europe. See www.coe.int (accessed 11 May 2009).

3 See http://conventions.coe.int/ (accessed 11 May 2009).

the Schengen Acquis to the Treaty of Amsterdam extended the convention to all EU member states (Official Journal, 2000a). It contains provisions for the direct exchange of information between the police forces and for cross-border pursuit, cross-border surveillance, and police 'sting' operations involving the controlled delivery of illicit drugs. It also provides a formal framework for the exchange of police liaison officers.

Fourth, in May 2000, the 'Convention on Mutual Assistance in Criminal Matters between the Member States of the European Union' was signed (Official Journal, 2000b). This time, the EU took the initiative instead of the Council of Europe because it had proven to be impossible to reach an agreement about an extension of the 1959 convention[4]. The Convention on Mutual Assistance in Criminal Matters includes an extensive framework for intercepting telephone conversations and contains provisions with regard to cross-border covert operations. Moreover, it formally introduced joint investigation teams as a means of enhancing operational police cooperation. The convention also extended existing provisions. Among other things, it enabled the interviewing of witnesses and experts by means of telephone or videoconferencing and extended the possibility of controlled deliveries to types of crime other than those involving illicit drugs.

Next, the Council Framework Decision on the European arrest warrant and the surrender procedures between member states (2002/584/JHA) adopted on 13 June 2002 is also worth mentioning (Official Journal, 2002a). A national judicial authority may issue such a warrant if the person whose return is sought is accused of an offence for which the maximum period of the penalty is at least a year in prison or if he or she has been sentenced to a prison term of at least four months. A decision by the judicial authority of a member state to require the arrest and return of a person should be executed as quickly and as easily as possible in the other member states of the European Union. The European arrest warrant therefore accelerates and simplifies surrender procedures and eliminates political involvement. It also means that member states can no longer refuse to surrender to another member state their own citizens who have committed a serious crime or who are suspected of having committed such a crime in another EU country, on the grounds that they are their own nationals[5].

Sixth, Germany, France, the Benelux countries, Spain, and Austria signed the Treaty of Prüm in 2005[6]. To begin with, the treaty was intended to facilitate the

---

4 However, already in 2001 the provisions of the Convention on Mutual Assistance in Criminal Matters were also adopted by the Council of Europe, by means of an additional protocol to the European Convention of 1959.

5 See http://ec.europa.eu/justice_home/fsj/criminal/extradition/fsj_criminal_extradition_en.htm (accessed 5 May 2009).

6 For an English version of the Treaty, see: Council of the European Union, Treaty of Prüm, 10900/05, Brussels, 7 July 2005. Available at: http://www.statewatch.org/news/2005/aug/Prum-Convention.pdf (accessed 23 March 2009).

exchange of information by allowing the parties online access to databases of DNA profiles and to trace evidence on a hit/no-hit basis. In other words, the police can check online if a matching DNA profile or fingerprint is available abroad. If this is the case, the competent authority can send a request for mutual legal assistance to ask for further details. The treaty also enables online access to vehicle registration data. Moreover, it lists a number of sources from which the police can directly request information. Finally, the Treaty of Prüm also contains articles specifically concerning public order policing.

After the original seven countries had signed the Treaty of Prüm, discussion started about incorporating the convention into the legal framework of the EU. In 2008, this resulted in the Framework Decision on the stepping up of cross-border cooperation, particularly in combating terrorism and cross-border crime, which incorporates the larger part of the original Treaty of Prüm[7]. The European Council accepted the decision (2008/615/JHA) on 23 June 2008 (Official Journal, 2008).

Finally, the Council Framework Decision 2006/960/JHA on simplifying the exchange of information and intelligence between law enforcement authorities of the member states of the European Union is particularly noteworthy (Official Journal, 2006). This decision updated Articles 39 and 46 of the Schengen Implementation Convention on information exchange between the police and also provided for intelligence sharing and specified the periods for responding to information requests. For example, the police need to reply to urgent requests within eight hours.

All this illustrates that there is a substantial legal framework in place for police and judicial cooperation within Europe. The common aims of the various conventions have been, first, to create a uniform basis for police and judicial cooperation in the light of an increasing number of cases of cross-border crime with the emphasis on serious and organised crime and, second, to speed up the exchange of requests for mutual legal assistance.

In the past, the national authorities, usually the ministry of justice, had to review virtually all requests. Nowadays, the local prosecution services or the police may directly handle almost all of them. The ministry of justice becomes involved only if questions arise for which there are no specific provisions in the legal framework. An example of this is the case of a Dutchman who allegedly murdered his wife and then hid the body in a forest in the Belgian Ardennes. After several months, he recovered the badly decomposed remains, put them in his car, and drove to Germany, where he was apprehended. The Dutch authorities thereupon asked the Germans to deliver the car, with the victim's body still in it, to the Netherlands for forensic examination. As might be expected, none of the conventions covered such a request. Legal experts of the German Ministry of Justice decided that the request should be complied with.

---

7 Some provisions with regard to cross-border public order policing were omitted, especially those Articles enabling police officers to provide assistance on foreign territory on their own initiative.

The legal framework for police and judicial cooperation outside Europe

In contrast to the legal framework for law enforcement cooperation within the context of the European Union and the Council of Europe, there are few multilateral conventions involving other countries of the world. From a European viewpoint, this is probably because most requests for mutual legal assistance are exchanged between nearby countries. For example, empirical research conducted in the Netherlands had shown that only about 10% of all the requests for mutual legal assistance handled by the Amsterdam prosecution service in 2002 originated from countries outside Europe (Fijnaut et al., 2005: 114)[8].

Multilateral conventions worth mentioning here are the United Nations convention against illicit traffic in narcotic drugs and psychotropic substances of 1988; the UN convention against transnational organised crime of 2000; and the Commonwealth Scheme for Mutual Assistance in Criminal Matters of 1990, which applies to member states of the Commonwealth of Nations.

The UN Convention of 1988 enables the parties to afford one another the widest measure of mutual legal assistance in investigations, prosecutions, and judicial proceedings in relation to criminal offences with regard to narcotic drugs and psychotropic substances listed by the UN (Article 7). This includes the production, manufacture, extraction, preparation, offering for sale, distribution, sale and delivery on any terms whatsoever, brokerage, dispatch and dispatch in transit, transport, importation or exportation (Article 3). The Convention also provides for mutual legal assistance in the case of conversion or transfer of property derived from these actions. The forms of assistance available include taking evidence or statements from persons, effecting the service of judicial documents, executing searches and seizures, examining objects and sites, and providing information and evidentiary items. Finally, there are provisions made for the transfer of proceedings (Article 8) and controlled delivery (Article 11).

The UN adopted the convention against transnational organised crime on 15 November 2000. The provisions with regard to mutual legal assistance (Article 18) are comparable to those listed in Article 7 of the 1988 convention. This convention, however, covers only transnational serious crime involving an organised criminal group. The UN defines serious crime as a conduct constituting an offence punishable by a maximum deprivation of liberty of at least four years or a more serious penalty. Applicability of the convention to crimes involving tourists may, therefore, be limited, as most tourists involved in crimes abroad will not qualify as an organised criminal group. However, members of organised criminal groups may well mix business with pleasure when on holiday. In one case examined by the

---

8 Most letters rogatory were sent by the United States and Israel. This is because, at that time, ecstasy was being trafficked from the Netherlands to the United States on a large scale largely by Dutch, American and Israeli citizens.

present author, a member of a Dutch criminal group producing ecstasy regularly took short vacations in Thailand during which he met with customers.

Provisions for mutual legal assistance are included in the Commonwealth Scheme for Mutual Assistance in Criminal Matters (or Harare Scheme). The member states adopted this convention in 1990 and extended it in 2002 and 2005.[9] The Commonwealth of Nations now includes 53 member states, with 1.9 billion inhabitants. The Scheme provides for the giving of assistance by the competent authorities of one country in respect of criminal matters arising in another country. It includes assistance similar to the UN conventions described above but also provides for facilitating the personal appearance of witnesses; for the temporary transfer of persons in custody to appear as a witness; for tracing, seizing and confiscating the proceeds or instrumentalities of crime; and for the preservation of computer data. The latter includes retrieving subscriber information, traffic data and content data (Article 15).

Apart from engaging in multilateral conventions, countries can also agree to bilateral arrangements on mutual legal assistance. The Netherlands, for instance, have adopted conventions with Germany, Belgium, Luxembourg, Canada, Australia, the Hong Kong Special Administrative Region of the People's Republic of China, and Surinam. Finally, if no treaties or applicable provisions exist, the national authorities of the countries involved can decide upon providing mutual assistance in individual cases subject to specific agreed-upon terms and conditions.

The organisational framework for police and judicial cooperation

Effective international law enforcement cooperation requires an organisational infrastructure for handling requests for mutual legal assistance. Hence, countries have made arrangements within the police and prosecution services in the form of specific departments charged with handling requests for mutual legal assistance. In the Netherlands, for instance, local Centres for Legal Assistance (*Internationale rechtshulpcentra*), of which there are six, are the focal points for requests for legal assistance. The public prosecution service and the police operate these centres jointly. The actual execution of requests is the responsibility of the local prosecution services and police. Individual countries have also made bilateral arrangements. An example is a joint police and customs station operated by France and Belgium in the border area of Lille, where information is exchanged directly. Finally, multilateral arrangements have been established at the international and EU levels. This includes Interpol, Europol, police-liaison networks, and, finally, the European Judicial Network and Eurojust.

---

9   See http://www.thecommonwealth.org (accessed 12 May 2009).

Interpol

The International Criminal Police Organization, more commonly known as Interpol, was founded in 1923 in Vienna. At present, 187 countries across the world are associated to Interpol. Although this organisation is not based on a treaty, it has comparable status. Interpol is primarily an information exchange network. To this purpose, national central bureaus have been set up in every member state through which requests for information may be sent. These bureaus can be reached 24 hours a day, seven days a week. In addition, Interpol provides data services, maintains databases of police information, and operates a command and coordination centre that member states may use in support of international police operations. Finally, Interpol also provides training and support to the police with regard to fighting cross-border crime[10]. However, contrary to what the public may think, Interpol itself has no executive investigative powers.

Europol

Europol is a young organisation relative to Interpol, as the Europol convention only came into effect in 1999. The idea, however, for creating a European criminal investigation department first emerged in the 1970s (Oberleitner, 1998: 99). In June 1991, the Council of the EU adopted a proposal to create a form of Europol in this sense (European Council, 1991: 20). In February 1992, however, Article K.1.9 of the Treaty of Maastricht referred to Europol only as the 'organization of a Union-wide system for exchanging information within a European Police Office'. The Europol Drugs Unit (EDU) was set up in 1995 as a forerunner of Europol (Official Journal, 1995a) The EDU was charged with exchanging information and intelligence affecting at least two member states and with helping the police and other competent agencies to combat illicit drug trafficking. In the years to follow, the mandate of the EDU was extended to trafficking in radioactive and nuclear substances, crimes involving clandestine immigration networks, trafficking in human beings and in illicit vehicle, and criminal organisations involved in money-laundering[11]. The EU adopted the Europol Convention on 18 July 1995, but it took another four years before it came into effect (Official Journal, 1995b).

Europol's office is in The Hague in the Netherlands. Europol acts as a clearing house for information with regard to organised crime and terrorism within the European Union. It operates liaison bureaus in each of the member states comparable to the National Central Bureaus of Interpol. In 2005, Europol processed 260,463 requests for information (Europol, 2007: 32). Furthermore, the organisation operates an information system (EIS, Europol Information System) and maintains analysis workfiles (AWF) in support of criminal investigations involving two or more member states. Europol opened 16 AWFs in 2007 (Europol, 2007: 26). Like Interpol, Europol has no executive powers.

---

10 See www.interpol.int (accessed 12 May 2009).

11 See http://europa.eu/scadplus/leg/en/lvb/l14005a.htm (accessed 23 March 2009).

Police liaison officers

Networks of police liaison officers have an important role in law enforcement cooperation. The Schengen Implementation Convention provides for the exchange of police liaison officers between the member states of the EU (Article 47). There is also a network of such officers in the context of the Commonwealth of Nations. The exchange of liaison officers may also result from bilateral agreement. Spain, for instance, has liaison officers presently stationed in eight EU member states, ten South-American countries, five African countries, and Russia, the United States, Turkey and Ukraine.[12] In return, 18 countries have stationed liaison officers in Spain itself. The exchange of police liaison officers often mirrors lines of criminal cooperation. The Netherlands, for instance, already had a liaison officer in Thailand in the 1970s because, at that time, South-East Asia was a major source of heroin sold on the Dutch market.

The primary role of police liaison officers, as stated in Article 47 of the Schengen Implementation Treaty, is to provide assistance in the form of the exchange of information for the purposes of combating crime by means of both prevention and law enforcement and with regard to responding to requests for mutual police and judicial assistance in criminal matters. Liaison officers have no executive powers and cannot undertake independent action on foreign territory. For instance, if a British investigation team wants to obtain traffic data of a cell phone from the Portuguese authorities, a police liaison officer may be contacted to act as an intermediary but also to determine if a request for mutual legal assistance meets the specific requirements set by the recipient country. The requesting country may approach its own police liaison officer in the country in which assistance is sought and vice versa. If agreed upon, liaison officers of third countries may also provide help. If, for instance, the Dutch police need to cooperate with Kyrgyzstan and do not have a liaison officer there, it may be possible to make use of one who is working there on behalf of another country.

The European Judicial Network and Eurojust

The European Judicial Network (EJN) started its activities in 1998 (Official Journal, 1998). This network consists of the national judicial authorities of the EU member states, each of which has assigned one experienced public prosecutor to the EJN. The primary aim of the EJN is to support the exchange of requests for mutual legal assistance. For instance, the EJN can assist public prosecutors who want to contact an authority in another member state and assist in formulating letters rogatory. Finally, the EJN has developed instruments intended to ease law enforcement cooperation, an example of which is a template form with regard to the European Arrest Warrant, which the EJN has made available online.

---

12   See www.interpol.int (accessed 12 May 2009).

The final important international institution is Eurojust, the office of which is also in The Hague. This organisation was founded in 2002 in order to facilitate law enforcement cooperation between the EU member states especially with regard to organised crime (Official Journal, 2002b). Each of the member states has assigned one experienced public prosecutor or police officer to Eurojust. Its main task is to support the competent authorities of two or more member states in criminal investigations. In 2007, Eurojust was asked for support in 1085 cases (Eurojust, 2007: 13). If needed, Eurojust can host meetings between criminal investigators from two or more member states working on cross-border cases for which it has facilities for simultaneous interpretation. In 2007, prosecutors used the facility 74 times (Eurojust, 2007: 21).

Investigation of crime involving tourists

This section focuses on practical police and judicial cooperation during the investigation of crime involving tourists. This is necessary only in a minority of cases as the local police and prosecution service of the country where the offence took place will usually be able to handle the investigation by themselves. In most cases, therefore, the exchange of requests for mutual legal assistance will be limited in scope. For instance, if a tourist has been victim of a crime and the police have not been able to identify an offender, there is no point in law-enforcement cooperation. In specific situations, however, close cooperation will be necessary.

The observations below are derived from the study of nine empirical cases handled by the Centre for Legal Assistance responsible for the southern part of the Netherlands from 2006 to 2008. One further case arose in an earlier research project (Van Daele et al., 2008). From this, it can be concluded that crimes involving tourists requiring extensive law enforcement cooperation are relatively rare[13]. In addition, we have examined public information on cases that have drawn much attention in the past years, particularly the disappearances of Madeleine McCann in Portugal and Natalee Holloway in Aruba. Based on the empirical data, police and judicial cooperation in cases involving tourists can be categorised as follows. First, the police may successfully conclude the investigation while the tourists involved are still on holiday. In these cases, the prosecutor or the defence may summon them to appear in court months, or even years, after the event took place. Second, investigation by the police may still be ongoing or not even started before the tourists involved returned home. In these cases, letters rogatory may be sent to request further interviews of victims or witnesses. If the tourist is suspected of the crime, investigation may well be required in his or her home country. Finally, there is the specific situation in which a tourist disappears on holiday. Although these cases are rare, they attract massive media attention and are, therefore, of interest in terms of law enforcement cooperation.

---

13 The Centre for Legal Assistance handles approximately 900 requests for mutual legal assistance annually that require further investigative action, excluding traffic offences (Spapens, 2008).

The three scenarios will be addressed in further detail below.

Scenario 1: The investigation is concluded while the tourists are still on holiday

If the investigation of a crime involving a tourist is successfully concluded while the persons involved are still on holiday, law enforcement cooperation will usually be limited. The police, of course, will have been able to take the necessary statements from both the victims and perpetrators. In cases of serious crime involving a tourist as a suspect, the police and judicial authorities will usually request information about the background and criminal record of the person involved.

Tourists who have been the victim of a crime or are suspected of having committed a crime may be summoned to appear when the case is brought before the court. In many instances, this will be several months, or even years, after the event took place. Usually, the competent authorities will send a request only a few weeks before the scheduled court session. In one of the cases examined, the Croatian authorities summoned a Dutch couple who had been the victim of an armed robbery on holiday to appear as witnesses on 17 December 2008. The Dutch authorities, however, received the letter rogatory only on 4 December.

Understandably, if notice is short, it is often difficult for a person to take time off work and to make the necessary travel arrangements. The extent the requesting country will reimburse expenses is also unclear, since there are as yet no uniform rules in this regard, even within the EU. The case studies show that witnesses often see no point in having to repeat statements before the court already given to the police at the time and refuse to appear. In some countries, however, this is in itself punishable by law, so the person in question runs the risk of apprehension or a fine on a subsequent visit.

Scenario 2: Investigative action is necessary after the tourists returned home

In cases that require investigative action after the tourists have returned home, the need for legal assistance will usually be greater than in the cases described above. To begin with, if the local police were unable to conclude the investigation whilst the tourists, either the victim or the perpetrator, were still in the country, requests for further enquiries may be sent.

One example concerns a case where two groups of Dutch nationals had been involved in a bar fight in Austria during a skiing holiday. At the time, the Austrian police had apprehended and interrogated the persons involved, but their statements proved to be inconclusive, not in the least because of drunkenness when the fight took place. Therefore, a request was sent to the Dutch authorities several months later asking for further interrogation in order to clarify what precisely had happened. However, no new facts emerged. In another case, a Dutch citizen had been involved in a traffic accident in Spain and was identified as a suspect by the Spanish police. The Spanish authorities wanted additional interrogation of this person and three Dutch witnesses by videoconference. The Dutch authorities, however, partly denied the request because the Convention on Mutual Assistance in Criminal Matters between the Member States of the European Union excludes suspects from being interrogated by videoconference. My third example refers to requests for compensation of damage inflicted by Dutch citizens during leisure activities. In one case, members of a student fraternity had caused €14,000 worth of damage to three bungalows rented in Belgium. In the second case, the mayors of three French municipalities requested Dutch organisers of a quad race to compensate for €11,000 worth of environmental damage caused by the participants. In both cases, the police knew the identity of the persons involved, and asked the Dutch authorities to determine whether they were willing to take responsibility and pay for the damage.

In other cases, the authorities may not yet know about the involvement of a tourist before he or she has returned home. Tourists who were the victim of a crime will probably report to the police. Therefore, in cases where identification needs to take place afterwards, the tourist has usually been the perpetrator. From the available information, it becomes clear that the majority of such cases refers to a traffic offence registered by cameras, such as speeding or driving through a red traffic light. In criminal cases, the police may identify a tourist in the course of a criminal investigation.

If a camera photographed a foreign licence plate, the authorities will usually file a request for identification of the person who drove the car. He or she will then personally receive a letter requesting that a fine be paid. If a traffic violation is prosecuted as a criminal offence, the offender also needs to be interrogated as a suspect by the police. In Switzerland, for example, motorists already run the risk of a jail sentence when exceeding speed limits in built-up areas by 15 kilometres or more per hour. The Dutch authorities receive thousands of requests annually with regard to the identification of Dutch drivers following traffic offences abroad. In a district along the Dutch–Belgian border, more than 50% of the requests for interrogation of suspects received in 2001 concerned traffic violations (Fijnaut *et al.*, 2005: 199).

The system for law enforcement cooperation is designed primarily with serious and organised crime in mind, and critics think it is, to some extent, improperly burdened by the large number of requests concerning traffic violations (Fijnaut et al., 2005). Recently, some improvements have been made. The Treaty of Prüm provides for automated searching of vehicle registration data, which might lead to a decreasing number of requests for identification of traffic offenders[14]. The most

---

14 In the case of vehicles not registered to private persons, however, identification of the driver who committed the offence will still be necessary.

practical solution, however, would be a system in which the authorities of the home country of the offender impose the fine or conduct the prosecution themselves under their own laws.

Apart from traffic violations, tourists may also commit crimes during their holiday and be able to return home before being identified or apprehended. In these situations, the need for law enforcement cooperation will usually be the most pressing, particularly when the crime is serious. An example concerns three rapes committed in 1987, 1994, and 1997 in the province of Zeeland, in the Netherlands. At the time, the police obtained DNA material of a possible suspect. Because of the quality of the material, however, forensic experts were only recently able to extract workable samples by employing new techniques, which revealed that the same person had committed all three crimes. Therefore, a 'cold case' team was set up and investigation restarted. During the initial investigation, witness statements led to the conclusion that the perpetrator might be from Germany. The police had interrogated a German suspect at the time, but he was not prosecuted because the evidence was insufficient. He had since moved to Switzerland. The first action taken by the investigation team was to send a letter rogatory to the Swiss authorities asking them to determine whether this person would voluntarily agree to have a sample of his DNA taken for comparison. He complied with this request, and the sample did not match the DNA material obtained at the crime sites. Thus, he was definitively cleared. Next, the Dutch prosecutor issued a request for mutual legal assistance to the German authorities. There, the DNA sample was compared with the national database, and this time there was a hit: the person whose DNA matched the sample was already serving a prison sentence in Germany. Further enquiries revealed that he had visited Zeeland on holiday in the years the crimes took place. Subsequently, the Netherlands sent a European Arrest Warrant to Germany. The Germans, however, refused to extradite the suspect because, in their opinion, he needed to serve his sentence first, which would end in 2011. However, this put the Dutch prosecutor in a quandary. The term of limitation of the rape committed in 1987 had already expired and this would also apply to the 1994 case by the time the suspect had completed the sentence. Therefore, Dutch authorities decided to transfer the proceedings to the German prosecution service in order to have the suspect tried even though he was already in custody for another offence.

This is but one example of a cross-border investigation involving a tourist. In practice, every case is unique and requires specific solutions as a function of the available legal framework.

Scenario 3: A tourist disappears abroad

Finally, tourists may disappear while on holiday abroad. Of course, in these cases, investigation will be the responsibility of the police and judicial authorities of the country where this occurred. Usually, contact will also be established with the police in the home country of the missing person, at least to serve as intermediaries with family members. If a local investigation renders no results, help may also be offered from the country of origin of the missing person.

In the summer of 2003, two Dutch youngsters of 17 and 19 years old, who had been on holiday in Thailand, were reported missing after they did not return home on their scheduled flight. After this date, the parents were no longer able to establish contact with their sons by e-mail or otherwise. The Dutch police had Interpol send out a Yellow Notice to help locate missing persons[15]. Pictures of the two were sent to the Dutch police liaison officer in Bangkok, who then contacted the Thai police. The pictures were also posted on a Dutch missing persons website. A week later, however, the youngsters were still not found, and their families contacted the press. As a result, the case received extensive coverage on television and radio and in national newspapers. Nine days after the disappearance, one of the boys contacted his parents and friends by MSN and gave a vague explanation for the events that had occurred. The Dutch police examined the possibility of tracing the IP address in Thailand, but this proved to be impossible at the time. The missing youngster also mentioned that he and his friend were trying to book onto another flight to Europe scheduled to leave three days later. This statement was checked with the airline but with a negative result. Next, the police were informed that the stepmother of one of the boys, who was a Thai national, intended to travel to Thailand herself, in the company of two journalists from a Dutch newspaper. Now, however, the other missing youngster also contacted friends in the Netherlands via MSN and mentioned the name of a Bangkok hotel where the two were staying. This information was immediately relayed to the Dutch police liaison officer, who phoned the hotel and received confirmation that they were indeed staying there. The liaison officer visited the hotel the next day, met with the two, and assured himself that no criminal offence had been committed. The Dutch Embassy was contacted to help the two youngsters make travel arrangements for their return home.

Not all cases of disappearance have happy conclusions. Examples are the disappearances of Natalee Holloway in Aruba in 2005 and of Madeleine McCann in Portugal in 2007. If the case remains unsolved, the local authorities may come under increasing pressure to accept operational assistance from the police of the victim's country of origin. The FBI, for example, provided assistance in the search for Natalee Holloway, and, in September 2006, Aruba called in the Dutch National Criminal Investigation Squad to assist with the investigation[16]. The English police, for instance, sent specially trained tracker dogs to Portugal in the Madeleine McCann case. Despite these efforts, the police failed to discover either Natalee Holloway or Madeleine McCann.

---

15   Interpol uses a noticing system where different colours refer to specific topics. See http://www.interpol.int/public/Notices/default.asp (accessed 12 May 2009).

16   Aruba is an independent region within the Kingdom of the Netherlands where the Dutch police does not have independent jurisdiction.

Public order policing in tourist areas

An interesting development in police cooperation with regard to tourism is the exchange of police officers who then participate in joint patrols in areas frequented by tourists. The main purpose is to assist in public order policing of these areas. In the Dutch province of Zeeland, this has been commonplace since the mid-1990s. The Treaty of Prüm and the subsequent Council decision 2008/615/JHA, however, further extended the legal framework for setting up joint operations aimed at public-order policing. I will briefly describe these initiatives.

In 1996, German police officers first came to the Province of Zeeland to work together with their Dutch counterparts in policing the town of Renesse during the summer season. Each year, thousands of German youngsters stay there on holidays. This, understandably, generates nuisance problems, usually following alcohol abuse. Therefore, the Dutch and German authorities concluded a bilateral agreement for exchanging personnel to participate in joint patrols. In the first years, however, the Dutch authorities did not allow the Germans to wear uniforms or carry any armament. These patrols proved to be very effective, particularly because communication between German police officers and tourists was much easier than with the Dutch, who usually do not speak German very well. The tourists appreciated contact with a police officer from their own country. They were, however, no longer able to get away with the excuse that certain behaviour, such as urinating in public, was supposedly allowed at home. Nuisance problems have substantially decreased since, but Renesse also lost some of its popularity among German youth. From 2000 onwards, the German police officers no longer operated in civilian clothes but were allowed to wear their own uniforms. After 2005, the Treaty of Prüm also allowed for carrying the standard armament of the German police. The exchange of police officers during the summer season continues to this day[17].

The French Police Nationale also experimented with provisions offered by the Treaty of Prüm, in particular with regard to joint operations (Article 24). In July 2008, German, Dutch and Spanish police officers were invited to assist the French police in Versailles for a month. The primary goal of this experiment was to become acquainted with each others' working methods. The Dutch police officer, however, also participated in an action against illegal souvenir sellers. Moreover, he was able to help in a case involving Dutch tourists staying on a camping site. A 14-year-old had been photographed with a cell phone by a 17-year-old whilst showering. The French police were called to the scene and interpreted the situation as a case of possible child pornography. Police officers immediately took the 17-year-old into custody, and asked the Dutch exchange police officer to assist them. He quickly established that the case was merely an act of mischief on the

---

17 In return, Dutch police officers are sent to Germany every December to help policing large-scale Christmas markets in Krefeld and Düsseldorf, which are frequented by many Dutch visitors.

part of the 17-year-old. The 14-year-old was called to the station to be interviewed by the police. The Dutch police officer picked up the boy at the campsite and acted as an interpreter for the French police. In the end, apologies were made, and the 17-year-old was released with only a warning.

Tackling drug tourism in the Dutch border areas

Earlier, I addressed the subjects of police and judicial cooperation with regard to tourists as victims or perpetrators of crimes abroad and police cooperation in public order issues involving tourists. Tourists, however, may also be involved in victimless crimes, such as persons travelling to the Netherlands in order to buy narcotic drugs. Over the past few decades, the Netherlands have developed into a major marketplace for foreign customers wanting to buy illicit drugs. The drug-dealing problem manifests itself especially in border areas. Individual customers from Belgium, Germany, and France, mostly from towns relatively close to the Dutch border, buy narcotics in 'coffee shops' and drug-dealing houses. The drug problem is the result of a complex development, the roots of which are to be found in the drug policy introduced by the Dutch government in the mid-1970s. From then on, a distinction was made between 'soft drugs' (marihuana, hashish) and 'hard drugs' (heroin, cocaine, synthetic drugs, etc.). The main policy goal of the government was to separate the markets for soft and hard drugs, and thus to prevent users of marihuana or hashish from easily crossing over to heroin or cocaine and the like. As a result, however, the selling and use of soft drugs gradually became more and more accepted by the public. Coffee shops emerged to sell marihuana and hashish. In many places, local authorities gradually chose to allow a number of these shops, although policy differed between municipalities. Generally, in the Netherlands itself, the drug policy was long considered a success because the number of heroin addicts stayed relatively low, and the prevalence of soft drugs use was not exceptional when compared to other European countries. However, since the second half of the 1990s, it started to become clear that this policy had produced unforeseen side effects.

First, coffee shops in towns close to the border started to attract customers from abroad in increasing numbers over the years. Economic prosperity, for instance, enabled many young people to buy their own cars and drive for tens or even hundreds of kilometres in order to buy drugs. Moreover, crossing the border became much easier after the abolition of fixed border controls in the Schengen Area in 1995. It is estimated that over 10,000 drug tourists now visit the Dutch border areas every day. Second, the amount of soft drugs sold in coffee shops is limited to 5 grams per customer. Of course, some of the users travelling to the Netherlands want to acquire larger amounts of soft drugs or to buy hard drugs as well. Hence, an infrastructure of drug-dealing houses has also developed. For example, in the border district of South Limburg, the number of drug-dealing houses is currently estimated at 150 (Fijnaut and de Ruyver, 2008: 149). Dealers operating from these premises also employ 'drug runners,' mostly youngsters of Moroccan descent, who will approach anyone they consider a potential customer already on the motorways leading to the border towns.

Reducing the number of drug tourists has proved to be a major problem. Local authorities in Dutch border towns have opted for relocating coffee shops nearer to the border in order to reduce the nuisance caused by drug tourists in the city centres. However, this infuriated their counterparts in the Belgian border areas, who saw it as a scheme aimed at shifting problems their way. Plans to limit the sale in coffee shops to Dutch citizens were judged to be in violation of EU regulations, although there has been no definitive answer to the question of whether or not the axiom of free movement of goods also applies to illegal goods. Furthermore, municipalities decide for themselves whether to allow coffee shops, and local authorities can therefore choose to revoke licences issued. Indeed, in one case, the local authorities decided to close all the coffee shops. The main problem so far has been that all the actions taken have merely shifted the nuisance problems to towns further away from the border or to the neighbouring countries.

In order to tackle the growing problems caused by drug tourists visiting drug-dealing houses, special police teams called Joint Hit Teams (JHT) have been formed. These teams also focus upon drug runners. JHTs are active on the main motorways leading to the Dutch part of the Meuse-Rhine Euro-region. A team of police officers from the Netherlands, Belgium, Luxembourg, and France covers the roads to Belgium and France. A German–Dutch JHT concentrates on the smuggling routes to Germany. The JHTs follow foreign buyers of illicit drugs to dealing houses and stop them as they return home. Subsequently, the police will raid the dealing house. However, in reaction to actions undertaken by the joint teams, drug dealers have started to set up dealing houses in Belgium. Once again, problems shifted elsewhere instead of disappearing.

The Dutch authorities are presently in the process of evaluating the foundations of the drug policy that they had pursued over the past 15 years.

Concluding remarks

This chapter has shown that an extensive legal and organisational framework for law enforcement cooperation has been created since 1959, particularly within Europe and especially with regard to the member states of the EU. In recent years, the development of these frameworks has accelerated because the crime problems have themselves rapidly become internationalised further over the last few decades due to increasing mobility, economic prosperity, and, within most of the EU, the abolition of fixed border controls. Outside Europe, however, mutual legal assistance remains largely dependent on bilateral arrangements made in specific investigations. An exception to this is the Commonwealth of Nations, where provisions for mutual legal assistance are comparable to those in the context of the Council of Europe.

In crime cases involving tourists, mutual legal assistance is usually limited, even in cases attracting substantial media attention. Sovereignty remains the leading principle in investigation and prosecution. In cases involving tourists as victims, the police and judicial authorities of the country where the crime was committed will conduct the investigation. The same applies to cases where a tourist is the perpetrator and in which the investigation was concluded while he or she was still on holiday. Law enforcement cooperation is required particularly when a tourist has been the perpetrator but has returned home before he or she could be apprehended of identified. With the exception of traffic offences, such cases remain relatively rare.

An interesting development is cooperation in policing tourist areas. For this purpose, the Netherlands and Germany have been exchanging police officers since the mid-1990s to patrol jointly the areas frequented by tourists. The results have been positive. The Treaty of Prüm and the Council Framework Decision 2008/615/JHA have recently extended the possibilities for this type of cooperation. Joint operations have also been mounted successfully against drug tourism, although involving the so-called 'waterbed effect'. This means that whenever problems are given specific attention in one place. they will shift and pop up elsewhere, just like when one is putting pressure on one part of a waterbed.

References

Eurojust (2007) *Annual Report 2007*, The Hague.

European Council (1991) Luxembourg, 28 and 29 June 1991, Presidency Conclusions, SN 151/2/91.

Europol (2007) *Annual Report 2007*, The Hague.

Fijnaut, C., Spapens, T. and van Daele, D. (2005) *De strafrechtelijke rechtshulpverlening van Nederland aan de Lidstaten van de Europese Unie*. Zeist, Uitgeverij Kerckebosch.

Fijnaut C., and de Ruyver, B. (2008) *Voor een gezamenlijke beheersing van de drugsgerelateerde criminaliteit in de Euregio Maas-Rijn*. Maastricht, Euregio Maas-Rijn.

McClean, D. (2002) *International Cooperation in Civil and Criminal Matters*, 2nd edn, Oxford: Oxford University Press.

Oberleitner, R. (1998) *Schengen und Europol, Kriminaliätsbekämpfung in einem Europa der inneren Sicherheit*, Vienna: Manzsche Verlags- und Universitätsbuchhandlung.

Official Journal of the European Union (1995a) L 62, 20 March 1995.

Official Journal of the European Union (1995b) C 316, 27 November 1995.

Official Journal of the European Union (1998) L 191/4, 7 July 1998.

Official Journal of the European Union (2000a) L 239, 22 September 2000.

Official Journal of the European Union (2000b) C 197, 12 July 2000.

Official Journal of the European Union (2002a) L 190/1, 18 July 2002.

Official Journal of the European Union (2002b) L 63/1, 6 March 2002.

Official Journal of the European Union (2006) L 386/89, 29 December 2006.

Official Journal of the European Union (2008) L 210/12, 23 June 2008.

Spapens, T. (2008) *Georganiseerde misdaad en strafrechtelijke samenwerking in de Nederlandse grensgebieden.* Antwerp/Oxford: Intersentia.

Van Daele, D., Spapens, T. and Fijnaut, C. (2008) *De strafrechtelijke rechtshulpverlening van België, Duitsland en Frankrijk aan Nederland.* Antwerp/Oxford: Intersentia.

9 The Preventive Turn in Crime Control and its Relationship with Tourism

Gordon Hughes

This chapter includes the following elements:

♦ A discussion of definitions of 'crime prevention' in the criminological literature

♦ An analysis of the emergence of crime prevention policy from the 1970s onwards

♦ An overview of the 'preventive turn' of recent decades and the development of an institutional architecture of prevention beyond the criminal justice system

♦ A discussion of forms of 'situational' and 'social' crime prevention, and how these might relate to tourism

♦ An account of the emergence of community safety and partnership working.

Introduction

Previous chapters in this collection have illustrated both the considerable risks and realities of criminal victimisation for tourists whilst also emphasising that significant numbers of tourists also appear to worry little about issues of insecurity and danger. There are then urgent questions regarding the prevention, or at best reduction, of such risks associated with both the places and people who make up the worlds of tourism. In turn there are quite specific challenges for crime prevention policies associated with tourist spaces and activities. Let us not forget that tourists and tourist localities may also be 'hot-spots' for violent and anti-social behaviour, as notoriously illustrated by both the UK's weekend night-time economy areas and further afield in holiday resorts such as Falaraki, Rhodes. In terms of responding to these problems and in a similar manner to the fears many schools have in publishing exclusion rates for unruly children in a competitive environment of school recruitment targets and league tables, the overt discussion of the dangers and risks of criminal victimisation in sites of tourism as well as the promotion of preventive, anti-crime measures may literally be 'bad for business'. That noted, the importance of crime prevention issues for any criminological discussion of contemporary experiences of tourism (whether this be the 'edgework' thrills of the surfer or the more sedate pursuits of the caravanner) cannot be underestimated. Accordingly, this chapter offers an overview of the major trends in crime prevention in contemporary late modern societies. Our major empirical focus will be on preventive initiatives associated with British developments although, given the global reach of tourism, our discussion cannot be restricted to trends and issues defined narrowly by a national frame.

The chapter is structured as follows. Following an initial discussion of the possible definitions of crime prevention in the criminological literature in the following section, we then turn to the institutional emergence of crime prevention in the decades since the 1970s across many jurisdictions. In the second section the key institutional features of the 'preventive turn' in late modernity (Garland, 2001) are discussed across the increasingly blurred boundaries of the public and private realms of the governance of security. In the third and fourth sections, the governmental rationales and techniques of what have been termed 'situational' and 'social' crime prevention programmes are presented and assessed. Finally, the fifth section discusses the rise of community safety partnership working in the UK as representative of a new form of multi-agency governance, drawing on both situational and to a lesser degree, social interventions. Throughout this overview of developments in crime prevention in late modernity, relevant links with the tourism studies literature will be drawn.

Defining crime prevention

Across the world, the last four decades have witnessed both a growth of interest in and heightened political and policy salience of crime prevention and increasingly that of community safety. This growing interest spans the varied constituencies of criminological researchers, practitioners in the crime control system, private sector knowledge brokers, politicians and a range of the 'publics'. Indeed the terms 'prevention', 'safety' and increasingly, that of 'security' and 'risk management' have become key referents, alongside if not prioritised over criminal justice, in crime control policy circles across many countries of the world. The impact of both these discursive and institutional shifts are clearly manifested in the formal policy and practice developments in the management of tourism as is evident more generally in the world of business and commerce. Furthermore, their impact is evident in the mass of individual decisions, calculations and activities taken up by consumers of tourism, processes themselves constituted by often 'risky' mobilities and flows of populations across time and space. Given the focus of this text it is impossible to understand the criminogenic features of tourist practices and their management without taking account of the preventive measures and strategies generated by both public and private agencies.

We begin with a seemingly simple question: what specific activities and allied techniques come to mind when you hear the words 'crime prevention'? I expect that different readers may come up with quite a number of different examples of activities which could be placed under the umbrella term of crime prevention, not least depending on where they live and who they are (in terms of gender, 'race', age, class, nationality, etc.). Perhaps the image of the notion of the police officer 'on the beat' came to mind, or the activities of a local Neighbourhood Watch group. Alternatively you may have thought of the installation of one of the oldest of all techniques of crime prevention, the household lock. Others may have envisaged the ever more popular 'hi-tech' surveillance technology of closed-circuit television (CCTV) which is now commonly found in the tourist 'hot-spots' of shopping malls, airports, car parks, leisure theme parks and public spaces in city centres (see also Jones, this volume, and Morgan and Pritchard, 2005). Given the renewed emphasis on the individual citizen looking out to protect him or herself, some readers may have thought about the 'self-help' preventive strategy of not walking out alone at night whilst holidaying in exciting but risky locations. Probably and tellingly, it is doubtful that many people would come up with examples of crime prevention initiatives targeted at business and corporate crime (that is, crimes chiefly *by* business or corporations rather than crimes against them) (see Bott, this volume), or crimes between intimates (such as domestic violence and child abuse), or crimes of the state (such as those against the human rights of their citizens or of other peoples). It may be helpful to bear in mind Sandra Walklate's important distinction between what she terms 'crime of the streets', 'crime of the suites' and 'crime behind closed doors' (Walklate, 1996: 296). It is understandable then that business crime ('crime of the suites'), crime between intimates ('crime behind closed doors') and, I would add, 'crime by states' rarely get onto our everyday, commonsensical 'agenda' of what crime prevention is because the simple truth is that crime prevention strategies in countries like the USA and the UK have been targeted primarily at predatory street crimes rather than the full gamut of crimes and social harms in society. These neglected areas of research represent a fascinating new study area for the criminology/tourism studies interface.

What is clear from all these possible forms of crime prevention is that there is a great plethora of activities and initiatives associated with the term 'crime prevention'. It is then a chameleon concept. In a recent spot of 'Googling' on my PC, for example, I discovered a total of 7,960,000 entries classified under the label of crime prevention on the Internet.

Unpacking the concept of crime prevention

Crime prevention is a difficult area to pin down both conceptually and empirically given the different meanings which are historically associated with it. To this day, it remains a profoundly 'slippery' and free-floating signifier in the competing discourses on law and order (Hughes, 1998: 17–18). To this end, it is important to unpack very carefully the models of crime prevention, from the deterrence model to the currently popular versions based on what are generally termed 'situational' and 'social' approaches to the prevention of both criminality and crime events. In pursuing this goal, it is vital to look at crime prevention both historically and comparatively.

What is crime prevention? Unless one answers with the tautology (that is, the use of words that merely repeat elements already conveyed) that the aims of crime prevention are the prevention of criminal acts(!), it will soon become evident that there is no one simple answer to the question. Accordingly, for example, crime prevention may be aimed at 'reforming' or 'deterring' the predatory offender or 'protecting' the individual tourist victim or the wider community. Furthermore, crime prevention strategies may be geared towards addressing quite distinct dimensions to the phenomenon of crime whether it be the context of the crime act, the criminal motive, problems in the environment or the unprotected, 'at risk' victim. Indeed, all correctional ideologies can be legitimised by the rhetoric of prevention, ranging from ideologies of incapacitation, deterrence and retribution to those of restitution, reparation and rehabilitation right through to those of diversion, decriminalisation and finally abolition! There is no simple answer then to the question 'what is crime prevention?' Instead we encounter a large body of both contested scholarly writing and policy oriented research and evaluations over the course of this idea's history.

According to Walklate, most understandings of prevention entail the possibility of both predicting an outcome and intervening in that process to change this pre-dicted outcome (Walklate, 1996: 297). It is further argued by Walklate that this basic starting point implies two distinct processes if the aim of preventive policy is to make some difference to human behaviour. First, in the case of crime preven-tion, it assumes we can agree and identify the causes of crime. Second, it presumes we know and agree on the policy responses which will prevent crime. However, such a consensus on causation and appropriate preventive policy responses is far from clear-cut. One of the leading experts on the evaluation of crime prevention initiatives, Ken Pease, has recommended caution towards any attempt to look for universality in the techniques of prevention since, when we consider the prevention of crime, we are in fact looking at a set of events joined only in their proscription by statute (Pease, 1994: 659). In a similar fashion, we may note that crime preven-tion itself is made up of a diffuse set of theories and practices. Caution over the existence of a single unproblematic definition of crime prevention may therefore be wise.

That noted, one of the most popular working definitions has been articulated in terms of 'the total of all private initiatives and state policies, other than the enforcement of criminal law, aimed at the reduction of damage caused by acts defined as criminal by the state' (Van Dijk and De Waard, 1991). This definition clearly excludes the enforcement of criminal law (and thus legal punishment) from its conceptualisation of the meaning of crime prevention. Yet it is the case that enforcement has played historically an important part in crime prevention and remains of major importance for contemporary strategies of crime control. As Garland (1990: 18) makes clear, legal punishment arising out of legal enforcement has been justified in preventive or reductive terms:

> Although legal punishment is understood to have a variety of aims, its pri-mary purpose is usually represented as being the instrumental one of reduc-ing or containing rates of criminal behaviour. It is thus possible to conceive of punishment as being simply a means to a given end – to think of it as a legally approved method designed to facilitate the task of crime control.

We also need to remain conscious that if crime prevention is viewed as covering every aspect of criminal justice, there is the danger of a form of crime prevention 'imperialism', colonising all aspects of the criminal justice system. This would risk 'crime prevention' becoming what Stan Cohen has referred to as a 'mickey mouse concept', like social control, which can have a range of meanings from infant socialisation to the death penalty (Cohen, 1985). As Lowman et al. (1987: 4) also note with regard to the concept of social control, it has become 'a skeleton key opening so many doors that its analytical power has been drained'. There are therefore limitations as well as merits in moving beyond the restricted definition of crime prevention as employed by Van Dijk and De Waard (1991).

Towards a working definition of crime prevention

Having 'unpacked' some of the differing interpretations of what crime prevention might entail, a 'dose' of conceptual pragmatism may be in order at this point. Indeed the present author when pressed to provide a 'good enough' or satisfac-tory dictionary definition of the term settled on 'any action taken or technique employed by private individuals and groups or public agencies aimed at the prevention and reduction of damage caused by acts defined as criminal by the state' (Hughes in McLaughlin and Muncie, 2001: 63). In similar vein, Crawford (2007: 871) defines crime prevention as including all pre-emptive interventions into the social and physical world with the intention, at least in part, of altering behaviour or the flow of events in a way that reduces the likelihood of crime or its harmful consequences. In turn, compared to traditional notions of criminal justice and punishment, it is concerned primarily with 'proactive' rather than reac-tive practices, is forward-looking rather than retrospective. Taken to its logical extreme it is about preventing things happening in the first place: whether this be designing out opportunities to commit burglary in tourist resorts or diverting groups of young men from entry into a criminal career through educational or recreational programmes. This offers the prospect of crime prevention offering a distinct policy alternative to the 'new punitiveness' evident in many contemporary societies (Sutton et al., 2008: 30). However, this preventive logic also means that the success regarding 'what works' is notoriously difficult to measure. The following humorous vignette (adapted from Currie, 1996: 13) captures the difficulties of crime prevention initiatives and interventions meeting the seeming 'holy grail' for governments and corporations of experimental scientific evaluation of what works based on 'before' and 'after' measures.

> A fellow is walking down a busy street in London wearing a suit of protective armour and waving a large club over his head, all the while shouting 'Get back! Get back!' much to the alarm and bemusement of the array of foreign tourists. So a police officer comes along and says, 'Excuse me sir, but what exactly are you doing?'. The guy says, 'I'm doing tiger prevention. I'm doing this to keep tigers away'. The puzzled cop scratches his head and says, 'But sir, no tigers have been seen on the streets of London in my lifetime'. And the guy says, 'See, it works!'.

The complexities inherent in evaluating a 'non-event' such as the prevention of crime or tiger-disorder (!) are clearly not to be underestimated. As Crawford (2007: 867) has observed, 'evaluation remains the weakest aspect of crime prevention studies'. The meaning of 'success' is itself highly contested. Debates about 'what works' are often struggles over the status of different criteria and public values that are not easily reducible to a universally accepted component of efficiency. Despite such empirical equivocation over any certainty over what can be proven to 'work' in scientific circles, there is a near complete consensus among criminological researchers (as well as many criminal justice practitioners) in questioning the validity and veracity of the claim that incarceration is the best crime prevention measure. As long ago as 1971 the respected criminologists Leon Radzinowicz and Marvin Wolfgang stated what has since become a criminological truism:

> Paradoxically, the more widespread crime becomes, the more essential it is to use criminal procedures and penal sanctions sparingly. A society with only a few criminals can perhaps afford to prosecute them all, to send them all to prison; a society with as many criminals as ours must increasingly use such measures only in the last resort.
>
> (1971: 3)

Nor is the criminological critique of the 'short-termism' of punitive 'prisons work' rhetoric and policy of populist pundits and politicians new. As long ago as the 1930s the American 'positivist' criminologists Glueck and Glueck (1936, cited in Hughes, 1998: 15), for example, wrote of the analogy between dominant methods of crime control (namely reactive policing and incarceration) as being akin to a policy of controlling fires by putting out flames: short-sighted and wasteful when policy should address the means of preventing fires in the first place.

It is also widely claimed by British criminologists that the discourse of crime prevention is now the dominant 'expert' paradigm for understanding how best to reduce crime rates (Jones *et al.*, 1994). According to the new paradigm, practical methods of reducing crime that are completely unconnected with punishment or even law enforcement must be found. The growth of interest in crime prevention thus 'arises from a paradigm shift that allows us to see the reduction of crime as a separate objective from the punishment of offenders' (Jones *et al.*, 1994: 302). Furthermore, Jones *et al.* (1994: 106) have argued that 'crime prevention policy has largely been the product of a specialised political and administrative elite' and so may be viewed as a professional rather than popular discourse. This emphasis on the state-based expertise of much preventive thinking and policy remains true in large measure although we should not underestimate the growing influence of what Garland (2001) has termed 'the new criminologies of everyday life' whose origins often lie in the sites of commerce and business. In turn such 'instrumental' private security rationalities differ from the more 'moral' notions of crime prevention associated with strengthening the levels of 'social capital' in more communitarian modes of crime prevention (Hughes, 2007, and see Jones, this volume). Readers are referred to Shearing and Stenning's fascinating account of this preventive logic in such tourist spaces as theme parks (Disneyworld) and their routinely embedded crime and disorder preventive measures (Shearing and Stenning, 1985).

The Australian criminologist Adam Sutton (1994) has noted that the major promise of crime prevention for criminologists is that it offers 'renewed relevance' versus the 'nothing works' pessimism of the period during the decline of the rehabilitative ideal in the 1960s and 1970s. Sutton (1994: 6) goes on to suggest that crime prevention initiatives may also offer the promise of a move away from punitive, divisive and exclusionary models of social control to more inclusionary and integrative ones. This remains a powerful normative and political appeal of crime prevention. Let us now examine the actual institutional features associated with 'the preventive turn' (Garland, 2001; Hughes, 2007) in many contemporary societies.

The preventive turn and its institutionalisation in late modernity

As long as two decades ago it was claimed by some US criminologists, with no little hubris, that crime prevention had become a major organising principle of almost all Western criminal justice systems (Roberts and Grossman, 1990: 76). More modestly, the leading UK criminologists Bottoms and Wiles have claimed that during the last three decades of the 20th century in many Western societies there has been a largely government-led movement for the development of an organised set of activities under the general heading of crime prevention (Bottoms and Wiles, 1996: 1). According to Bottoms and Wiles, it is possible to delineate a typology of crime prevention activities specifically associated with broader trends associated with late modernity[1]. Bottoms and Wiles' typology is not meant to be exhaustive and it is explicitly restricted to the contemporary situation of late modernity. As a result of their typology, the same authors suggest that there is clear evidence that crime prevention is no longer solely the province of the state. More specifically Bottoms and Wiles (1996: 7–10) distinguish four major types of contemporary crime prevention activity, namely:

1 *Defensive strategies* (such as car steering locks, rape alarms, private policing of private property, Neighbourhood Watch)

2 *Guardianship and monitoring* (such as the targeted policing of likely victims or offenders, information monitoring, CCTV, responsiveness to customer needs)

3 *The creation of new forms of social order* (such as multi-agency forms of order, public and private partnerships which have become a defining feature of contemporary crime control, exclusions of potentially troublesome individuals, public safety initiatives)

4 *Criminality prevention* (such as pre-school enhancement programmes, diversion schemes for young offenders and pre-emptive targeting of youth at risk of offending).

This typology is especially important in alerting us to the extent and variety of crime prevention in recent decades and to show how taken for granted they have become in our everyday lives, both at home and work and in our 'escape attempts' from the daily routines of life epitomised by the holiday trip.

In turn a growing number of criminological commentators have noted the centrality of the 'preventive turn' to much of the routine work of adaptive problem solving in the new 'culture of control' famously mapped out by Garland (2001). The relatively new policy field of community safety and its institutional infrastructure of multi-agency partnerships, spanning public and private agencies, targeted at both the reduction of crime and disorder and the promotion of safety and quality of life as public goods for local communities is the tangible expression of these increasingly salient features of the local governance in the UK and beyond (Hughes and Edwards, 2005; Edwards and Hughes, 2008). In Garland's (2001: 16–17) words:

> Over the past decade, while national crime debates in Britain and America have focused upon punishment, prisons and criminal justice, a whole new infrastructure has been assembled at the local level that addresses crime and disorder in quite a different manner. ... The new infrastructure is strongly oriented towards a set of objectives and priorities – prevention, security,

---

1 The late modernity thesis has emerged out of the sociological theorising on the major social transformations of the late 20th and early 21st centuries. In the work of Giddens and as adapted by Hughes (1998) and Garland (2001) among others in criminology, it focuses on both the growth of new forms of trust, new risks and critical reflexivity and the concurrent decline of old certainties such as tradition and deference to 'experts' (including that of the 'sovereign' state). The thesis also points to the consequences of the processes of globalisation for social relations.

harm-reduction, loss-reduction, fear-reduction – that are quite different from the traditional goals of prosecution, punishment and 'criminal justice'.

It also needs to be emphasised that there has been a massive increase in the production of, and trade in, private security, situational anti-risk techniques of crime prevention, from locks and alarms to the use of capitalist companies, such as the security corporation of Group 4 for crime control functions previously set aside for state agencies (see Jones, 2007 and Chapter 10 in this book). The acknowledgement and recognition of these important shifts in the nature of governance across both the 'public' and 'private' sectors is difficult to refute. It is certainly the case that in recent decades there has in turn been a 'boom industry' in criminological writing and research concerned with the plethora of policy and practice initiatives centred around crime prevention and community safety.

Mapping situational crime prevention

One of the most influential means of understanding crime prevention strategies and interventions in policy debates in contemporary Western societies has been in terms of the distinction between situational and social strategies of prevention. To complicate matters further, the social strategies are often sub-divided into 'developmental' and 'community' crime prevention. Tonry and Farrington define the key contemporary crime prevention strategies as follows:

> By developmental prevention, we mean interventions designed to prevent the development of criminal potential in individuals, especially targeting risk and protective factors discovered in studies of human development. By community prevention, we mean interventions designed to change the social conditions that influence offending in residential communities. By situational prevention, we mean interventions designed to prevent the occurrence of crimes, especially by reducing opportunities and increasing risks.
>
> (1995: 2–3)

Of these strategies, situational crime prevention has been the most influential in routine practices in both the public and private sites in the preventive sector. Much of the latter's appeal lies in its often 'quick fix' techniques and ability to measure the impact of situational modifications upon behaviour. It has also gained support for its emphasis, in these market-driven, neo-liberal times, that the prevention of crime is no longer, if it ever was, a monopoly service owned and undertaken by the state. Rather the prevention of crime is the responsibility of all private and prudential citizens and institutions. Put simply it is part and parcel of routine, everyday good governance.

Situational crime prevention is focused on 'the management, design, or manipulation of the immediate physical environment to reduce the opportunities for specific crimes (Crawford, 2007: 872). It chiefly concerns opportunity reduction, by making the targets of crime harder to get at, increasing the risks of detection, and reducing the anticipated rewards of crime (Cornish, and see Hughes, 1998: 65–67). Typical examples include the installation of surveillance technology in both private and public spaces, like car parks and shopping areas, to reduce the opportunities for the theft of vehicles or crimes against victims.

Situational crime prevention's theoretical roots need not detain us long here. Suffice to note that its analyses are largely premised on rational actor and economic models of human behaviour (offenders like other humans are basically hedonistic, pleasure maximisers). In criminological terms situational crime prevention is associated with research influenced by rational choice theory, crime as opportunity and routine activities theory (Hughes, 1998: 58–74). However, it is also vital that we attribute much of these ways of thinking and acting to the many managers and security staff who are tasked to arrive at practical solutions to counter or reduce the problem of crime as it affects their enterprise (Garland, 2001: 161). And of course the rise of crime prevention has gone hand in hand with the commercialisation and privatisation of security and associated panoply of preventive technologies and hardware (Jones, 2007). In turn, insurers have played an axial role in preventive, risk-averse ways of thinking, not least in disseminating actuarial logics and governmental technologies of prediction (Ericson and Doyle 2004).

Much of situational crime prevention's attraction across commerce and government lies in the simplicity of its analysis, unlike the complexities and qualifications of much sociologically-driven criminological theory of crime causation (see Botterill and Jones, Chapter 1, this volume). Crucially it offers practical solutions to problems in the here and now. 'Criminogenic situations, 'hot products', 'hot spots' – these are the new objects of control. It aims to embed controls in the fabric of normal interaction, rather than suspend them above it in the form of sovereign command' (Garland, 2001: 129). As Young (1994: 91) has noted, 'it has hammered home the earthy facts of space and actual experienced choice at a particular time to a criminology all too content to live in abstractions'. Politically and ideologically it also speaks the same language as that characterising neo-liberal governments across much of the West. It also chimed with the wider concerns over what Garland (2001: 106) has described as 'the normality of high crime rates and the acknowledged limitations of the criminal justice state in the last decades of the 20th century.

It is evident across the globe, and more specifically for our purposes here, across the ever expanding sites of tourism that situational crime prevention measures and techniques have been the most influential of all crime prevention techniques (and of all criminological theorising) in the decades following the 1970s on the policies and practices of crime prevention. In Downes and Rock's (2007: 322) terms:

> Situational control theories, more than any other approach, have helped to fashion the character of late modernity. While lacking any explicit concern with theorising root causes, its principal focus is very much to analyse the

temporal, spatial, and technical aspects of crime prevention in a rapidly changing world, to wrong-foot the offender by reducing opportunities and enhancing detection capture. Every target hardened, every space rendered defensible is a criminological gain.

Try to imagine a holiday resort without its guardians in the shape of uniformed officers of the corporation, even if dressed in Disneyworld fashion (Shearing and Stenning, 1985), CCTV cameras in resorts, or swipe cards for access to internal lifts and bedrooms in hotels. These are the routine manifestations of the 'new criminologies of everyday life' (Garland, 2001).

Garland (2001: 161) has neatly summarised the effects of these new preventive and security mentalities, especially those targeted at risky 'situations' across both cultural industries like organised tourism and the tourists' own routines of everyday life:

> The present day world of private-sector crime prevention exists in a reflexive relationship to the theories and prescriptions of situational crime prevention. It is in this interchange – between the practical recipes of the commercial sector managers and the worked-out rationales of criminologists and government policy-makers – that one must locate the strategy of preventive partnership and the habits of thought and action upon which it depends.

For all its influence and current hegemony in policy circles, situational crime prevention has been subject to sustained critique from both within established criminology and its critical wings (Hughes, 1998: 67–73; Crawford, 2007: 881–882). Among its Achilles heels are the following:

◆ Given that it fails to address the root causes of crime it merely deflects crime from one situation to another

◆ In turn, selective target hardening may raise normative issues around equity and the problem of a have and have-not society ('the rich in his castle, the poor at his gate' or, for our times, the affluent in their secure, hi-tech gated private communities and marginalised in public housing estates and on the insecure streets)

◆ Many situational measures are intrusive and invade traditional notions of privacy as well as civil liberties and human rights

◆ Its emphasis on target hardening and changing places rather than people has encouraged government policy to ignore the up-stream and longer-term conditions which give rise to crime and thus an imbalance in intervention has occurred

◆ Finally the new criminologies of everyday life offer an impoverished view of the social and may be better understood perhaps as the 'new anti-social criminologies of everyday life' (Hughes, 2007).

Social crime prevention and the rise of community safety programmes

Social crime prevention is focused chiefly on changing social environments and the motivations of offenders. These two areas of intervention are commonly known as community and developmental crime prevention. Unlike situational crime prevention, developmental crime prevention focuses on interventions aimed at addressing the causes of crime and dispositions (especially identified 'risk factors') of both individuals, and groups of people, who offend. Meanwhile community crime prevention measures tend to focus on the development of schemes, such as youth clubs summer camps and activity-based projects, to deter potential or actual offenders from future offending.

Much of social crime prevention's focus across the developmental and community distinctions noted above is aimed at strengthening socialisation agencies and community institutions in order – to influence those individuals, families and groups that are most at risk of offending (Bright, 1991: 64). Such interventions tend to be offender or potential offender focused – aiming to affect the dispositions of offenders and whole neighbourhoods potentially, over time. Social crime prevention is longer-term in its goals when compared to situational techniques which are aimed at crime events in the here and now. For example, social crime prevention interventions might ask 'how might young people, often from deprived and desperate communities adjoining overtly prosperous and privileged tourist locations and 'gated communities', be discouraged from seeing minor predatory theft such as pickpocketing as an attractive if illicit option for illegitimate entry to the good times?' Projects ranging from education and job training classes to organised sports activities have been deployed to try and give potential and actual offenders a sense of 'stake' in the local community.

Social crime prevention interventions have had much less influence in recent decades in both the public and private sectors when compared to the situational technologies of control associated with the new criminologies of everyday life. In particular, they have often been criticised for lacking focus and an inability to 'prove' an positive impact on the prevention of crime among its targeted populations. Despite these criticisms of social crime prevention's failure to prove that its interventions evidentially 'work', they remain a recurrent feature of preventive partnership working, as epitomised by the rise of statutory local community safety partnerships in the UK.

Community safety and the hybridisation of situational and social interventions[2]

Both situational and social crime prevention approaches tend to be what is termed inter-or multi-agency in orientation, rather than being driven by one agency alone, such as the police. Jock Young has defined multi-agency crime prevention as follows: 'Multi-agency intervention is the planned, co-ordinated response of the major social agencies to problems of crime and incivilities' (Young, 1991: 155). Also common to both situational and social crime prevention is their claim to be less damaging than traditional (retributive) justice approaches. The institutional form most commonly taken by multi-agency partnership working in the UK, deploying a mix of situational and social interventions is termed the local crime and disorder reduction partnership or community safety partnership. Its nomenclature may differ in other jurisdictions across late modern societies but similar institutional developments are evident especially in Anglophone countries across the world (Hughes *et al.*, 2002, Sutton *et al.*, 2008). In tourist areas across the UK the statutory local community safety partnership will the key governmental locus for all the relevant agencies, public and private, to come together to address the crime and disorder issues and safety and preventive solutions to problems generated by different modes of tourism and leisure-based consumption. Typically these local issues in tourist locations range from illegal beach parties and raves, drunken behaviour and violence in the night-time economies (Hobbs *et al.*, 2003) to property thefts and acts of violence against tourists (see Mawby, Chapters 2 and 3 in this volume) and accidents happening to often naive and transient 'outsiders' (tourists as victims).

Community safety as a policy approach sits at the intersection of attempts by the state to deliver social welfare and improved quality of life, and policing and control in local communities. Community safety emerged in the 1980s as a local governmental strategy which sought to move beyond the traditionally police-driven agenda of crime prevention. Apart from seeking to involve other 'social' agencies in crime prevention (i.e. moving from single to multi-agency activities), community safety has also been associated with more aspirational claims both to generate greater participation and possibly leadership from all sections of the local community, geographically defined, in crime prevention. As a long-term outcome, community safety across the Western world is often linked in government discourse and policy aspiration to the 'communitarian' and 'social capital' oriented ambition of replacing fearful, insecure communities with 'responsibilised' safe and secure ones. In the national politics of the contemporary UK in the 1990s and 2000s, for example, local community safety strategies have been a crucial component of the mantra 'tough on crime, tough on the causes of crime'. Once again, we see that community safety sits at the fault line of repressive crime control ('tough on crime') and more preventive and welfare strategies ('tough on the causes of crime').

---

2 Parts of this section first appeared in Edwards and Hughes, 2008

For the purposes of governance, community safety is associated largely with public actions aimed at a broad range of crimes and, increasingly, 'disorder' or acts of 'anti-social behaviour' and 'incivilities' in specific localities and communities. As noted above, at the more rhetorical level, community safety is a form of both crime prevention and safety promotion involving 'policing' in the broadest sense of the word, seeking the participation of community members alongside formal agencies of the local state and quasi-formal voluntary and private agencies. In this sense community safety is a clear example of the broad shift from 'government' to 'governance' (Rhodes 1997).

Between 1998 and 2008 all 376 statutory partnerships in England and Wales were legally obliged and empowered to:

◆ Carry out audits of local crime and disorder problems
◆ Consult with all sections of the local community
◆ Publish three-year crime and disorder reduction strategies based on the findings of the audits
◆ Identify targets and performance indicators for each part of the strategy, with specified time scales
◆ Publish the audit, strategy and the targets
◆ Report annually on progress against the targets.

Such locality-based approaches to crime prevention naturally 'miss' anything to do with reducing the risks on British residents abroad. Rather the reduction of crime risks for British residents abroad will be dependent on the tourism-receiving localities and regions to carry out similar processes. The opportunities for comparative research between tourist generating and receiving regions of the world in respect of crime prevention practices are considerable.

Most Crime and Disorder Reduction Partnerships (CDRPs) and Community Safety Partnerships (CSPs) have been characterised by very similar formal organisational structures. For example, there is normally a formal strategic/operational division; there are usually specific thematic or geographically based 'action' teams; the key statutory partners or 'responsible' authorities are made up of public agencies ranging from the local authority, police, probation, fire, police authority and health alongside co-opted agencies from both the statutory and voluntary sector. The 'community' is usually presented in the local strategies as a spatial and moral concept, emphasising locality and belonging and unity (albeit across consensual diversity, including 'well-behaved' tourists). However, there is also a common tendency to place certain groups outside the community due to their 'anti-social' activities, pointing to the key role of boundary and exclusion in representations of community (including 'anti-social' tourists). In turn, the community is usually 'passively' present in terms of being 'consulted' rather than an active participant in the planning and delivery of community safety (Hughes, 2007), for example, drunk driving campaigns associated with holiday periods .

There continue to be ongoing reforms of CDRPs/CSPs as the vehicles for community safety at the time of writing this chapter which have the stated aim of improving further their performance at the local level. However, such partnership work remains substantively determined by the evolving central government agenda of targeted, 'evidence-based' and measurable crime and disorder reduction, linked to specific negotiated priorities.

The following priorities are taken from the published strategies of the 22 CSPs in Wales for 2005–08 but they also reflect the typical priorities shared across partnerships across England and Wales. Research shows that those marked with an asterisk were consistently the top priorities in local CSP strategies (Edwards and Hughes 2008):

♦ Anti-social behaviour*

♦ Arson

♦ Burglary

♦ Domestic abuse

♦ Fear of crime*

♦ Hate crime

♦ Home safety

♦ Prolific and persistent offenders

♦ Property/business crime

♦ Road safety

♦ Rural crime

♦ Substance abuse*

♦ Vehicle crime

♦ Violence

♦ Youth offending*.

The primary focus of community safety partnerships in terms of their stated priorities since the Crime and Disorder Act 1998 has thus been on crime and disorder reduction. On the surface this suggests that they are primarily engaged in local crime control rather than social policy work. However the actual outcomes of such control work may be preventive in character rather than purely repressive and enforcement-oriented when examined in terms of its problem-solving orientation and when studied empirically 'on the ground' (Hughes, 2007).

The centrally-propelled and Home Office-directed drive towards the institutionalisation of community safety and crime and disorder reduction remains strikingly apparent across every local government authority in England and Wales. Such processes have seen an ever increasing number of multi-agency community safety teams – managers, officers, project workers, police secondees, 'drug action/ substance misuse teams', anti-social behaviour units, etc. – which now form an increasingly salient, if still fragile, part of local government structures and processes. As a relatively novel set of institutions and experts, community safety work is set to remain a key feature of the local governance of crime, disorder and security in England and Wales. However, there are major challenges that lie in wait, not least those associated with innovations in the local policing of the terror threat (especially in high-profile tourist spots) and 'radicalisation'; additionally, tensions exist in the nature and form of neighbourhood policing and the uneasy and unstable relations between such police-oriented initiatives and local community safety policy (see Hughes and Rowe, 2007).

Readers may find it instructive to discuss how these institutional developments associated with public/private partnership working are manifested in the published strategies and initiatives in both well-established tourist resort areas across the UK as well as in the burgeoning tourist business associated with cities and their reshaping and regeneration as 'pleasure-dromes' for both foreign and domestic visitors. Certainly many cities now compete to offer safe but exciting spaces for consumption and such entrepreneurial urban marketing draws extensively on the new technologies of prevention.

Summary and conclusions

This chapter may be best viewed as an initial mapping exercise which aims to help the reader understand the main features of crime prevention measures today when viewed criminologically. The main focus throughout the chapter has been on the institutional development of crime prevention and the pertinence of its associated interventions and technologies for understanding crime and its control with regard to the different worlds of tourism. The discussion has been less concerned with assessing different theories of what might work in preventing crime and victimisation among tourist populations. Given the paucity of available research studies on crime prevention and tourism, it is evident that there remains a dearth of empirical research – with a few notable exceptions – on the particular challenges for strategies of crime prevention with regard to tourism and its consuming subjects. It is a gap that criminologists and tourism studies researchers should attend to with some urgency and do so in partnership.

References

Bottoms, A. and Wiles, P. (1996) 'Crime prevention and late modernity', in T. Bennett (ed.), *Crime Prevention: The Cropwood Papers*, Cambridge: Cropwood. pp. 6-22

Bright, J. (1991) 'Community safety, crime prevention and the local authority', in P. Wilmott (ed.), *Policing and Community*, London: Policy Studies Institute. pp. 45-53.

Cohen, S. (1985) *Visions of Social Control*, Cambridge: Polity.

Crawford, A. (2007) 'Crime prevention and community safety', in M. Maguire R. Morgan, and R. Reiner. (eds), *Oxford Handbook of Criminology*, Oxford: Oxford University Press. pp. 866-909.

Currie, E. (1996) 'Is America really winning the war on crime and should Britian follow its example?', NACRO 30th annual lecture, London: National Association for the Care and Resettoement of Offenders

van Dijk, J. and de Waard, J. (1991) 'A two-dimensional typology of crime prevention projects', *Criminal Justice Abstracts*, September, 483–503.

Downes, D. and Rock, P. (2007) *Understanding Deviance*, Oxford: Oxford University Press.

Edwards, A. and Hughes, G. (2008) 'Resilient Fabians: community safety officers and anti-social management in Wales', in P. Squires (ed.), *ASBO Nation*, Bristol: Policy Press. pp. 57-72.

Ericson. R and Doyle, A. (2004) *Uncertain Business: Risk, Insurance and the Limits of Knowledge*. Toronto: University of Toronto Press.

Garland, D. (1990) *Punishment and Modern Society*. Oxford: Oxford University Press.

Garland, D. (2001) *Culture of Control*, Oxford: Oxford University Press.

Hobbs, D., Hadfield, P., Lister, S., and Winlow, S. (2003) *Bouncers: Violence and Governance in the Night Time Economy*. Oxford: Oxford University Press

Hughes, G. (1998) *Understanding Crime Prevention: Social Control, Risk and Late Modernity*, Buckingham: Open University Press

Hughes, G. (2007) *The Politics of Crime and Community*, Basingstoke: Palgrave Macmillan.

Hughes, G. and Edwards, A. (2005) 'Comparing the governance of safety in europe: A geo-historical approach', *Theoretical Criminology*, 9(3): 345-363.

Hughes, G. and Rowe, M. (2007) 'Neighbourhood policing and community safety: Researching the instabilities of the local governance of crime, disorder and security in contemporary UK', *Criminology and Criminal Justice*, 7 (4), 317–346

Hughes, G., ,McLaughlin, E., and Muncie, J. (eds) (2002) *Crime Prevention and Community Safety: New Directions*. London: Sage.

Jones, T (2007) 'The governance of security' in M. Maguire. R. Morgan and R. Reinder (eds), *Oxford Handbook of Criminology*. Oxford: Oxford University Press. pp.841-865.

Jones, T., Morgan, R. and Newburn, T. (1994) *Democracy and Policing*, London: Policy Studies Institute

Lowman, J., Menzies, R. and Palys, T. (1987) *Transcarceration*, Aldershot: Gower.

McLaughlin, E. and Muncie, J. (2001) *Sage Dictionary of Criminology*, London: Sage.

Morgan, N. and Pritchard, A. (2005) 'Security and social "social" sorting: traversing the surveillance–tourism dialectic', *Tourism Studies*, 5 (2), 115–132.

Pease, K (1994) 'Crime prevention', in M. Maguire, R. Morgan and R. Reiner (eds), (*Oxford Handbook of Criminology*, Oxford, Oxford University Press pp. 949-79.

Radzinowicz, L. and Wolfgang M. (1971) *Crime and Justice*, vol. 2, New York: Basic Books.

Rhodes, R. (1997) *Understanding Governance: Policy Networks, Governance, Reflexivity and Accountability*, Buckingham: Open University Press.

Roberts J. and Grossman M. (1990) 'Crime prevention and public opinion', *Canadian Journal of Criminology*, 32 (1), 75–90.

Shearing, C. and Stenning, P. (1985) 'From the Panopticon to Disney World: The development of discipline', in A. Dobb and E. Greenspan (eds), *Perspectives in Criminal Law*, Aurora, Ontario: Canada Book Co. pp. 335-349.

Sutton, A. (1994) 'Crime prevention: promise or threat?', in P. O'Malley and A. Sutton (eds), *Crime Prevention in Australia*, Sydney: Federation Press.

Sutton, A., Cherney, A. and White, R. (2008) *Crime Prevention*, Cambridge: Cambridge University Press.

Walklate, S. (1996) 'Community and crime prevention', in E. McLaughlin and J. Muncie (eds), *Controlling Crime*, London: Sage. pp. 152-83

Young, J. (1991) 'Left realism and the priorities of crime control', in D. Cowell and K. Stenson (eds), *The Politics of Crime Control*, London: Sage. pp. 147-160.

Young, J (1994) 'Incessant chatter: Recent paradigms in criminology' in M. Maguire, R. Morgan, and R. Reiner (eds), *Oxford Handbook of Criminology*, Oxford: Oxford University Press. pp. 69-124.

10 Governing Security in Tourist Spaces

Trevor Jones

This chapter includes the following elements:

♦ An overview of the key themes in criminological literature on the changing ways in which security is conceptualised, organised and delivered in contemporary societies

♦ A discussion of specific examples of 'tourist spaces' that pose particular problems and solutions for the governance of security

♦ An analysis of four specific features of contemporary security governance that have particular relevance for policing and security provision/authorisation in these kinds of tourist spaces: diversification, the growth of risk-based approaches, social polarisation, exclusion and expansion

♦ A discussion of the normative implications of these changes in security governance and a consideration of implications for future research.

In this chapter, we examine the policing (and more generally, the 'governance of security') of a range of 'tourist spaces' such as enclave resorts, large hotel complexes, cruise liners, airports, and so on. In such spaces, security is often authorised and delivered primarily by 'non-state' policing agents. The chapter therefore speaks to some important themes in recent criminological discussion of changes in the organisation and delivery of security in contemporary polities (Jones, 2007). A key element within this work concerns the 'pluralisation' of policing, meaning that contemporary policing is increasingly authorised and delivered by a complex range of public, private and community agencies and organisations, as well as the public police (Crawford, 2008; Crawford *et al.*, 2005; Jones and Newburn, 2006). Tourist spaces provide particularly interesting case studies of such trends, and present opportunities to consider the wider implications for security provision and governing more generally. The chapter is divided into three main sections. The first provides the conceptual and empirical context, summarising the main themes from the criminological literature on the 'pluralisation' of policing, and briefly touching on literature from tourism studies/sociology of tourism regarding the 'tourist spaces' to be discussed in later sections. The second section reviews the key dimensions of security governance in tourist spaces with a particular focus on diversification, the growth of risk-based approaches, polarisation/exclusion, and expansion. The final section considers some of the normative implications of these conceptual and empirical developments, and draws some general conclusions from the issues considered in the chapter.

Conceptual and empirical context

From 'policing' to 'security governance'

From the birth of the 'New Police' in the early 19th century until the latter part of the 20th century, policing became firmly associated with the formal institutions of the state and viewed as a quintessentially 'public' service. This mindset has until recently dominated scholarly treatments of policing, which for the most part have focused upon the activities of the specialist state bureaucracy – 'the police' – tasked with law enforcement, crime investigation, public reassurance and peace-keeping. Such 'state-centric' ways of thinking about policing have been increasingly challenged on conceptual, empirical and normative grounds (Shearing, 2006).

Defined as the organised provision of peace-keeping, rule enforcement and investigation, it is clear that policing can be delivered by a range of individuals and agencies, and should not therefore be conceptualised in ways that exclusively focus upon state-organised arrangements (Johnston, 2000). Recent work has sought to deploy definitions of policing that capture the full range of 'policing' activities and agencies involved and do not restrict the conceptual gaze to the activities of state policing bodies (Newburn and Reiner, 2007; Jones, 2008). This broadening of conceptual focus has been accompanied by – indeed, emerged as a direct result of – a growing body of empirical research that explores the 'policing' activities of a range of public, commercial and voluntary agencies as well as the public police (Johnston, 1992, 2000; Bayley and Shearing, 1996; Jones and Newburn, 1998). Indeed, it has been suggested that these important conceptual and empirical shifts should be reflected in a change of terminology (Johnston and Shearing; 2003). For a group of influential writers (see Wood and Dupont, 2006), the term 'policing' is too closely associated with state institutions and its usage contributes to an ongoing scholarly 'myopia' about policing beyond the police (Shearing, 2006). For this reason, the term 'security governance' is suggested as capturing more effectively the fundamental changes that have occurred in recent decades (Johnston and Shearing, 2003). This draws upon the broader language of 'governance' that has emerged in political science, and challenges traditional conceptions of the way that governing power is exercised in contemporary polities. As Rhodes (1997) argued, governing power increasingly operates via 'self-organising inter-organisational networks'. The central state has a far more fragile grasp on the shaping and implementation of policy than has generally been assumed. Relationships between the various parties within policy networks are characterised by 'power dependence' (Stoker, 1998). Since policy actors have access to different types and levels of resources –

financial, political, legal or administrative – the policy process is characterised by negotiation and bargaining between a myriad of bodies, both state and non-state. Governmental authorities rule via attempting to steer networks in the required direction, through a process of negotiation and bargaining rather than central command. Thus, it is suggested that we have seen a shift from 'government' to a more diffuse notion of 'governance', which involves the mobilisation of governing mentalities and capacities beyond the realm of the state (see Jones, 2007 for further discussion).

It remains open to debate whether or not we agree that the term 'policing' has outlived its usefulness, or more broadly that the idea of 'governance' reflects a dramatically changed set of developments in the ways that societies are governed as we move into the 21st century. But there is now wide agreement that regulation, order maintenance, and law enforcement activities are increasingly 'pluralised' in contemporary societies and the public police are one among many 'policing' bodies (Jones and Newburn, 2006). Several elements to this pluralisation can be identified. Perhaps the most important has been the expansion – numerically, functionally and spatially – of the commercial security sector across many nations (Johnston, 1992; Jones and Newburn, 1998). Commercially-provided guarding, security and surveillance equipment and investigatory services have seen very significant growth across the globe over recent decades. The growth of domestic security sectors within nation states has been accompanied by a burgeoning trans-national security industry, engaged in the provision of military hardware and per-sonnel, corrections and policing operating above and across national boundaries (Bowling and Newburn, 2006). Various factors have contributed to the expansion of 'policing for profit', including ever-growing demands on public providers, the deliberate privatisation of policing functions, and a range of broader structural changes in contemporary industrial societies that exacerbate concerns about risk and insecurity (Jones and Newburn 2006). A key factor contributing to private security growth – and one which is of vital importance in this chapter – is changes in the nature of urban (and other) space. It has been argued that there has been a significant growth in the kinds of spaces which form the 'natural habitat' of private security rather than the public police, a development which is discussed in more detail in the next sub-section.

In addition to, and partly in response to, the growing visibility and influence of commercial policing, many countries have seen the emergence of new forms of public sector policing provision which have pluralised further the policing landscape. These include local authority patrol forces and municipal police forces (Loader, 2000), the creation of new auxiliary ranks within public police organisations (such as 'Police Community Support Officers' (PCSOs) in England and Wales or *politiesurveillanten* in the Netherlands) (Jones *et al.*, 2009). These relatively new forms of 'policing' have supplemented longer-established law enforcement and regulatory agencies operating largely within the public sector including special police forces (e.g. The British Transport Police (BTP)), specialist investigatory/

regulatory bodies attached to national and local government (e.g. the Health and Safety Executive (HSE), environmental health officers, trading standards officers, and benefit fraud investigators). In addition, some authors have highlighted the development of informal policing forms such as voluntary citizen patrols or even vigilantism (Johnston, 1996), and the emergence of transnational policing forms above the nation state (Sheptycki, 2000). In sum, therefore, policing has become pluralised within, beyond, below and above the nation state (Loader, 2000).

Private spaces and 'private governments'

As noted above, one important explanatory factor in the growing visibility of commercial policing has been the changing nature of urban spaces. The leading writers on private policing, Clifford Shearing and Philip Stenning, coined the term 'mass private property' to describe large, geographically-connected holdings of commercially-owned property to which access is open to large numbers of people, such as shopping centres, retail parks, educational campuses, and private residential complexes (or 'gated communities') (Shearing and Stenning, 1981, 1987). Shearing and Stenning suggested that the re-birth of private policing in the latter part of the 20th century was closely linked to the expansion of these kinds of spaces. They argued that these developments were tantamount to the emergence of a new corporate feudalism, whereby 'private governments' emerge within the broader jurisdiction of state government. This means that not only is the delivery of security privatised, but the more fundamental responsibility for defining the social order in such communal spaces shifts from the state to corporate entities (Shearing, 1992: 425). In sum, people increasingly live, work, shop, and – crucially for our purposes here – spend their holidays and leisure time in commercially-governed (and privately-policed) spaces. Although such spaces may appear to be 'public', in the sense of their size and accessibility to large numbers of people, they remain 'private' in terms of property ownership with important legal implications for rights of exclusion and the governing of behaviour in such places. The tourist sector provides a number of important examples of such spaces, in the form of hotel complexes, leisure parks and 'enclave resorts' (Shmid, 2008). Although laws of private property provide the owners/managers of such spaces with some autonomy to define and enforce rules within them, ultimately, of course such spaces usually fall within the overall legal control of sovereign nation states (Jones and Newburn, 1998). However, some examples of the tourist spaces we are considering here routinely operate outside the territorial jurisdiction of individual states, such as cruise liners in international waters and passenger jets in international airspace. This jurisdictional issue renders the policing and governance of such spaces potentially even more complex.

As noted above, it is not just the provision of security that is increasingly a matter for non-state actors. There has also been an expansion of the various auspices under which security is authorised (Bayley and Shearing, 2001). This reflects a more fundamental shift outlined earlier – from government to governance – with the expansion of domains of non-state governance that not only can contract-in security provision themselves (sometimes from state providers), but are themselves key definers of the nature of the order to be protected, the number and type of rules required to do this, and the manner in which compliance is to be achieved. There are, therefore, growing numbers of communal spaces which are not only privately policed, but are subject to forms of 'private government' (Macaulay 1986). These are defined as 'non-state entities that operate not simply as providers of governance on behalf of state agencies but as auspices of government in their own right' (Shearing, 2006: 11). Thus, sovereignty itself – the authority to govern – is increasingly exercised by corporate 'private governments'. Such developments call into question the involvement of the state not only in security provision, but in governing social life more generally, a point to which we will return later. Some such developments arise from deliberate government policies of privatisation, but many have emerged independently of any state strategies. Given the allegedly expanding influence of 'private governments', it has been argued that we should view people as 'denizens' of a range of distinct governmental domains, rather than as 'citizens' of a single, territorially-defined, sovereign state (Shearing and Wood, 2003).

There is no doubt that the spatial configuration of the contemporary built environment has important implications for the governance of security. Recent work has indicated a growing degree of spatial complexity in many countries, with a continuum of spatial types varying in terms of legal ownership and openness (Wakefield, 2003; Kempa et al., 2004). In England and Wales, for example, case law has confirmed the right of the owners of mass private property to arbitrarily exclude people from their land (Wakefield, 2003). Crawford (2006) has argued that the courts in England and Wales have provided private property owners with an almost unqualified right to exclude, with major implications for the powers of private governments over citizens' lives. The use of 'banning' powers in this way can exclude some citizens from a major part of public life, given the extensive range of employment, retail and leisure facilities that are located in such spaces (von Hirsch and Shearing, 2000). The right to exclude from such spaces is not subject to due process safeguards that limit the application of the criminal law, and can often constitute disproportionate 'punishment' in relation to the original 'offence'. Indeed, the grounds for exclusion can be quite broad and have no need to involve the breaking of any civil or criminal legal code at all.

The extent to which privately-governed spaces have increased in contemporary societies has been the subject of some debate. For example, Roberts has argued that the 'size of these shifts should not be exaggerated... [t]hese spaces are always there in centralized polities...this configuration is certainly not a unique feature of late capitalism, even if it takes on distinctive forms' (2005: 16). However, there is certainly evidence of substantial growth in such spaces in many countries, particularly those with high levels of land availability relatively liberal planning regulations (MacLeod, 2003; Glasze et al., 2006). In other countries – such as the

UK and some continental European countries – the limited data available suggest that these trends are less marked, but are certainly still significant, particularly in the retail sector (Minton, 2002; Jones and Newburn, 1999). Recent research has also suggested that there has been an expansion of such spaces in the residential sector with a growth of 'gated' developments (Atkinson *et al.*, 2003; Atkinson and Flint, 2004) It is also important to note that the apparent expansion of commercial private government has occurred at the same time as the collapse of other forms of governance 'below the state' over the past century, relating to industrial decline and the shrinking influence (or complete disappearance) of a range of mid-level institutions that played an important role in ordering social life, including trade unions, workers' institutes, religious organisations, and participation in clubs and societies (Mount, 2005). 'Private' forms of governance in themselves are therefore far from new, but in recent decades have taken on distinctive forms. Many of the new communal spaces that are discussed in the literature on private security are now established and governed (in a day-to-day sense) by commercial profit-making organisations (as compared with the greater influence of non-market forms of private government for earlier generations, such as chapels/churches, trade unions, community clubs and organisations, etc.). Much contemporary 'private government' is concerned primarily with promoting a safe and pleasant environment for the consumption activities of the better-off. Members of disadvantaged communities are more likely than the affluent classes to be directly or indirectly excluded from many kinds of corporate space. A further important development has been the globalisation of 'private government', which reflects growing corporate influence over social life more broadly. Many of these zones of governance – and particularly those on which we focus in this chapter – operate not only within nation states, but across and outside of national boundaries (Shearing, 2006).

Tourist spaces

Whilst analysis of security and policing within the broader literature of tourism studies and the sociology of tourism remains rather sparse to date, there is increasing discussion of distinctive spatial forms relating to tourism. Spaces which cater, or are designed explicitly, for tourism (and more broadly, the consumption of leisure activities), share a number of important characteristics with the new communal spaces discussed above, including the particular issues relating to security governance. Examples of such spaces include 'tourist enclaves' (gated or otherwise), cruise liners, theme parks and sports stadia, airports and passenger jets, and the reconfigured spaces of town and city centres.

Tourist enclaves

There is a growing literature on the development and impacts of 'tourist enclaves' (Schmid, 2008). These are spaces which emerge from a process of spatial and social segregation of tourists from local residents. This can occur in relatively fixed geographical spaces. Schmid (2008) provides an interesting ethnographic analysis of the operation of tourist enclaves in Luxor, Egypt and also highlights how tourist enclaves in this area emerged partly as a result of the deliberate actions of major tourist companies such as Thomas Cook. The process of tourist 'enclavisation' has been particularly noted with the emergence of tourist destinations in developing countries, with the perceived security of tourists being a major stimulus to such phenomena (Shaw and Shaw, 1999). Although the development of such enclaves is often promoted on the grounds of potential economic benefits to indigenous populations, there is evidence that such benefits are often exaggerated (Frietag, 1994). Large enclosed hotel complexes, gated 'tourist communities' such as the golfing communities on the Florida coast (Blakeley and Snyder, 1997), and even non-gated tourist villages or resorts, can all be viewed in this sense as tourist enclaves, which emerge from and continue to operate, at least in part, on the basis of distinctive forms of policing and security governance.

Cruise liners

Another form of 'tourist space' which has attracted the attention of tourism researchers is the ultimate 'enclavic space' of the cruise liners – in effect floating and enclosed mini-cities – where passengers are contained for long periods and day-to-day governance and regulation of behaviour is conducted primarily by the company that owns the ship and the officers and crew that staff it (Atkinson and Blandy, 2009; Weaver, 2005; Jaakson, 2004). Worldwide, the cruise industry has experienced very substantial growth in recent decades (Dowling, 2006). For example, industry reports predicted a doubling of annual totals of cruise passengers, from 9.8 million to 20.7 million, in the decade to 2010 (World Travel and Tourism Council *et al.*, 2002). The notion of an independent floating 'sovereign' space is not just an interesting way of conceptualising cruise liners, but is something that is explicitly promoted by the media and by cruise operators themselves. For example, November 2009 saw widespread media coverage of the launch of Royal Caribbean's new cruise liner, *Oasis of the Seas*. With a passenger capacity of over 6000 plus a staff complement of about 2300, the *Oasis of the Seas* is the world's largest passenger liner and has been widely reported as a floating metropolis: 'The ship is sold as an urban experience, a city on the ocean, and on a preview voyage out towards the Caribbean that is what most people seemed to enjoy: getting a cappuccino in one of the ship's seven distinct "neighbourhoods" and indulging in some serious consumption' (Adams, 2009). Royal Caribbean International advertisements refer to their cruise liners as 'The Nation of Why Not', further playing on the image of an independent sovereign entity. Of course, in formal legal terms there are times when these ships are in port and under the jurisdiction of particular territorial states, but even then the legal position is complicated, as will be discussed below. At times when such ships are in international waters, they are to a degree beyond the reach of the criminal and civil law of individual sovereign states (Bloor and Sampson, forthcoming).

Theme parks and sports stadia

Another important form of tourist space to consider is the 'theme park', which has been growing in popularity globally over recent decades (Blank, 1998; Milman, 2008). Perhaps the emblematic example of a theme park was the focus of a fascinating analysis by Shearing and Stenning (1985, 1987). Their account of the policing of Disneyworld draws out many of the defining features of 'private policing' and what distinguishes such forms from state organised arrangements. These spaces raise particular issues for access control and behaviour, and also for the regulation of health and safety laws. In the UK, for instance, there have been a number of tragic incidents in which people have been killed or injured during rides in leisure parks. In 2006, a 16-year-old girl was killed after falling 100 feet from a ride in the Oakwood Leisure Park in South Wales. The park's owners subsequently pleaded guilty to a charge brought by the HSE of contravening health and safety laws, and were fined £250,000 plus costs (South Wales Argus, 2008). Sports stadia are another important site of leisure consumption, and example of 'mass private property' where very large crowds of people gather. They raise particular issues for policing and security. The regulation of sports fans within stadia has, since the 1980s, been undertaken primarily by privately employed stewards contracted by the sporting clubs themselves, with the public police taking on an advisory 'backstage' role with regard to what happens within the private space of the stadium. In addition, most sports stadia now have sophisticated CCTV systems to aid in crowd control and regulation of behaviour. Problems of football hooliganism have largely moved to the areas outside (and transport links to and from) football grounds, although outbreaks of crowd trouble within grounds do occasionally still occur.

Airports and passenger jets

Another form of space that has received increasing sociological attention is that of the airport. Indeed, the airport has been described as the archetypal 'non-space' (Auge, 1995). Such views present airport spaces as sharing a number of characteristics with a range of other kinds of mass private property that have proliferated in recent decades such as supermarkets, service stations, shopping centres etc. They are seen as non-places because there is little to distinguish one from the other, and, despite the physical presence of large numbers of people, social interaction between them is limited in important ways. In short, they are spaces 'where people coexist or cohabit without living together' (Urry, 2007: 146). However, Urry goes on to argue that to categorise airports as 'non-places' fails to recognise the increasingly complex and vibrant social life that occurs in such spaces. Such a term also overlooks the increasing resemblance between the design and operation of such spaces and those outside. In particular, social life in cities is becoming more like that in airports (and other mass collective spaces), as the contemporary urban environment is increasingly subject to new forms of ordering and surveillance (Urry, 2007: 147–148). Airports also provide an important exception to the general lack of scholarly attention given to the policing of tourist spaces. As will be outlined below, this is one kind of tourist space that has seen a major scholarly focus on issues of security and surveillance, especially since the terrorist attacks of 9/11 and subsequent terrorist plots to attack airlines (see, for example, Morgan and Pritchard, 2005). The policing of passenger behaviour once the airplane is in flight provides another area of interest. For example, recent years have seen a number of media reports of 'air rage' during flights, where it has fallen to the air stewards to intervene, and on occasion, physically restrain passengers who have become violent. A particularly remarkable incident occurred in 2006, when a senior British diplomat was reportedly drunk and aggressive on an international flight to Heathrow, and broke three pairs of plastic handcuffs when air stewards and other passengers attempted to restrain him. He was arrested at Heathrow Airport and subsequently acquitted at a Crown Court trial of being drunk on an aircraft, on grounds of the fact that he had been taking anti-depressant drugs which had reacted with alcohol to cause his aggressive behaviour (BBC News Online, 2006). The renewed concerns about terrorist attacks, following 9/11, have also turned the spotlight upon the provision of in-flight security. After the attacks on New York and Washington in 2001, there were reports of increased numbers of armed federal 'air marshals' being deployed, undercover, on flights to and from the USA. In January 2010, in response to the failed Christmas Day attempt to bomb an airline as it came to land in Detroit, President Obama announced an expansion of Federal Air Marshals on US aircraft.

Town and city centres

Most of the 'tourist spaces' considered above are privately-owned and managed (with the exception of some enclave resorts). However, it is worth noting here a growing trend of surveillance and securitisation of public spaces in the town and city centres of contemporary Western societies. Whilst concerns have been raised about the polarising effects of the emergence of new private communal spaces, it is argued that security governance in the remaining public spaces increasingly follows the exclusionary and risk-based policies of 'private governments'. The spread of crime prevention by environmental design, exclusionary use of 'anti social behaviour orders' (ASBOs) and other such interventions (such as youth curfews) have, in effect, privatised public spaces (Crawford, 2006). The advent of 'town centre management', the spread of state-of-the-art CCTV systems in public spaces, the employment of private security guards (or similar kinds of personnel) to patrol town and city centres, and the exclusion of beggars and the homeless from particular areas, can be seen as part of this general trend. One justification for this has been to make towns and city centres more pleasant and amenable spaces for leisure and consumption activities, including tourism. But one interpretation of such trends sees the 'sanitisation' of public spaces as part of a broader neo-liberal strategy that seeks to maximise the potential for consumption in urban environments (Coleman, 2003). However such trends are viewed, it is clear that, in an important sense, town and city centres can be considered as examples of 'tourist spaces' alongside the various forms of mass private property that cater for tourists.

Key dimensions of security governance in tourist spaces

In this section, we draw upon the broader literature on private policing to explore some key characteristics of the provision of security and ordering in new communal places, and their particular relevance to such developments in the context of tourism.

Diversification

Tourist spaces of the kind outlined above provide important examples of the diversification of security authorisers and providers that has been highlighted by research on the pluralisation of policing. For example, the literature on particular forms of tourist spaces indicates clearly how such spaces are subject to forms of 'private government' outlined above. For example, hotel complexes and private gated resorts are primarily policed by private security agents, and thus form classic examples of 'mass private property' outlined above. In such areas, a degree of sovereignty passes to the property owners, in so far as many of the rules of behaviour are decided by the property owners and enforced, in so far as they need to be, by their agents, including private security personnel. In such cases, a significant source of power for private policing agents is that they can exclude non-compliant visitors from the space. This is true of theme parks such as Disneyworld, an unambiguously privately-owned space within which the rules that are to be enforced, and the enforcement of them, falls in the first instance to the property owners and their representatives. Another interesting analysis of the application of informal rules of behaviour in tourist spaces can be found in Andrews' (2009) analysis of the gendering of social relations among tourists in Magaluf. This work highlights how rules of dress and acceptable behaviour vary significantly between male and female tourists. Large cruise liners are another example of 'privately' governed tourist spaces, which have been described as 'floating gated communities' (Atkinson and Blandy, 2009: 94). Weaver (2005) outlines some of the ways in which 'ship rules' – such as forbidding passengers from bringing on board of cheap alcohol purchased on-shore – are 'policed' by ship personnel. There are also rules that restrict social contact between ship employees and passengers, which are enforced by supervisors and can result in formal sanctions for the staff involved (Weaver, 2005).

Thus, analysis of some tourist spaces has strong parallels with the policing of 'mass private property' outlined in the criminological literature. However, a consideration of other tourist spaces provides some interesting contrasts with the literature on mass private property and policing. Much of the general literature on mass private property (shopping malls, gated communities, etc.) emphasises the growing extent and influence of private policing as compared with public policing. However, some of the key tourist examples considered here show the continued importance of public policing forms, often in partnership with corporately-employed security personnel. Tourist enclaves such as Luxor are policed by – indeed, in some ways owe their existence to – a coalition of state and non-state policing forces. The state – in its formulation and enforcement of local regulations about tourist guides – plays a key strategic role in the process of enclavisation and the maintenance of social and spatial boundaries once such a process is complete. The local 'tourist police' (part of the state policing forces) play a central role in creating and maintaining the segregation of tourists from locals (Schmid, 2008). It is reasonable to assume that whilst the tourist police maintain boundaries in public space, the owners of the private 'enclavic' spaces such as the cruise ships and hotel complexes, organise their own security and rely on their own staff to control access and regulate behaviour within such spaces. Although Schmid does not discuss such issues in detail, it may be that such areas see similar forms of co-operation and information exchange between public and private policing agencies as has been noted in other studies of commercial security and public safety (Jones and Newburn, 1998).

There are other examples of places where both public and private policing works in tandem to support the tourist economy. In some jurisdictions, the public police forces are increasingly encouraged to engage with the 'tourist industry' and participate in policing networks that maximise the safety (and the revenue capture) from tourists in particular areas (Muehsam and Tarlow, 1995). Whilst established tourist resorts clearly raise issues for the policing of public space, tourist 'enclaves' clearly include other spaces that are privately-owned and to which general access is restricted. The complex nature of some tourist spaces renders inevitable the intermingling of state and private security functions. To take an example, security staff in airports and staff working on airlines have additional legal powers, over and above those of private citizens, to restrict the liberty of citizens if they are felt to pose a threat to order or safety (see earlier references to 'air rage' cases). The strategic and symbolic importance of airline travel, and in particular the major terrorist incidents involving airlines in recent years, have led to a renewed focus of state authorities on the policing of airports and air travel. In some cases, it has led to a reversal of broader trends towards the privatisation of policing (for example the nationalisation of airport security in the USA by the Department of Homeland Security, following the 9/11 attacks). The expansion of undercover Federal Marshals on flights to and from the USA can be seen in the same light, although the extent of this policy is unclear. There is also a growing inter-connectedness of various forms of surveillance, covering both 'public space' and 'private data'. The growing web of surveillance over international travel was already well advanced by the turn of the new millennium, but the new terrorist threat has given this further impetus (Morgan and Pritchard, 2005). Once again, this demonstrates how international air travel – and the spaces through which many tourists much pass – is now subject to an extraordinarily complex network of surveillance and policing, involving a diverse range of state, commercial and other private actors.

The growth of risk-based security

Security governance in tourist spaces is not only diversified in its authorisation and provision, but in its fundamental essence it contrasts in some important ways with more traditional public policing approaches. In the privatised 'security bubbles' of the better-off, at least, there has been a marked shift way from traditional reactive and punitive approaches and towards proactive and risk-oriented ones (Loader and Sparks, 2007). The commodification of security has encouraged forward-looking loss reduction mentalities that do not sit comfortably with traditional criminal justice approaches based on the retrospective punishment of past wrongs. As in the classic account of the policing of Disneyworld (Shearing and Stenning, 1987), security provision is low-key, embedded and consensual, in order to maximise the comfort of the consumers and their likelihood of spending more money. Unlike the overt, expressive, backward-looking and punishment-oriented nature of traditional public police activities, the policing of the theme park is covert, instrumental, proactive and focused entirely on loss reduction (and profit maximisation). It is 'built in' to the physical architecture of the space, with visitor movements and spending opportunities carefully marshalled via planned routing and environmental design.

This analysis of a key type of tourist space is consistent with broader theories suggesting that contemporary social life is increasingly organised around attempts to predict and prevent (or at least ameliorate) future harms (Beck, 1992). Within criminology, there has been a huge focus on the emergence and spread of risk-based mentalities, discourses and practices. For example, it has been argued that an actuarial 'new penology' has emerged in which formerly dominant approaches based on the retrospective punishment and/or the rehabilitation of offenders is being displaced by instrumental approaches that focus on pragmatic forms of managing risk in the most cost-effective ways possible (Feeley and Simon, 1994). Such developments have been linked to the growing influence of 'criminologies of everyday life' (such as 'rational choice' and 'routine activities' theories) that underpin the idea of 'situational' crime prevention (Garland, 2001; Hughes, this volume, 2010). This approach seeks to manipulate the physical environment to minimise opportunities for crime and disorder, reduce the perceived rewards or increase the potential risks of such behaviour (Clarke, 1997). Developments in the corporate sector are central to all these trends. Shaped by the instrumental objective of loss reduction, Johnston and Shearing (2003) show how risk-oriented forms of thinking have a certain fit with market sensibilities. This has resulted in a proliferation of different kinds of security provision, which are more hidden and consensual than traditional forms. For example, they place more emphasis on surveillance (often using new technologies such as CCTV), and deploy a range of other interventions to modify behaviour. On this view, security is increasingly embedded, both occupationally and functionally, throughout organisations. It is also designed into the physical structure of premises, so that the architecture and layout of the built environment reduces the possibility of non-compliance (Newman, 1972; Coleman, 1985).

As the analysis of tourist space examples demonstrates, however, risk-based mentalities and practices exist alongside more traditional punishment-oriented activities (Loader, 1999; Johnston, 2000). Some of the tourist spaces discussed above have always been policed by networks of public and private policing agents, and some arenas have seen the state reasserting control over security provision. In airports, the complex intermingling of commercial and state security interests behind the scenes show how new hybrid forms of security provision are emerging. The policing of the liminal spaces through which international tourists travel – seaports, airports, and international rail terminals – provide perhaps the most clear examples of the cross-fertilisation of public and private security approaches. As Morgan and Pritchard remark, 'the most diverse forms of surveillance are to be found in these betwixt places of arrival and departure, themselves marginalized "non-spaces" largely ignored in the social sciences' (2005: 116).

Polarisation and exclusion

A noted characteristic of contemporary security governance of tourist spaces relates to its exclusionary and polarising tendencies. The growth of actuarial mentalities and practices, as outlined above, widens the gaze of those concerned with promoting security. Risk-based approaches go well beyond the retrospective gathering of evidence about past offences. They casts their nets wider, to cover all those whose behaviour might cause harm in the future. At the same time, the focus upon traditional suspect populations – the poor, unemployed, homeless people, and ethnic minorities – is intensified. They are the prime candidates against whom security-oriented measures are deployed, partly because of their perceived 'threat' to the established order and the safety of the better off. Morgan and Pritchard (2005) provide an extensive account of how such developments are making themselves felt in the surveillance and security policies relating to air travel. There is substantial evidence that particular groups are subject to intensive security measures, based primarily on stereotypes relating to physical appearance or nationality. The major concerns about terrorist threats have been used to focus surveillance on particular national or ethnic groups, in ways that are often perceived as discriminatory (Curry, 2004).

Thus, the proliferation of privatised tourist spaces contributes to the polarisation of security experiences. Traditional punitive controls are increasingly applied to certain categories of the population, whilst the better off are more likely to experience the embedded and consensual forms of security governance. Although the rich are increasingly protected within commercially-governed safe spaces, the less advantaged are banished to increasingly dangerous 'public' spaces, policed by an increasingly militarised public police force (Davis, 1990). Increasingly effective crime prevention in these protected tourist spaces, along with the spread of commercial forms of private governance, exclude the poor both directly and indirectly whilst simultaneously displacing further crime and disorder to disadvantaged areas. In addition, in those public spaces that remain outside the privatised tourist bubbles of security, policing and security provision increasingly adopts elements of the exclusionary and risk-based policies of private government. As noted above, crime prevention by environmental design, and policies such as 'anti social behaviour orders' (ASBOs) and youth curfews in effect privatise public spaces (Crawford, 2006). Whilst the spread of 'gated communities' in Britain is significantly less than has been the case in the USA, nevertheless there is some evidence of increasing residential segregation of this type (Webster, 2002; Atkinson and Flint, 2004). Whilst such developments clearly help to foster social polarisation, in part on the basis of attempts to increase security, they have the paradoxical effect of heightening fear of crime (and crime itself) in the longer term, an issue to which we turn now.

The expansionary dynamic

The growing role played by the commercial (and other) sectors in security governance has not been accompanied by a parallel fall in state provision. On the contrary, the state security and penal apparatus has been expanding more rapidly than ever. In many countries, public police forces now employ record numbers of staff. Public expenditure on the police, courts and penal system has spiralled, as have prison populations, community sentences and the numbers of people experiencing other forms of penal supervision. As Stan Cohen (1985) predicted over two decades ago, the privatisation (and 'communitisation') of policing and punishment has not replaced state provision, but has added to it. The two developments are, of course, linked in a number of important ways. As noted, privatisation has been an addition to, not a replacement for public policing and punishment, and has facilitated the expansion of surveillance. Incidents that would previously have been dealt with informally are now subject to official attention and processing. There are more CCTV cameras, private security guards, and other functionaries to notice and record incidents and direct police attention towards them (Jones, 2007).

Furthermore, a possible unintended effect of the rise of actuarial approaches to security and crime control may be an enhanced public thirst for symbolic and expressive punishment (Garland, 2001). It may be also be the case that the growing visibility of both public and private security personnel, public awareness-raising campaigns about crime prevention, and the range of target hardening measures that are now an established part of the urban landscape, actually all work to sharpen subjective feelings of insecurity. Thus, attempts to feed the monster of insecurity via more policing – public and private – is rather like scratching an itch that simply gets worse.

The notion of 'private security' has been described as an 'oxymoron', in that attempts to package and sell security via the market are inherently expansionist (Loader, 1997). For example, Loader suggests that private security companies help to construct their own demand, by deliberately playing upon public fears and insecurity. These trends, along with a range of other structural/cultural changes, have contributed to what has been termed an 'insatiable demands' for more security (Morgan and Newburn, 1997). Nils Christie (2000) has highlighted the self-generating dynamic of commercial crime control in capitalist societies. On this view, the global expansion of prison populations (and more broadly, the numbers of people under state penal supervision) has been driven by a 'prison-industrial complex', an international alliance of commercial penal and industrial interests that makes profits from expansionist penal policies. The spatial polarisation – which the growth of privatised tourist spaces both reflects and helps to shape – is itself part of this expansionary dynamic. Such developments displace crime and disorder towards disadvantaged areas, encourage further social disorganisation in disadvantaged neighbourhoods, and thus increase the likelihood of crime and disorder. These trends also increase social distance, and the tendency to perceive people from other social and economic groups as a threat (Zedner, 2003).

Finally, it should be noticed that the expansion of security concerns is situated within a broader range of structural and cultural shifts that have gathered pace in the latter part of the 20th century. Such developments include: labour market restructuring; the growth of social and spatial mobility that has weakened the individual's ties with local places; the decline of participation in intermediate level institutions such as trade unions, local shops, community groups, religious organisations and clubs; growing economic inequality and social polarisation; and increasing financial and environmental instability. Such trends have perhaps contributed to a more fundamental sense of 'ontological insecurity' (Giddens, 1991) that leads to heightened awareness of, and anxiety about, the 'other' (Garland, 2001). Such understandings of insecurity are particularly interesting when applied to the field of tourism, given that the 'tourist gaze' (Urry, 2002) often involves encounters between people of different nationalities and cultures. Tourism often involves an uneasy combination of a fascination with, and fear of, 'the other'. This mirrors the paradox of contemporary societies that are awash with anxieties about crime and disorder, and yet have an apparently unquenchable thirst for more attention to such phenomena in popular culture and news media.

Conclusion

The governance of security has changed in very significant ways over recent decades, and a focus upon 'tourist spaces' provides numerous potential opportunities to understand better the complex nature and possible impacts of such developments. The fragmentation that characterises contemporary security governance more generally is now clearly visible within the realm of tourist spaces. Indeed, the proliferation of such spaces has made an important contribution to these wider developments. However, much research and writing in both tourism studies and criminology has yet to reflect these shifts. An important challenge for future research is to develop further the analysis of security governance within the tourist realm, and its implications for considerations of security more generally. An improved conceptual and empirical understanding of what is happening to security governance in tourist spaces should also help inform normative debates about security governance. As well as challenging dominant empirical understandings of what policing is, the literature on plural policing has stimulated normative debates about how policing should be. Much of the above discussion has resonated with general concerns about the possible negative impacts of the growth of non-state policing of the type found in many tourist spaces. Such concerns include reports of the low service standards of non-state policing forms, and about the emergence of unaccountable 'private armies' that promote the interests of the rich and powerful. The growth of privately policed spaces can exacerbate social polarisation and stimulate rather than neutralise feelings of insecurity. However, some of the leading writers on private policing have argued that in some circumstances non state-forms of security provision and governance may allow for the development of more equitable and effective forms of security provision in local communities (Johnston and Shearing, 2003; Shearing, 2006). On this view, governments should seek to facilitate the participation of disadvantaged groups in security markets, and encourage communities to develop their own locally-designed forms of private governance (Wood, 2006). In this sense, the multi-faceted nature of policing of tourist spaces (for example) may contain positive lessons for the improvement of policing and security provision more generally. There is not the space to consider such arguments in more detail here. For now, we can simply conclude that studying how security is governed in tourist spaces holds much promise for conceptual, empirical and normative work that combines the insights both of criminology and of tourism studies.

References

Adams, T. (2009) 'Titanic times five: Oasis of the Seas aims to leave cruise rivals in huge wake'. *The Guardian*, 25 November 2009.

Andrews, H. (2009) '"Tits out for the boys and no back chat": Gendered space on holiday', *Space and Culture*, **12** (2), 166–182.

Atkinson, R. and Blandy, S. (2009) 'A picture of the floating world: grounding the seccessionary affluence of the residential cruise liner', *Antipode*, **41** (1), 92–110.

Atkinson, R. and Flint, J. (2004) 'Fortress UK? Gated communities, the spatial revolt of the elites and time–space trajectories of segregation', *Housing Studies*, **19**, 875–892.

Atkinson, R., Blandy, S., Flint, J. and Lister, D. (2003) *Gated Communities in England*, London: Office of the Deputy Prime Minister.

Auge, M. (1995) *Non-Places: Introduction to an Anthropology of Supermodernity*. London: Verso.

Bayley, D. and Shearing, C. (1996) 'The future of policing', *Law and Society Review*, **30** (3), 585–606.

Bayley, D. and Shearing, C. (2001) *The New Structure of Policing*, Washington, DC: National Institute of Justice.

BBC News Online (2006) 'Diplomat cleared over "air rage"', 24 January, http://news.bbc.co.uk/1/hi/england/hampshire/4644022.stm Accessed 14 December 2009

Beck, U. (1992) *Risk Society: Towards a New Modernity*, London: Sage.

Blakeley, E. and Snyder, M. (1997) *Fortress America: Gated Communities in the United States*, Washington DC: Brookings Institution Press.

Blank, C. (1998) 'Parking it for fun'. *American Demographics*, April 1998

Bloor, M. and Sampson, H. (forthcoming) 'Regulatory enforcement of labour standards in an outsourcing globalized industry: the case of the shipping industry', *Work, Employment and Society*.

Bowling, B. and Newburn, T. (2006) 'Policing and national security'. Paper presented at London-Columbia Police, Community and the Rule of Law Workshop, London, 16-17 March.

Christie, N. (2000) *Crime Control as Industry*, 3rd edn, London: Routledge.

Clarke, R. (1997) *Situational Crime Prevention: Successful Case Studies*, 2nd edn, Albany, NY: Harrow and Heston.

Cohen, S. (1985) *Visions of Social Control*, Cambridge: Polity.

Coleman, A. (1985) *Utopia on Trial: Vision and Reality in Planned Housing*, London: Hilary Shipman.

Coleman, R. (2003) 'Images from a neo-liberal city: the state, surveillance and social control', *Critical Criminology*, **12** (1), 21–42.

Crawford, A. (2006) 'Policing and security as "club goods": the new enclosures?', in J. Wood and B. Dupont (eds), *Democracy, Society and the Governance of Security*, Cambridge: Cambridge University Press. pp. 111-138.

Crawford, A. (2008) 'Plural policing in the UK: policing beyond the police', in T. Newburn (ed.), *The Handbook of Policing*, 2nd edn. Cullompton: Willan. pp. 147-181

Crawford, A., Lister, S., Blackburn, S. and Burnett, J. (2005) *Plural Policing: The Mixed Economy of Visible Patrols in England and Wales*, Bristol: Policy Press.

Curry, M. (2004) 'The profiler's question and the treacherous traveller: narratives of belonging in commercial aviation', *Surveillance and Society*, **1** (4), 475–499.

Davis, M. (1990) *City of Quartz: Imagining the Future in Los Angeles*, London: Verso.

Dowling, R.K. (2006) 'The cruising industry', in R.K. Dowling (ed.), *Cruise Ship Tourism*, Wallingford: CAB International. pp. 3-17.

Feeley, M. and Simon, J. (1994) 'Actuarial justice: the emerging new criminal law', in D. Nelken (ed.), *The Futures of Criminology*, London: Sage. pp. 173-201.

Frietag, T. (1994) 'Enclave tourism development: for whom the benefits roll?', *Annals of Tourism Research*, 21 (3), 538–554.

Garland, D. (2001) *The Culture of Control: Crime and Social Order in Contemporary Society*, Oxford: Oxford University Press.

Giddens, A. (1991) *Modernity and Self-Identity: Self and Society in the Late Modern Age*, Stanford, CA: Stanford University Press

Glasze, G., Webster, C. and Frantz, K. (eds) (2006) *Private Cities: Global and Local Perspectives*, London: Routledge.

Hughes, G.(2010) 'The preventive turn in crime control and its relationship with tourism' in Botterill, D. and Jones, T. (eds) *Tourism and Crime: Key Themes*. Oxford: Goodfellow Publishers.

Jaakson, R. (2004) 'Beyond the tourist bubble? Cruise ship passengers in port', *Annals of Tourism Research*, 31 (1), 44–60.

Johnston, L. (2000) *Policing Britain: Risk, Security and Governance*, London: Longman.

Johnston, L. (1996) 'What is vigilantism?', *British Journal of Criminology*, 36(2), 220-36.

Johnston, F. (1992) *The Rebirth of Private Policing*. London: Routledge.

Johnston, L. and Shearing, C. (2003) *Governing Security: Explorations in Policing and Justice*, London: Routledge.

Jones, T. (2008) 'Private Policing', in T. Newburn and P. Neyroud (eds) *The Dictionary of Policing*. Cullompton: Willan. pp. 223-225.

Jones, T. (2007) 'The governance of security: pluralization, privatization and polarization in crime control', in M. Maguire, R. Morgan and R. Reiner (eds), *The Oxford Handbook of Criminology*, 4th edn, Oxford: Oxford University Press. pp. 841-865.

Jones, T. and Newburn, T. (1998) *Private Security and Public Policing*, Oxford: Clarendon Press.

Jones, T. and Newburn, T. (1999) 'Urban change and policing: mass private property reconsidered', *European Journal on Criminal Policy and Research*, 7 (2), 225–244.

Jones, T. and Newburn, T. (eds) (2006) *Plural Policing: A Comparative Perspective*, London: Routledge.

Jones, T., van Steden, R. and Boutellier, H. (2009) 'Pluralisation of policing in England & Wales and the Netherlands: Exploring similarity and difference', *Policing and Society*, **19**(3), 282-299.

Kempa, M., Stenning, P. and Wood, J. (2004) 'Policing communal spaces: a reconfiguration of the mass private property hypothesis', *British Journal of Criminology*, **44** (4), 562–581.

Loader, I. (1997) 'Private security and the demand for protection in contemporary Britain', *Policing and Society*, 7, 143–162.

Loader, I. (1999) 'Consumer culture and the commodification of policing and security', *Sociology*, **33** (2), 373–392.

Loader, I. (2000) 'Plural policing and democratic governance', *Social and Legal Studies*, **9** (3), 323–345.

Loader, I. and Sparks, R. (2007) 'Contemporary landscapes of crime, order and control: governance, risk and globalization', in M. Maguire, R. Morgan and R. Reiner (eds), *The Oxford Handbook of Criminology*, 4th edn, Oxford: Oxford University Press.pp. 78-101.

MacLeod, G. (2003) *Privatizing the City? The Tentative Push Towards Edge Urban Developments and Gated Communities in the United Kingdom*, Report for the Office of the Deputy Prime Minister, Durham: University of Durham.

Macaulay, S. (1986) 'Private government', in L. Lipson and S. Wheeler (eds), *Law and the Social Sciences*, New York: Russell Sage Foundation. pp. 445-518.

Milman, A. (2008) 'Theme park tourism and management strategy', in A. Woodside and D. Martin (eds), *Tourism Management: Analysis, Behaviour and Strategy*, Wallingford: CAB International. pp. 218-231.

Minton, A. (2002) *Building Balanced Communities: the US and UK Compared*, London: Royal Institute of Chartered Surveyors.

Morgan, N. and Pritchard, A. (2005) 'Security and social "Sorting": traversing the surveillance–tourism dialectic', *Tourist Studies*, **5** (2), 115–132.

Morgan, R. and Newburn, T. (1997) *The Future of Policing*. Oxford: Oxford University Press.

Mount, F. (2005) *Mind the Gap: The New Class Divide in Britain*, London: Short Books.

Muehsam, M. and Tarlow, P. (1995) 'Involving the police in tourism', *Tourism Management*, **16** (1), 9–14.

Newburn, T. and Reiner, R. (2007) 'Policing and the police', in Maguire, M., Morgan, R., and Reiner, R. (eds) *The Oxford Handbook of Criminology*, 4th edn, Oxford: Oxford University Press. pp. 910-952.

Newman, O. (1972) *Defensible Space: Crime Prevention through Urban Design*, New York: Macmillan.

Rhodes, R. (1997) *Understanding Governance: Policy Networks, Governance, Reflexivity and Accountability*, Buckingham: Open University Press.

Roberts, S. (2005) 'After government? On representing law without the state', *Modern Law Review*, **68** (1), 1–24.

Schmid, K. (2008) 'Doing ethnography of tourist enclaves: boundaries, ironies and insights', *Tourist Studies*, **8** (1), 105–121.

Shaw, B.J., Shaw, G. (1999) '"Sun, sand and sales": enclave tourism and local entrepreneurship in Indonesia', *Current Issues in Tourism*, **2**, 68–81.

Shearing, C. (1992) 'The relation between public and private policing', in M. Tonry and N. Morris (eds), *Modern Policing*, Chicago: University of Chicago Press. pp. 399-434

Shearing, C. (2006) 'Reflections on the refusal to acknowledge private governments', in J. Wood and B. Dupont (eds), *Democracy, Society and the Governance of Security*, Cambridge: Cambridge University Press. pp. 11-32.

Shearing, C. and Stenning, P. (1981) 'Modern private security: its growth and implications', in M. Tonry and N. Morris (eds), *Crime and Justice: An Annual Review of Research*, vol. 3, Chicago: University of Chicago Press. pp. 193-245.

Shearing, C. and Stenning, P. (eds) (1987) *Private Policing*, Newbury Park, CA: Sage.

Shearing, C. and Wood, J. (2003) 'Nodal governance, democracy and the new "denizen", *Journal of Law and Society*, 30 (3), 400–419.

Sheller, M. (2004) 'Returning the tourist gaze: Caribbean gender and racial encounters', paper presented at the annual meeting of the American Sociological Association, San Francisco, 14 August 2004.

Sheptycki, J. (ed.) (2000). *Issues in Transnational Policing*. London: Routledge

South Wales Argus (2008) 'Oakwood death: theme park fined £250,000 after teen's death'. *South Wales Argus*, 18 December 2008.

Stoker, G. (ed.) (1998) *The New Politics of British Local Governance*, Basingstoke: Macmillan.

Urry, J. (2002) *The Tourist Gaze*, 2nd edn, London: Sage.

Urry, J. (2007) *Mobilities*, Cambridge: Polity Press.

Von Hirsch, A. and Shearing, C. (2000) 'Exclusion from public space', in A. von Hirsch, D. Garland and A. Wakefield (eds), *Ethical and Social Perspectives on Situational Crime Prevention*, Oxford: Hart. pp. 77-96.

Wakefield, A. (2003) *Selling Security: the Private Policing of Public Space*, Cullompton: Willan.

Weaver, A. (2005) 'Spaces of containment and revenue capture: "super-sized" cruise ships as mobile tourism enclaves', *Tourism Geographies*, 7 (2), 165–184.

Webster, C. (2002) 'Property rights and the public realm: gates, green belts, and Gemeinschaft', *Environment and Planning B: Planning and Design*, 29, 397–412.

Wood, J. (2006) 'Research and innovation in the field of security: a nodal governance view', in J. Wood and B. Dupont (eds), *Democracy, Society and the Governance of Security*, Cambridge: Cambridge University Press. pp. 217-240.

Wood, J. and Dupont, B. (eds) (2006) *Democracy, Society and the Governance of Security*, Cambridge: Cambridge University Press.

World Travel and Tourism Council, International Hotel and Restaurant Association, International Federation of Tour Operators, International Council of Cruise Lines and United Nations Environment Programme (2002) *Industry as a Partner for Sustainable Development: Tourism*, Paris: United Nations Environment Programme.

Zedner, L. (2003) 'Too much security?', *International Journal of the Sociology of Law*, 31(3), 155-84.

11 Tourism, Image and Fear of Crime

Martin Selby, Helen Selby and David Botterill

In this chapter we:

♦ Consider the interrelationships between tourist destinations, place image, crime and the fear of crime

♦ Conduct a review and extend the orthodox view that there is a negative relationship between crime and tourism

♦ Introduce Schutz's 'stock of knowledge' as a way of understanding the relationship between tourist destination image and tourist behaviour

♦ Provide examples that demonstrate the battleground of tourism destination image

♦ Suggest a radical reconceptualisation of the crime/tourism nexus through a consideration of the 'fear of crime' concept.

Introduction

This chapter considers the interrelationships between tourist destinations, place image, and fear of crime. We do this in two sections. First, it has long been acknowledged that place or destination image plays a significant role in consumer decision-making. An increasing number of researchers have also recognised the significance of images of safety and security in travel decision-making. Conversely, negative images of crime in localities are assumed to deter the attraction of not only visitors, but also inward investment and inhabitants. Several place image studies also suggest a link between images of crime and mass media representations. What is not clear, however, is how specific incidents of criminal behaviour are factored into tourist decision-making. In the chapter we draw upon cultural and humanistic studies in order to offer a conceptual framework for analysing how specific forms of mass media representations, and specific 'textual communities', are associated with both positive and negative images relating to crime, danger, safety, and security. It is agued that Schutz's 'stock of knowledge' (e.g. Schutz, 1972) concept provides a means of understanding the relationship between representations of crime and tourist decision-making. Furthermore, that the 'stock of knowledge' not only influences the choices of destinations, but also influences the behaviour of tourists during a visit to a particular tourist destination.

A second strand of analysis in this chapter offers an integration of the destination image literature with the fear of crime literature found in criminology. Whilst many place image studies point to interrelationships between images of crime and travel decision-making, less is known about the relationship between perceptions of crime and tourist behaviour within a destination. This takes on a particular significance in considering the relationship between destination image and crime when we incorporate our arguments about the sources of destination imagery. In our conceptual schema, destination image is not only formed through 'impressions' but is shaped by actual experience of a destination or, vicariously, the reporting of tourist experiences by others. The flow of information surrounding destination imagery is, importantly and despite the best efforts of the agencies of tourism promotion, not uni-directional. Of at least equal significance are the parallel flows of information from tourist to tourist that derive from actual experience. These 'private' narratives have reinforced habitual and inter-generational tourist behaviours in perpetuity but recent advances in information technology have converted private narratives into public ones. Expanded flows of information through travel blogs, consumer rating devices, reality TV holiday programmes and 'youtube-type' websites have made a conceptual connection between image and behaviour an imperative.

In order to better understand these phenomena in the context of criminology, we also visit the 'fear of crime' concept. The difficulties associated with defining 'fear of crime' are noted. A brief history of the fear of crime debate is then documented. Attention is drawn to the various stages and developments in policy and academic debate. This allows an understanding of how the concept has emerged as an object of study and as a priority for policy-making. Our intention here is to begin to sketch out how the fear of crime concept might inform a reinterpretation of the tourism destination/crime nexus. We discuss a range of factors that appear to be associated with variations in fear of crime, such as gender, age, ethnicity; and assessments of the seriousness of consequences and personal risk. Attention once again turns to representations and discourses relating to crime in tourist destinations. Representations and discourses appear to be salient to images of crime prior to visiting tourist destinations, the fear of crime whilst visiting, and also responses to crime in tourist destinations. Significantly, however, despite the complex relationships between the concepts, Schutz's 'stock of knowledge' acts as an important conduit or hub.

Place image and crime

Introducing the relationship

A substantive contribution of place or destination image studies relates to the crucial role of images in an individual's decision-making before they visit a locality. Place image is also believed to influence levels of satisfaction or dissatisfaction resulting from first-hand experience of localities. The significance of place image has long been recognised by tourism authorities, and it is interesting that some of the most notable examples of place marketing were instigated in order to counteract negative images of crime, violence, lack of safety, and social problems. According to researchers such as Sonmez (1998), perception of risk associated with a destination can disrupt the usual decision-making process. Despite the fact that Mawby *et al.* (2000) found that 45 per cent of respondents had 'never' thought about crime when choosing a destination, 42 per cent admitted that they had ruled out at least one destination due to crime. Conversely, it is widely acknowledged that safety, security and peace are essential prerequisites of a tourist destination (Pizam and Mansfeld, 1996). It is assumed that a potential visitor initially acts upon their image of a locality, rather than the objective 'reality' of the destination. However, as we argue later in this chapter, image and reality have become more entangled as sources of information and representations of a destination proliferate via new information technologies.

A decision to visit a locality is believed to be influenced less by quantifiable characteristics, than by the consumer's overall expectations regarding levels of satisfaction and well-being. An image is conceptualised as the net result of a person's beliefs, ideas, feelings, expectations, and impressions (Chon, 1990). Dichter (1984: 76) states that 'an image is not just individual traits or qualities, but the total impression an entity makes on the minds of others'. Consumers choose to visit one locality over another because of the locality's perceived attributes, using their perceptions of attributes as input factors to estimate the satisfaction that they will gain. As Jenkins (1999: 2) argues, destination images influence both the decision-making behaviour of potential tourists, and levels of satisfaction upon experiencing the destination first-hand. It is significant that images are conceptualised as changing throughout the travel experience, as more information is acquired by the individual (see Ashworth and Goodall, 1988).

Numerous pieces of research, including Pearce (1982) and Woodside and Lyonski (1990), indicate that the destination's image influences travel behaviour both positively and negatively. This is also recognised by tourism practitioners, exemplified by the frank admission by the South African Tourism Minister that more than 22 million potential visitors have been lost over a five-year period due to South Africa's reputation for violent crime (Starmer-Smith, 2008). This assertion was based upon the South African Tourism Brand Tracker, analysing eight key markets (DEAT, 2005). The complexity of the place product is considered to make image even more critical (Ashworth and Goodall, 1988), as decisions are mainly based upon images rather than 'facts' or first-hand experience. It would also appear that some of the most significant negative images of a locality relate to crime, violence, and a lack of safety (see Madsen 1992; Selby 1995, 2004a; George, 2003). In a UK study (see Selby, 2004b), repertory grid analysis was used to build up an intersubjective language of how urban tourists distinguish between attractive and unattractive urban tourism destinations. The research, conducted in UK cities, revealed 'safe–unsafe' to be a crucial construct used in deciding whether or not to visit a city for leisure purposes.

The orthodox way of thinking about crime and tourist destinations, therefore, is to view the relationship in a negative form. This is evidenced when we examine official sources of information that name and shame destinations for their criminal records, ostensibly warning against travel or at least raising questions in the potential tourist's mind. Travel advisories provide official advice for tourists about a range of risks associated with travelling abroad. On the UK Government's Foreign and Commonwealth Office website, British residents (and other English-language speakers) are provided with a regularly updated review of the conditions in most countries of the world. The production of these services can be controversial, however, particularly in the area of safety and security where travel restrictions can be put in place. In June 2002, attacks on tourist hotels in Kenya led the UK and US governments to issue an 'all but essential travel' warning against travelling to Kenya. In response, British Airways cancelled all flights to the country (BBC, 2003a). This situation was exacerbated by further warnings to US citizens in December 2003 leading to complaints by the Kenyan government of alleged breaches in diplomatic procedures by US consular staff in Nairobi (BBC, 2003b). More recently, in June 2009, the same two governments have clashed over the sudden cancellation of what was to be an inaugural flight of a direct link from Atlanta to Nairobi provided by Delta Airlines, the first direct flight between the two countries for 20 years. 'The US Department for Homeland Security was said to have taken the decision because of "security vulnerabilities" in Nairobi. Kenyan Foreign Affairs Minister Moses Wetangula said the move would dampen prospects for a recovery in the tourism sector, "It amounts to a travel advisory against the country"' (BBC, 2009a).

In another recent example, the threat of attacks against foreigners in Sabah, Malaysia, an area popular with British tourists, led to a travel advisory being issued by the US Government in which it claimed that 'There are indications that both criminal and terrorist groups are planning or intend acts of violence against foreigners in Eastern Sabah' (as cited in Henderson, 2010). In response, the Sabah Tourism Board issued an immediate response disputing the US travel notice through its spokesperson Senator Datuk T. Murugiah, a deputy minister in the prime minister's department, claiming that extensive measures had been put in place to combat terrorist attacks on tourists. The protection of tourists is not just a matter of policing and security as there are clearly significant economic interests at stake, as these two examples show. Official information is clearly contradictory in these instances and tourists confronted with divergent opinions often turn for advice to other tourists and residents of the destination through the platform of Internet discussion boards.

Whilst there are enduring negative associations between crime and tourist places we also acknowledge a possible, positive synergy. This can take several forms. First, criminal behaviour, or the possibility for it given lax legal frameworks or culturally acceptable or economically-driven sanctioning of deviance, can be a motivation for tourists. Consequentially, as Montgomery notes in Chapter 5, the destination image of parts of East Asia is suggestive of the easy availability of sexual encounters providing a cover for paedophile activity. In Chapter 6, Shiner reports research studies of tourists who choose destinations dependent on the availability of drugs and in Chapter 8, Spapens provides a case study of drug tourism on the borders of the Netherlands. While the tourist activities cited in these chapters are more obviously deviant, several studies report on the more ambivalent situation where visitation results in the raucous and sometimes uncivil behaviours associated with the night-time economy (Hobbs *et al.*, 2003). Second, we acknowledge the arguments of Lennon in Chapter 12 and other authors who document the many sites of crime that constitute parts of the tourist product. Indeed, the assumption that the association between destination image and crime is primarily negative begins to be challenged by the growing list of criminal behaviour perpetuated by tourists and evidenced in this book.

Crime and tourist decision-making

According to authors such as Gunn (1972: 120), the different stages of the decision-making process result in a variety of place images, depending on the amount, source, and objectivity of information available. Gunn, in a seven-phase decision-making model (Figure 11.1), makes a useful distinction between the official 'projected image' of the tourism authorities, and the 'organic image', from non-tourist sources. The term 'organic image' is given to the formation of images based on non-commercial sources, such as art, literature, education, family and friends, and the mass media. More commercial sources of information and representations are conceptualised as contributing to an 'induced image'. The induced image is formed from advertisements, brochures, guidebooks, and the activities of intermediaries such as travel agents, destination marketing organisations, and marketing consortia. The 'modified induced image' is formed with the addition of first-hand experience of the destination, and may itself be changed by return travel and reflection following the visit.

Such models, therefore, consist of a hierarchy of images, consisting of initial perceptions based on organic sources, and a modification of the image upon visiting the destination. This modification results in a much more 'realistic, objective, differentiated and complex image' (Echtner and Brent-Richie, 1991: 4). Naive images – the images of consumers who have not visited a destination – consist of representations from a wide variety of sources. Possible sources include promotional literature, word of mouth, visual representations, and representations from a diverse range of texts. It would seem that organic images, from unofficial sources such as the mass media, may be particularly strong and persistent.

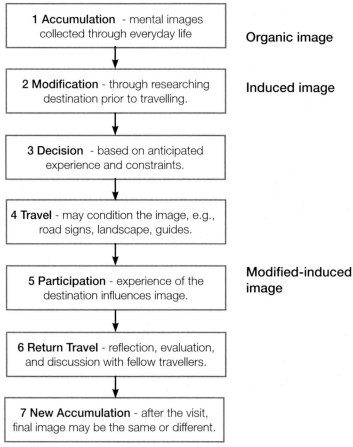

Figure 11.1: Destination image and tourist decision-making
Source: After Gunn (1972:120)

The consumer behaviour literature, however, (see, for example, Assael, 2003) asserts that different types of decision-making can be identified. In particular, a distinction is made between 'habitual' and 'complex' decision-making and both are evident in tourist behaviour. The majority of studies of tourist decision making, including Gunn (1972), adopt the complex model where consumers actively gather information to inform their decisions. But it is also true that a significant amount of tourist behaviour displays a form of habitual behaviour. Here, destination preferences are not so much subject to information searching, but are strongly influenced by inter-generational patterns of holiday taking and more structural influences, such as cultural familiarity, historical association and material resources such as second-home ownership. Incidents of crime may therefore provoke different reactions within the complex/habitual decision-making process and as we shall argue later in this section the extent to which tourists hold a 'stock of knowledge' about a particular destination will mediate the response.

Stock of knowledge

Humanistic geography has engaged with perceptions of fear (see Tuan, 1980), but an underrated contribution comes from Schutz (e.g. 1970, 1972). According to Schutz, experiences collected from childhood become sedimented in a stock of knowledge about localities. The stock of knowledge has a vital influence on future action, forming the basis of decision-making. The stock of knowledge can be considered to be a sedimentation of past experiences, some first-hand, and some socially transmitted (representations). Whatever the source of information, knowledge is arranged into 'types', and when little alternative information is available, stereotypes are formed. The stock of knowledge of tourists and hosts develops with new experiences, whether direct or mediated. In familiar situations, however, tourists can rely upon previously proven 'recipes' for acting, and these are likely to have been socially transmitted. Questioning the assumptions underlying many decision-making models, it is only when an individual is faced with contradictory information that an active attempt to seek further information is made (Schutz and Luckmann, 1974). Berger an Luckmann (1967) also assert that it is possible to 'seek the origins of the stock of knowledge.' This enables the researcher to trace the representations contributing to the stock of knowledge.

In the context of South Africa (see Ferreira, 1999), for example, it is possible to recognise a discourse in the mass media relating to high levels of crime, and this discourse may result in the formation of a stock of knowledge about crime in South Africa. The stock of knowledge of South Africa may be influenced by the recent debate regarding the FIFA World Cup, but also the advice of family and friends, television programmes, travel reviews, and newspaper articles over a long period of time. Knowledge of past atrocities may be influential, such as the murder of the dancer Daryl Kempster (Telegraph, 2008), the murder of a British tourist (The Independent, 2002) and reports on the BBC News Service of attacks against a pensioner in 2003 and the rape of a British tourist in 2002. Crucially, however, social relations and structures create intersubjective rather than individual stocks of knowledge, and consequently, intersubjective action. Applied in the context of tourism, the focus of attention becomes groups of consumers who intersubjectively acquire similar images and experiences of a destination (see Selby, 2004a). We can therefore conceptualise different social groups who have similarities in their contact with, and interpretation of, particular representations of a locality. Studies such as Selby (2004b) suggest that negative typifications concerning issues such as crime are shared by individuals with similar cultural, social, lifestyle, and personality characteristics.

Following Schutz, everyday life should be the focus of research into images of crime, as it is in everyday life that all kinds of experiences are accepted and taken for granted as common sense. It is also clear that the transmission of knowledge is influenced by the roles and credibility of the knowledge communicators, be they parents, teachers, politicians, journalists, or fellow tourists (Schutz and Luckmann, 1974). Action involves a process of projecting the likely consequences of a particular action into the future. The act of visiting a particular tourist destination, is thus projected into the future and then becomes the focus of reflective attention (Schutz, 1972). The same process may then be applied to another destination, and the projected consequences are evaluated and compared. If the stock of knowledge of a locality has been influenced by representations of crime, violence, and a lack of security, the locality is unlikely to be chosen as a place to visit. In contrast to most goods, where the characteristics are '...ready made and well circumscribed' (Schutz and Luckmann, 1974: 159), tourist decision-making draws heavily upon the stock of knowledge.

Types of images

It is significant that a study commissioned to evaluate images and first-hand experiences amongst visitors to South Africa revealed a modification upon visiting. Despite the very high levels of recorded crime in South Africa, positive perceptions about safety increased from 32% to 55% (Cape Town Routes Unlimited, 2008). Negative perceptions decreased from 35% to 14%, but there was little change in terms of the 'neutral' respondents (Cape Town Routes Unlimited, 2008). Conversely, George (2003) found that visitors to Cape Town who felt threatened or unsafe were unlikely to return. In a study of Cardiff, Wales (Selby, 2004b), naïve images amongst those who had never visited the city were compared with the 're-evaluated image' upon actually visiting. The latter were considerably more positive in general, but particularly for the construct 'safe–unsafe'. The research revealed strongly negative images of Cardiff as 'industrial' and 'unsafe', yet these images were significantly less frequent amongst visitors with first-hand experience of the city. Furthermore, factor analysis suggested that negative naïve images of crime were associated with mass media representations, particularly newspapers and television programmes. It is important that first-hand experience is influential only in the final stages, emphasising the initial importance of images formed without first-hand experience.

The emotive nature of crime and safety tends to increase both the number and influence of organic images, created through mediated or indirect experiences, particularly through mass media representations. Crime, therefore, may constitute an important component of what place image researchers term 'organic images'. Rio de Janeiro has high recorded crime rates, particularly for violent crime. However, it is relatively rare for tourists to be targeted for serious criminal acts, as gang-related crime in a limited number of problem favelas accounts for a disproportionately large share. These subtleties, however, may be lost on potential visitors from around the world, upon reading headlines such as 'Drugs gang shoot down police chopper near Rio de Janeiro' (Boyle, 2009), 'Brazil: crime against tourists increasing in Rio de Janeiro' (World Travel Watch, 2006), or 'Elite police head to crime-hit Rio' (Aljazeera, 2007). The award of the Olympic Games in 2016 has increased the intensity of debate about Rio's crime problem, with articles such as 'Can Rio's crime problem be solved before the Olympics?' (Time Magazine, 2009).

The award of the FIFA World Cup 2010 to South Africa would also appear to be a double-edged sword. Whilst a successful tournament from the perspective of spectators has the potential to challenge images of crime as visitors and television viewers re-evaluate their images, there has also been considerable analysis of crime in South Africa following the announcement. The figures certainly don't make pleasant reading, with South Africa rated second in the world for assault and murder per capita, and first for rapes per capita (United Nations Office on Drugs and Crime, 2009). Further compounding the problem, there has actually been an increase in recorded crime in the run-up to the event, with car-jackings increasing by 6%, residential robberies by 24%, and bank robberies by 118% (*Telegraph*, 2008). Not surprisingly, this has led to much debate about the appropriateness of South Africa as a venue, with headlines such as 'Crime fears grow as South Africa readies for football World Cup' (Smith, 2009), and 'South Africa's crime wave' (Reuters, 2009). As Cornelissen and Swart (2006) argue, the impacts of representations of crime are more severe in developing countries.

As Bramwell and Rawding (1996: 202) point out, the majority of place image studies focus on the received images of tourists. In effect, this is an individual's overall interpretation of numerous sources of information about a locality. However, researchers have increasingly sought to analyse the projected images of tourism authorities and destination marketing organisations. The Mersey Partnership in Liverpool (UK) is notable for its work in targeting stereotypical images of crime and violence. The city of Liverpool, along with its metropolitan county 'Merseyside', has a mid-table position with regards to recorded crime in British cities (see Home Office, 2009). Liverpool has less recorded crime than affluent London boroughs such as Kensington, yet stereotypes of crime and violence persist. Although the image of Merseyside has been central to the remit of The Mersey Partnership since its conception, the 'Make it Merseyside' Campaign in 2002 was an innovative and overt attempt at tackling stereotypes. One element of the strategy was to target key opinion-formers and decision-makers with 11 positive key facts about Merseyside, termed the 'Facts Campaign'. The positive facts challenged the stereotypes about Liverpool and Merseyside, drawing upon strengths such as the existence of 'more museums, theatres and galleries than anywhere in the UK outside London'. The most audacious, however, was the assertion that 'Merseyside is one of the safest city regions in the UK'. The adverts pointed out that Merseyside has similar rates of crime as counties such as Cambridgeshire, and were underscored with a Harvard-style reference to the latest Home Office Statistical Bulletin. The message was communicated through various media, but it was interesting that the bill-board version was carefully targeted at opinion-formers and investment decision-makers using City of London tube stations. The integrated 'Make it Merseyside' campaign aimed to build brand awareness through the full communications mix. The use of market research, market testing, and the use of advertising and public relations agencies were designed to target investment brokers, senior decision-makers and key opinion-formers. The Mersey Partnership also conducts annual Image Tracking Research, in order to monitor the image of the region amongst national business decision-makers. According to Burgess (1990), the source of information and the style of presentation significantly affect the credibility. Giletson and Crompton (1983) also emphasise the importance of non-official sources such as the advice of friends. It should be acknowledged, however, that there may be an increasing degree of blurring of the organic-induced categorisation, due to the contemporary sophistication of public relations aimed at developing 'credible' media such as travel writing (see Urry, 1995). For a comprehensive review of the destination image literature we recommend Gallarza et al. (2002).

Representations and discourses

Drawing upon cultural studies, it is significant that both tourist landscapes and representations of destinations can be read as texts. If texts signify that a locality will not even meet the basic safety and security needs of an individual, it is likely to have a powerful influence upon action and behaviour. Tourism represents an important cultural phenomenon, bound up in the ways that humans 'assess their world, defining their own sense of identity in the process' (Jackle, 1985: xi). Contemporary cultural approaches are particularly concerned with the codes through which meaning is constructed. As Duncan and Duncan (1988: 117) argued, literary theory provides a means of examining the text-like qualities of landscapes and their representations. Whether texts are in the form of tourist landscapes, promotional material, or mass media representations, their meaning are always contested and unstable. They can acquire meanings and consequences unintended by their authors, and it is these readings that have social, psychological, and material consequences. In the context of tourism, there can often be contradictions between the messages communicated by different agencies. The Open Golf Championship on the Wirral peninsula (UK) provides an interesting example. The destination marketing organisation the Mersey Partnership viewed the championship as a major opportunity to improve the image of the Liverpool City Region. Merseyside Police, which has seen the largest crime reduction nationally over the last three years, operated a pubic information promotional campaign. This included posters in Liverpool railway stations with strap lines such as 'Watch your wallet while you watch for birdies. Don't let a thief mark your card at the Open'.

It is possible to conceptualise a discourse within tourism that represents a collection of narratives, concepts, signs, and ideologies developed by a particular organisation or group. In the context of tourism, it is also important that representations of a destination can effectively replace the destination – with the objective reality of the destination effectively becoming redundant. The city of Liverpool does not have high rates of crime relative to comparable British cities (see Home Office, 2009), with less recoded crime than affluent London boroughs. Merseyside Police have also achieved impressive reductions in recorded crime. Despite this, a strong discourse persists in the UK, representing the city as dangerous and unsafe. The rather excessive and place-specific reporting, debate and analysis of several shocking murder cases has played a part in the discourse. So too has the economic and social history of a city that declined from being the world's most important port to the first-post-industrial city (see Urry, 1995). Yet the discourse also consists of a surprisingly diverse range of representations, including jokes and comedy sketches, and the comments of prominent politicians. The so-called comedy of Liverpudlian Stan Boardman provides an example, with his numerous jokes about car crime. One of the most popular sketches of comedian Harry Enfield depicts Liverpudlians (or 'Scousers') fighting at a wedding. Senior British politicians including Jack Straw and Boris Johnson have hit the headlines for making disparaging remarks about the city. Even positive news stories provide an opportunity to draw upon stereotypes, such as the announcement of the European Capital of Culture 2008 designation on the BBC's *Liquid News* satirical news programme. The announcement was accompanied by several minutes of footage of riots and burning cars. The 'soap opera' Brookside, which was set in Liverpool, ran for 21 years throughout the 1980s and 1990s. Devised by Phil Redmond, the series featured hard-hitting and sensational storylines, and almost every conceivable crime. Phil Redmond was later rewarded for his contribution to Liverpool's image with the role of Creative Director at the Liverpool Culture Company, the organisation responsible for promoting the city through the European Capital of Culture programme in 2008. As meaning is only created when texts are interpreted by readers, it is also significant that different groups of readers fall into different textual communities, each gaining different sets of meanings from their readings. The arguments of cultural researchers are especially convincing in the sphere of place consumption. As contemporary societies increasingly 'turn their citizens into image junkies' (Sontag, 1978: 24), the significance of representations increases and, as Shields argues in the context of urban tourism, 'a shroud of representations stand between us and even the concrete objects in the city' (Shields, 1992: 229).

In his 'circuit of culture' model, Johnson (1986) emphasises the transformation of meaning as representations are encoded and decoded over time and in different contexts. Meaning is therefore transformed at each stage of the circuit of culture, including the transformation upon reading, which depends on the social characteristics of the audience. The forms of reading may differ significantly between different groups of readers, or textual communities. It may even be the 'mis-readings' (ibid.: 284) that are more significant. Just as the various factors that influence 'fear of crime' will be discussed in the next section, it would seem that the interpretation of representations of crime is influenced by multiple 'demographic' variables. A factor analysis of tourist images and experiences of Cardiff, Wales (Selby, 2004b), suggested that lifestyle, personality, and previous travel experience influence the ways in which the same landscape or representation is interpreted. The act of reading a cultural text also makes an impression on lived cultures, shaping the environment in which fresh cultural texts are produced.

Tourism and fear of crime

Introducing the concept

In order to better understand perceptions of crime upon actually visiting a locality, we now turn to what can broadly be termed the 'fear of crime' literature. Although 'fear of crime' is a rather abstract concept that denotes a broad range of social and political concerns, a core of meaning may be reasonably identified: public concerns and worries about becoming a victim of crime, perceptions of the risk of victimisation, precautionary behaviours such as avoiding certain situations because of concerns about personal safety, and subjective judgements about the safety of our streets (Jackson, 2002). Whilst it has long been observed that tourist destinations have high rates of crime (see Mawby *et al.*, 2000), it would appear that the fear of tourist crime is rather more complex than recorded crime statistics would suggest.

The concept of 'fear of crime' first emerged with a series of surveys commissioned by the US government in 1967. Not only was there concern about the rising crime rates, but also public attitudes and responses (Jackson, 2003). The debate homed in on the relationship between fear, experience of crime, and 'objective' risk. The late 1970s and early 1980s saw crime and public concerns about crime in Britain become increasingly salient social and political issues. The British Crime Survey was established, as policy-makers and the public apparently needed facts and reassurance to calm excessive concern and elevated demands that were being stoked up by public debate (Jackson, 2009). This became known as the 'risk–fear paradox', and re-education and public involvement in community safety became important objectives. The risk-fear paradox has also been evident in the context of tourism, as the fear of crime in destinations is often disproportionate to the actual risk. For example, it is believed that media publicity of attacks on one British and one German tourist in Florida in 1992, led to a 22% decline in arrivals (Brayshaw, 1995; Brunt *et al.*, 2000). Surprisingly, Brunt *et al.* (2000) found considerably lower rates of fear of crime amongst British holidaymakers compared to fear of crime at home. It would seem, however, that fear of crime is considerably higher within specific social groups and environments, and averages are rather misleading.

During the 1980s, in the UK, the issue of fear of crime became infused with two other discourses and policy formations (Jackson, 2003). First, there was an increase in expenditure on the criminal justice system as 'law and order' emerged as a politically charged topic. Second, fear of crime became linked to crime prevention, and the government encouraged the public to be more responsible both for crime and for their fears concerning crime. Additionally, research publications, the mass media, and political rhetoric all had the effect of further sensitising the public to crime and 'fear of crime' (Lee, 1999). The 'broken windows' theory (Wilson and Kelling, 1982) also gained credibility. The theory asserts that perceptions of the physical and social environment and the behaviours of some individuals affected public perceptions of crime. In response, it would seem that local partnerships and tourism/destination management authorities have increasingly targeted visible signs of crime, through both discourse and intervention strategies. In the 1990s, emphasis was increasingly placed on considering public emotions as an indicator of the impact of the 'crime problem', rather than the management of fear through re-education. Fear of crime did however remain a salient issue in official Government statements, and became bound up with the idea that the public were rightly concerned and wanted action (Jackson, 2003). Emphasis also shifted to the role of disorder ('incivility'), and policy began to shift towards more strongly linking fear of crime, anti-social behaviour, and the incidence of crime.

Incivilities

The concept of 'incivility' was widened to include an indication of social disorganisation, a lack of social cohesion and trust, and an unstable neighbourhood in decline (Jackson, 2003). This concept would appear to be salient to tourist destinations in which visitors may rely upon superficial and fairly unreliable cues regarding levels of crime and personal safety. Visitors may be disproportionately influenced by the presence of beggars, hawkers, derelict buildings, rubbish or litter, vandalism, people using or dealing drugs, drunk or rowdy behaviour, graffiti, or 'slums'. It is possible, therefore, that localities where tourists are approached on the street or beach are perceived to have higher levels of crime. The 'faux-guides' in Morocco or the '*jineteras/os*' in Cuba, for example, may increase the perceptions of crime in general, and tourist scams in particular. Mawby *et al.* (2000) found that 'beggars pestering tourists' was the only incivility that tourists identified as a problem. However, it is unlikely that the other incivilities tested in the study, drawn from the British Crime Survey, are particularly salient to tourists.

Perceptions of incivilities have been found to be a significant predictor of both feeling unsafe walking alone at night and worries about crimes such as burglary and mugging (e.g. Hough, 1995). The British Crime Survey measures perceptions of antisocial behaviour by asking respondents to rate the seriousness in their neighbourhood of several factors such as teenagers hanging around, poor street lighting, noisy neighbours, vandalism, and litter. Taylor and Hale (1986) suggest that incivilities and antisocial behaviour increase anxiety because they signify the potential for victimisation and because they are seen to reflect social disorganisation, a lack of social cohesion and trust, and an unstable neighbourhood in decline.

A number of studies have found strong connections between individual differences in perceived incivilities and fear of crime, with effects remaining after controlling for neighbourhood crime rates and neighbourhood structure (Taylor, 2001). Interestingly, perceived incivilities appear to predict fear of crime more strongly than 'objective' measures. As Coleman (2005) argues, partnership networks have seized upon the apparent link between incivilities and fear of crime, creating both discourses and interventions aimed at ridding the streets of undesirable (and visible) threats to the tourism brand. In the UK, the homeless have been subjected to a range of interventions. In the city of Liverpool these include the training of Big Issue vendors to act as tourist information guides (Coleman, 2004), a £50,000 police operation targeting aggressive beggars, the temporary banning of *Big Issue* sales, and increased surveillance. Similar measures have been taken in Leeds, UK, under the slogan 'Shape up or Ship Out' (Coleman, 2005).

Recent studies have explored this apparent relationship between anti-social behaviour and fear of crime. In the UK, anti-social behaviour (ASB) has been defined as 'acting in a manner that caused or was likely to cause harassment, alarm or distress to one or more persons not of the same household as [the defendant]'(Crime and Disorder Act 1998). The concept is, therefore inherently subjective, as the same behaviour is likely to be interpreted differently by different individuals. Flatley *et al.* (2008), found significant variations in perceptions of ASB, according to both the socio-demographic characteristics of respondents, and environmental characteristics. Perceptions of ASB are likely to be higher in areas of deprivation, or 'hard pressed areas'. Such areas are characterised by low community cohesion, and a propensity for inhabitants to have been victims of crime. Perhaps surprisingly, perceptions of ASB have been found to be higher amongst younger people (Flatley *et al.*, 2008). Prior (2009) suggests, however, that the presentation of UK Home Office statistics on ASB can act as a self-fulfilling prophecy. For example, whilst there has been considerable emphasis on the role of young people as perpetrators, Wood's (2004) report actually indicated that speeding and illegally parked traffic was the most serious concern to 2003/04 British Crime Survey respondents. Interestingly, the traffic questions were subsequently removed from the survey. The following year, the 2004/05 British Crime Survey (Upson, 2006) identified perceptions of 'young people hanging around' to be the most serious ASB problem.

Analysis of the British Crime Survey by Millie (2007) suggests that ASB tends to be confined to deprived urban areas. Such areas are characterised by multiple deprivation, indicated by factors such as lack of qualifications, and predominantly rented housing. These findings suggest that ASB is likely to be experienced by visitors to inner city or 'down town' neighbourhoods in urban tourism destinations. Whilst Millie's research also suggests a correlation between ASB and black and minority ethnic communities, Taylor *et al.* (2001), found that it is material circumstances, and not ethnic heterogeneity that is associated with ASB. Friedrich *et al.* (2009) analysed the spatial distribution of ASB in two London boroughs. It was found to be lower in permeable (rather than gated) communities, which have both pedestrians and residential entrances on the street. This lends support to Jacobs' (1961) vision of social efficacy, with benefits derived from loosely defined social networks. It would also seem to be warning against assuming that the enclosed 'tourist bubble' (Judd and Fainstein, 1999) approach to tourism planning and development protects visitors from crime and anti-social behaviour. Millie (2007) suggests both spatial and temporal variations in perceptions of ASB. It would seem that ASB is also likely to be experienced by visitors to city centres at night, where alcohol consumption plays a major role. Policy responses, however, can often play on simplistic stereotypes, with the banning from city centres of 'youthful' activities such as skateboarding and congregating in groups, whilst drink-related acts of violence amongst older age groups are tolerated (Millie, 2007). Millie (2008) demonstrates how anyone whose behaviour is considered to be outside the norm may be labelled as anti-social. Furthermore, this labelling may be inconsistent with the perceptions of place consumers, particularly visitors. It would seem that urban aesthetics is influential to visitors, yet rarely understood by government agencies. Consistent with the 'broken windows' theory, graffiti has been vigorously eradicated from some urban localities, and graffiti artists have been prosecuted, yet in Bristol (UK), the work of local graffiti artist Banksy has been celebrated by local authorities, particularly due to its tourism potential. The progression of 'acceptable' forms of graffiti into popular and middle-class tastes is illustrated by the conviction of two men in Brighton (UK) for painting over a Banksy graffito.

Gender

A series of qualitative research projects have helped to re-conceptualise fear of crime (e.g. Girling et al., 2000). Such projects have addressed the bluntness of many survey tools, and instead used methods that underpinned theoretical development. Building on the earlier work of feminist researchers, qualitative researchers argued that listening to people talk about crime and the risk of crime using their own frames of reference, allowed for an understanding of the meanings associated with individuals' perceptions of the threat of criminal victimisation. Qualitative methods facilitated the investigation of the cultural meanings of crime, and were used in a number of studies to investigate individuals' descriptions of their perceptions, attitudes, and behaviours (e.g. Taylor et al., 1996; Pain, 1997; Hollway and Jefferson, 1997; Tulloch et al., 1998).

Gender is the strongest and most consistent socio-demographic covariate of fear of crime throughout the literature. This is the case whether the concept is operationalised as perceptions of safety, or worries or fears about becoming a victim of a specific crime. Hough (1995), for example, found that women were on average more worried about being burgled than men, although the effect was lower for personal crimes. Gendered differences in perceptions of danger also seem to be apparent in the context of travel, as Carr's (2001) study of young visitors to London indicated. Carr (2001) found a significant difference between men and women in terms of how they perceive dangers in public places, although only at night time. Women were more likely to perceive danger at night-time, and more likely to seek the company of single sex groups both during the day and at night. Interestingly, however, there was not a significant difference in perception of danger according to group composition, suggesting that personality also plays a strong role in perceptions of danger.

Gendered differences in perceptions of danger in leisure spaces have been recognised for some time. Rountree and Land (1996) found men significantly less likely to feel unsafe within public spaces, and authors such as Mowl (1994) and Feltes (1997) examined the constraining effect this has on women's leisure activities. The heightened perception of danger at night-time has been noted for some time (e.g. Whyte and Shaw 1994), and researchers such as Valentine (1989) found that women tend to seek the company of others at night, particularly men. Carr's (2001) study, however, suggested that single sex groups are an increasingly popular choice, at least amongst young people. Theoretical and empirical work has begun to examine the psychological nature of emotion and a number of interesting theoretical questions have arisen (Greve, 1998; Jackson, 2003; Gabriel and Greve, 2003). Such studies have highlighted the multidimensional nature of emotion including cognitive and behavioural features. With its utilisation of psychological research on worry, recent theoretical and empirical work carried out by Jackson (2003) has indicated feedback loops between worry about crime, risk perceptions, and interpretations of one's social and physical surroundings. In addition to the suggestion that personality and emotion plays an important role, it is important to recognise that gendered perceptions of danger are very culturally-specific, and generalising about the 'female tourist' is impossible.

Explorations of discussion boards developed alongside tourism promotion and travel services, such as that provided by Tripadvisor, illustrate how such feedback loops may be influencing tourist decision-making and behaviour within localities. According to the FCO travel advisory for Mexico, 'Drug-related violence affects many states and is a particular problem in Sinaloa, Chihuahua, US border states and Pacific states' (Foreign and Commonwealth Office, 2010). The Pacific coast region of Michoacán and the city of Acapulco are popular tourist areas in Mexico. This contrasts with the Tripadvisor webpage (Tripadvisor, 2010a) where Acapulco is characterised by 'Mountain views, raucous nightlife and a C-shaped bay with a plethora of beaches...' Beneath the enchanting description, one worried tourist raises the question 'What has happened to Acapulco?' (Tripadvisor, 2010b,) and posts the following message in November, 2009, 'Okay, I just read a creepy review under Hotel Elcano. The reviewer did not have a problem with the hotel, but talked about being constantly accosted on the streets by prostitutes and offered drugs at many bars. I will be traveling with my husband and two very attractive teenage daughters. Do I need to be worried? Was this reviewer for real? What are your thoughts?'. The majority of the 20 replies from recent tourists to, and current residents of, the city are reassuring in tone. While this example nicely demonstrates Jackson's feedback loops in relation to gendered perceptions of danger, it also suggests that individual and unsubstantiated tourist-to-tourist contributions to the stock of knowledge can be of limited validity. The advice given to the mother provided practical advice on how to behave on the street and when not to venture out. Despite the high profile coverage of the armed encounters between members of drug cartels in Acapulco in 2009 (BBC, 2009b) there was no mention on Tripadvisor of 'drug wars' nor of other warnings of violent civil unrest on official websites (Foreign and Commonwealth Office, 2010).

Age and ethnicity

There is a large volume of research indicating an increased fear of crime amongst the elderly, however, recent research suggest a more complex relationship. Some studies have found for example, that elderly people are no more afraid of crime than younger people (Pain, 1997). Furthermore, a closer examination of BCS data reveals that although elderly people are more likely to feel unsafe on the streets after dark, they are no more worried about burglary or assault than younger people. More research is needed in the context of tourism to evaluate both the perception and the avoidance strategies of older people in tourist destinations. Recent research, for example, has highlighted how the elderly population should be further differentiated along a number of factors in order to examine their anxieties, rather than amalgamated as a homogeneous population (Selby et al., 2003). In a study of perceptions of crime amongst visitors to Washington, DC, it was found that both the number of previous visits, and demographic variables such as gender, marital status and level of education were salient (Demos, 1992). Few studies have examined individual risk evaluations that incorporate the notion of vulnerability. In fact only one study (Ferraro, 1995) attempted to bridge the micro (individual vulnerability) and macro (aggregate) levels of analyses, by exploring whether certain groups worry more because they feel more vulnerable to crime and its effects. Indeed most studies have simply assumed this is the case (Jackson, 2002).

There also appears to be a need to explore the issue of race and fear of crime more fully. Hough (1995) reported significant variations in levels of concern about a range of crimes between different ethnic groups. It seems feasible that there will be variations in fear of crime between different ethnic groups whilst travelling, and this could be further complicated by the ethnic composition of the destination. There seems to be little doubt that racial stereotypes and prejudice will influence the fear of crime in particular tourist destinations. Racial stereotypes amongst European and US visitors, for example, may increase the fear of crime when visiting African and Middle Eastern destinations and poorer districts with high levels of ethnic diversity in their homeland cities. The effects found by Hough (1995), however, did not survive the introduction of a range of other socio-economic, perceptual, and experiential variables in a series of analyses. Socio-economic factors at the neighbourhood level are common predictors of the fear of crime. Individuals residing in less prosperous areas tend to feel less safe at night in their neighbourhoods (Hale *et al.*, 1994; Hough, 1995). Strong effects of area type (categorised as 'suburbs/rural', 'towns/cities', and 'inner-cities') have been reported on both worries about specific crimes, and perceptions of safety whilst alone after dark. Analysis of the 1994 BCS revealed significant effects from ACORN[1] categories on perceptions of safety (Pantazis, 2000). Research by Selby (2004a) in the UK suggested an association between socio-economic and lifestyle variables and particularly positive or negative perceptions of a tourist destination. A survey of visitors to Cardiff (Wales), and the use of factor analysis also suggested that the level of experience of travel (or previous travel career) was salient, with experienced travellers having higher expectations in terms of service, but also being more resigned to risks such as being a victim of crime.

Perceptions of risk and victimisation

One important dimension is perception of personal risk. A number of studies have found estimates of the likelihood of victimisation, and being afraid of becoming a victim of crime to be empirically distinct concepts (Ferraro, 1995; Rountree and Land, 1996; Jackson, 2002). Studies have found evidence that perceptions of the likelihood of victimisation plays a mediating role between socio-economic variables and interpretations of the environment (e.g. incivilities), and fear of becoming a victim of various crimes (e.g. Farraro, 1995; Sacco and Glackman, 1997). A study conducted in Orlando, Florida, suggested that tourists' previous exposure to crime affected their overall sense of safety (Milman and Bach, 1999). Part of the reason why perceptions of incivilities predict fear is that it raises perceptions of risk of victimisation, which in turn impacts on fear. Another example is gender. Research has found that a large proportion of the 'gender effect' could be explained by women's increased perceptions of the likelihood of victimisation (Ferraro, 1995). For a discussion of victimisation more generally see Chapter 4.

Research has also found support for the notion that perceptions of the seriousness of the consequences of victimisation strongly predicts fear. Warr (1997) for example, argues that men and women perceive different levels of seriousness in the consequences of victimisation, and that for this reason their levels of fear cannot be directly compared. However, the seriousness of consequences of victimisation is a complex issue that needs more study, and there are a number of possible hypotheses that could be tested. For example, having relatively low socio-economic resources may mean the material consequences of burglary or robbery are far more long-lasting than for individuals who are insured and/or can afford to replace stolen possessions. Back-packers, for example, may suffer a greater impact from burglary or robbery, if they are carrying all of their possessions in one piece of luggage and are also under-insured. Conversely, the social support offered by

---

1 ACORN profiling categorises areas into 54 types, which aggregate to 17 groups and six categories, by amalgamating data items from the Census, including occupation, education, and home ownership to provide a typology of areas according to socio-demographic and lifestyle characteristics.

back-packer hostels or home stays may provide a sense of belonging within a cohesive community and may provide a sense that one could cope with the potential effects of victimisation. In this context it is also likely that physical vulnerability is an important concern for the weak and the sick. As Jackson (2002) argues, there is currently a gap in the literature concerning the relationship between perceptions of the seriousness of consequences of victimisation, fear of victimisation, and the issues noted above such as the role of social support.

A related concept is that of perceived control over victimisation, which refers to estimates of the ability to avoid or control an outcome. For example, two measures of physical vulnerability related to perceived control over victimisation have been found to predict worries of mugging; physical size, and ability to defend ones self physically (Hough, 1995). Perceived control may operate on two levels, for example, men may tend to feel both more able to control whether they fall victim to certain types of personal crime than women, and may also feel more able to withstand the encounter if it were to occur. Goodey (1994) has argued that gender and socialisation are important to feelings of control, and subsequently to fear of crime. However, again there is a lack of evidence in relation to perceptions of control over risk and fear of crime, and further research is required to investigate these issues. In the case of tourism, there are also likely to be variations according to the perceived reputation of the inhabitants of the locality. These perceptions may relate to judgements concerning the average physical and psychological characteristics of inhabitants.

Numerous studies have examined the effect of victimisation experience on fear of crime. 'Direct' victimisation refers to one's own experiences, whereas 'indirect' victimisation is that which has been experienced by friends, family or neighbours, and denotes beliefs about criminal activity in a locality, stemming from information networks or the mass media. The evidence supporting a relationship between criminal victimisation and fear of crime is mixed. However, in general, indirect experience of victimisation appears to be a better predictor than direct. Hale (1996) argues that hearing about victimisation from a friend or relative may allow one's imagination full scope without the same urgency to find a coping strategy as one might with direct victimisation. This may explain the stronger relationship between fear and indirect (rather than direct) victimisation that is sometimes found (for example, Box et al., 1988).

Redefining crime in tourist destinations

There is a large literature on the effects of various discourses on a range of attitudes and beliefs concerning crime. As discussed in the context of images of crime, the media frequently sensationalise and shock through lurid and alarmist descriptions of rare events and by excessively reporting more banal episodes of crime (Jackson, 2002).There appears to be something of an obsession with crime within the mass media, and when exotic and distant localities are added to the equation, the appeal become even greater. In an interesting twist, in August 2009 two backpackers were charged in Rio de Janeiro for falsely reporting a crime in order to make an insurance claim. The arrest was reported on the website of the Policia Civil do Estado de Rio de Janeiro, along with claims that such incidents of fraud are common and inflate Rio's crime rate. The pair were later released on appeal due to the use of incorrect search procedures (Weaver, 2009). It may not be coincidental that in Rio, surveys use the term 'feelings of insecurity', rather than 'fear of crime' (Dirk *et al.*, 2004). Networks of agencies within tourist destinations develop discourses and interventions aimed at making localities more attractive to place consumers, particularly visitors. As suggested earlier in the chapter, it would seem that tourists develop an intersubjective 'stock of knowledge' (see Selby, 2004a) of crime associated with particular localities. This is largely formed through mediated knowledge (representations) rather than first-hand experiences, yet it can have a significant impact on both decision-making, and action within tourist destinations. In the case of contemporary tourism, travel reviews mediate the first-hand experiences of fellow tourists, and this knowledge may be credible and influential within the stock of knowledge, but not necessarily comprehensive.

There has been a redefinition of crime, fear, and security in tourist destinations by various agencies, and interventions aimed at reducing the visibility of crime to tourists. This has important implications for spatial ordering and social control. Coleman (2005) points out that this redefinition (or over-definition) has developed alongside more conventional urban tourism discourses such as the city as 'carnivalesque', a place of 'ordered disorder' (Featherstone, 1991: 82), a city on the edge, and a festival marketplace (Goss, 1993). Excitement, spontaneity, risk and a 'bustling city' are thus part of the brand (as long as they can be carefully managed), but 'non-performed difference' threatens to destabilise the city's place marketing. Coleman (2005) demonstrates how fear of crime, disorder, and incivility, drawing upon the 'broken windows' thesis, has legitimised the targeting of 'unconventional' and nuisance' behaviours that detract from the aesthetics of urban tourist destinations. Networks of institutional power in cities firstly define the 'problems' through a powerful discourse of fear, and then employ surveillance equipment, by-laws, private security guards, police operations, and promotional campaigns to rid the streets of undesirable elements.

In recent years, there have been some interesting contributions that question the appropriateness of the fear of crime concept, and these are particularly salient to tourism. Hutta (2009) points out the international variations in terminology, with 'feelings of insecurity' more common in France, and 'subjective feelings of safety' used in Germany. More substantively, Hutta (2009) critiques the *disposatif* of safety, which by positing the binary 'safety/fear' in the centre, facilitates a politics of fear and drives political agendas aimed at ridding entrepreneurial localities of undesirable obstacles to achieving the desired brand image and attracting capital. Hutta (2009) suggests the alternative concept of *Geborgenheit*. Although rather difficult to translate accurately into English, *Geborgenheit* is a positive and inherently spatial concept, referring to 'the atmospheric, perceptual, or intersubjective intensities of a place that provide shelter or enable someone to open up to it' (Hutta, 2009: 256). Of particular salience to studies of tourism, '*Geborgenheit*' denotes 'being at home with', rather than literally 'being at home'.

Conclusions

We began our chapter from the orthodox standpoint that criminal acts have a negative impact on tourist decision-making because tourists will avoid destinations with a high prevalence of crime. Furthermore, that destination image has a significant impact upon tourism consumption. As we have suggested in this chapter, the impact of fear of crime on both tourist decision-making, and behaviour within a locality, is rather more complex than any simple causal relationship. Whilst actual criminal incidents involving tourists are proportionally small in relation to total tourism flows, this has not halted the battle over the image of tourism destinations. As we demonstrate through a number of examples, destination images are the subject of contestation between major interests in tourism. National governments can come into conflict over travel advisories surrounding crime and security and the actions of major tourism corporations, such as the recent Delta Airlines case in Kenya, embroil other major players in the contest. We have shown how information technologies have further usurped the aspirations of agencies of tourism promotion to control or at least direct the image of a destination. Tourist-to-tourist 'chat' is now a regular part of the information gathering that supports complex decision making in holiday consumption.

We have also argued that destination image is not just a matter of impressions of a place formed through representations, but is also informed by actual behaviours. Of course, for first-time visitors to a place these are limited to the surrogate accounts of others. This is not a new phenomenon, given the established influence of travel writers and the importance of guide books in trip planning, but it is now enhanced by fast-moving information technologies. There would appear to be a complex relationship between representations of crime in tourist destinations, images of crime, experiences of crime, and fear of crime. It would seem, however, that the 'stock of knowledge' occupies the space between the four concepts, rather like the hub of a wheel.

In positing a much closer and dynamic relationship between representations, images, first-hand experiences, and perceptions than in previous models of destination image, we have invoked Schutz's concept of a 'stock of knowledge'. Through the assertion that the 'common sense' of individuals is informed by a plethora of influences – historical, ideological, cultural and behavioural – and shaped by many social agents and actions, including inter-generational narratives and behaviours, the 'stock of knowledge' is a powerful analytical concept in understanding the crime/tourism nexus. We suggest that it accounts much more satisfactorily for habitual patterns of tourist consumption, a mode of tourism consumption that is much more prevalent than the tourism research literature would suggest. Habitual patterns of tourist consumption seem to be particularly resilient to incidents of crime and threats to security and help explain the so-called 'resilience' of the tourism industry in the face of disruption.

These extensions to the orthodox accounts of tourism consumption, destination image and crime suggest some different avenues for future research. But in exploring the 'fear of crime' literature we have signalled a more radical break in studies of the tourism/crime nexus. As other authors in this book remind us, the shift in public policy away from reactive and punitive criminal justice systems to risk-averse and crime prevention measures has captured the rise in the 'fear of crime' milieu. Immediately, the scale of the tourism/crime nexus outstrips both the actual incidents of criminal behaviour and the events that shatter 'normal' secure tourist environments. Fear of crime seems both timeless and boundless. Thus, the imperative to extend tourism studies to directly engage with criminology becomes irresistible as the argument that crime is a relatively insignificant externality to mainstream tourism just melts away. As an initial offering we have discussed a range of factors that appear to be associated with variations in fear of crime, such as gender, age, ethnicity, and assessments of the seriousness of consequences and personal risk. Where possible, we have connected these to observations on the behaviour of tourists and changes in practice by agencies of tourism promotion and development. We would acknowledge, however, that this is only a start and there is much more work to be done to further understand the relationships between tourism, image and the fear of crime.

References

Aljazeera (2007) 'Elite police head to crime-hit Rio', 15 January, www.english. aljazera.net/news/americas, accessed 22 January 2010.

Arnold, H. (1991) 'Fear of crime and its relationship to directly and indirectly experienced victimisation: a bi-national comparison of models', in K. Sessar and H.J. Kerner (eds), *Developments in Crime and Crime Control Research*, London: Springer-Verlag.

Ashworth, G.J. and Goodall, B. (1988) 'Tourist images: marketing considerations', in B. Goodall, G.J. Ashworth (eds), *Marketing in the Tourism Industry*, Beckenham: Croom Helm, pp. 215–238.

Asseal, H. (1987) *Consumer Behavior and Marketing Action*, Boston, MA: PWS Kent.

Assael, H. (2003) *Consumer Behavior: A Strategic Approach*, Orlando, FL: Houghton Miffin.

BBC (2003a) 'Kenya protests at US warnings', http://news.bbc.co.uk/1/hi/world/ africa/3292121.stm, accessed 17 January 2010.

BBC (2003b) 'Kenyan anger at "panic measure"', http://news.bbc.co.uk/1/hi/world/africa/3033097.stm, accessed 18 January 2010.

BBC (2009a) 'Kenya anger as US cancels flight', http://news.bbc.co.uk/1/hi/world/africa/8082942.stm, accessed 18 January 2010.

BBC (2009b) 'Deadly gun battle rocks Acapulco', http://news.bbc.co.uk/1/hi/world/americas/8088131.stm, accessed on 18 January 2010.

Berger, P.L. and Luckmann, T. (19676) *The Social Construction of Reality: A Treatise in the Sociology of Knowledge*, New York: Anchor Books.

Box, S., Hale, C. and Andrews, G. (1988) 'Explaining the fear of crime', *British Journal of Criminology*, 28, 340–356.

Boyle, C. (2009) 'Brazilian drugs gangs shoot down police chopper near Rio de Janeiro: 2 officers dead', *New York Daily News*, October 17.

Bramwell, B. and Rawding, L. (1996) 'Tourism marketing images of industrial cities', *Annals of Tourism Research*, 23, 201–221.

Brayshaw, D. (1995) 'Negative publicity about a tourism destination: a Florida case study', *EIU Travel and Tourism Analyst*, no. 5.

Brunt, P., Mawby, R.I. and Hambly, Z. (2000) 'Tourist victimisation and the fear of crime on holiday', *Tourism Management*, 21, 417–424.

Burgess, J. (1990) 'The production and consumption of environmental meanings in the mass media: a research agenda for the 1990's', *Transactions of Institute of British Geographers* (NS), 15, 139–161.

Cape Town Routes Unlimited (2008) *Perceptions of International Visitors to South Africa on Safety and Security – Implications for the 2010 FIFA World Cup*, Cape Town: CTRU.

Carr, N. (1999) 'A study of gender differences: young tourist behaviour in a UK coastal resort', *Tourism Management*, 20, 223–228.

Carr, N. (2001) 'An exploratory study of gendered differences in young tourists' perception of danger within London', *Tourism Management*, 22, 565–570.

Chon, K.S. (1990) 'The role of destination image in tourism. A review and discussion', *Tourist Review*, 45 (2), 2–9.

Coleman, R. (2004) 'Watching the degenerate: street camera surveillance and urban regeneration', *Local Economy*, 19 (3), 199–211.

Coleman, R. (2005) 'Surveillance in the city: primary definition and urban spatial order', *Crime Media Culture*, 1 (2), 13–148.

Cornelissen, S. and Swart, K. (2006) 'The 2010 Football World Cup as a political construct: the challenge of making good on an African promise', *Sociological Review*, 54 (2), 108–121.

DEAT (Department of Environmental Affairs and Tourism) (2005) *2010 Soccer World Cup Tourism Organisation Plan Executive Summary*, Pretoria: South African Tourism.

Demos, E. (1992) 'Concern for safety: a potential problem in the tourism industry', *Journal of Tourism Marketing*, 1 (1), June, 81–88.

Dichter, E. (1985) 'What's in an image?', *Journal of Consumer Marketing*, 2 (1), 75–81.

Dirk, R.C., Pinto, A.S. and Vieira, A.L. (2004) Avaliando o sentimemento de inseguranca nos bairros de cidade de Rio de Janeiro', paper presented at the 28th Annual meeting of ANPOCS, Rio de Janeiro, www.comunidadesegura. org/

Duncan, J.S. and Duncan, N. (1988) '(Re)reading the landscape', *Environment and Planning D: Society and Space*, 6, 117–126.

Echtner, C.M. and Brent-Richie, J.R. (1991) 'The meaning and measurement of tourism destination image', *Journal of Tourism Studies*, 2 (2), December.

Featherstone, M. (1991) *Consumer Culture and Postmodernism*, London: Sage.

Feltes, L. (1997) 'Safety: the unspoken barrier to women's physical activity', *Melpomene Journal*, 16 (3), 9–11.

Ferraro, K.F. and LaGrange, R. (1988) 'Are older people afraid of crime?', *Journal of Aging Studies*, 2 (3), 277–287.

Ferraro, K.F. (1995) *Fear of Crime: Interpreting Victimization Risk*, New York: SUNY Press.

Ferreira, S.L. (1999) 'Crime: a threat to tourism in South Africa', *Tourism Geographies*, 1 (3), 313–324.

Flatley, J., Moley, S. and Hoare, J. (2008) *Perceptions of Anti-Social Behaviour: Findings from the 2007/08 British Crime Survey*, Supplementary Volume 1 to Crime in England and Wales 2007/08, Home Office Statistical Bulletin 15/08, London: Home Office.

Foreign and Commonwealth Office (2010) Mexico, http://www.fco.gov.uk/en/ travel-and-living-abroad/travel-advice-by-country/north-central-america/ mexico, accessed 16 January 2010.

Friedrich, E., Hillier, B.and Chiaradia, A. (2009) 'Using space syntax to understand spatial patterns of socio-environmental disorder', Proceedings of the 7th International Space Syntax Symposium, Stockholm: KTH.

Gabriel, U. and Greve, W. (2003) 'The psychology of fear of crime, conceptual and methodological perspectives', *British Journal of Crminology*, 43, 600-614.

Gallarza, M.G., Saura, I.G. and H.C. Garcia (2002) 'Destination image: Towards a conceptual framework', *Annals of Tourism Research*, 29, (1), 56-78.

George, R. (2003) 'Tourists' perceptions of safety and security whilst visiting Cape Town', *Tourism Management*, 24 (5), October, 575–583.

Giletson, G. and Crompton, R.J. (1983) 'The planning horizons and sources of information used by pleasure vacationers', *Journal of Travel Research*, 23 (3), 2–7.

Girling, E., Loader, I. and Sparks, R. (2000) *Crime and Social Change in Middle England: Questions of Order in an English Town*. London: Routledge.

Goodey, J. (1994) 'Fear of crime: what can children tell us?', *International Review of Victimology*, 3, 195–210.

Goss, J.D. (1993) 'Placing the market and marketing place', *Environment and Planning D: Society and Space*, **11**, 663–688.

Greve, W. (1998) 'Fear of crime among the elderly: foresight not fright', *International Review of Victimology*, **5**, 277–309.

Gunn, C. (1972) *Vacationscapes: Designing Tourist Regions*, New York: Van Nostrand.

Hale, S. (1996) 'Fear of crime: a review of the literature', *International Review of Victimology*, 4, 79–150.

Hale, S., Pack, P. and Salkeld, J. (1994) 'The structural determinants of fear of crime: an analysis using census and crime survey data from England and Wales', *International Review of Victimology*, 3, 211–233.

Henderson, B. (2010) 'Terrorism warning to Borneo tourists', *Daily Telegraph*, 16 January 2010.

Hobbs, D., Hadfield, P., Lister, S., and Winlow, S. (2003) *Bouncers: Violence and Governance in the Night Time Economy*, Oxford: Oxford University Press.

Holloway, W. and Jefferson, T. (1997) 'The risk society in an age of anxiety: situating the fear of crime', *British Journal of Sociology*, 48 (2), 255–266.

Home Office (2009) Total Recorded Offences 2008–2009 Rate Per 1000 Population by Local Authority District, http://www.homeoffice.gov.uk/rds/ia/atlas.html Accessed 22 January 2010.

Hough, M. (1995) 'Anxiety about crime: findings from the 1994 British Crime Survey', *Home Office Research Study No. 147*, London: Home Office.

Hutta, J.S. (2009) Geographies of Geborgenheit: beyond feelings of safety and the fear of crime', *Environment and Planning D: Society and Space*, **27**, 251–273.

The Independent (2002) 'Reward of £3000 after British tourist is killed in South Africa', 24 October 2002.

Jackle, J.A. (1985) *The Tourist: Travel in Twentieth Century North America*, Lincoln: University of Nebraska Press.

Jackson, J. (2002) 'Fear of crime: an examination and development of theory and method', PhD thesis, London School of Economics and Political Science, University of London.

Jackson, J. (20093) 'A psychological perspective on vulnerability in the fear of crime' *Psychology, Crime and Law,* 14 (4), 365-390.

Jacobs, J. (1961) *The Death and Life of Great American Cities*, London: Random House.

Jansson, K., Budd, S., Lovbakke, J., Moley, S. and Thorpe, K. (2007) *Attitudes, Perceptions and Risks of Crime: Supplementary Volume 1 to Crime in England and Wales 2006/2007*, Home Office Statistical Bulletin, 19/07, London: Home Office.

Jenkins, O.H. (1999) 'Understanding and measuring tourist destination images', *International Journal of Tourism Research*, **1**, 1–15.

Johnson, R. (1986) 'The story so far and further transformations?', in D. Punter (ed.), *Introduction to Contemporary Cultural Studies*, London: Longman, pp. 277–313.

Judd, D.R. and Fainstein, S.S. (eds) (1999) *The Tourist City*, New Haven, CT: Yale University Press.

Lee, M. (1999) 'The fear of crime and self-governance: towards a genealogy', *Australian and New Zealand Journal of Criminology*, **32** (3), 227–246.

Leiber, S.R. (1977) 'Attitudes and revealed behaviour: a case study, *Professional Geographer*, **29** (1), 53–58.

Madsen, H. (1992) 'Place-marketing in Liverpool: a review', *International Journal of Urban and Regional Research*, **16** (4), 633–640.

Mawby, R. Brunt, P. and Hambly, Z. (2000) 'Fear of crime amongst British holiday makers', *British Journal of Criminology*, 40, 468–479.

Millie, A. (2007) 'Looking for anti-social behaviour', *Policy and Politics*, **35** (4), 611–627.

Millie, A. (2008) 'Anti-social behaviour in British cities', *Geography Compass*, **2** (5), 1681–1696.

Milman, A. and Bach, S. (1999). 'The impact of security devices on tourists' perceived safety: the central Florida example', *Journal of Hospitality and Tourism Research*, **23** (4), 371–386.

Mowl, G. (1994) *Gender, Place and Leisure: Women's Leisure in Two Contrasting Areas of Tyneside*, Departmental Occasional Papers, Series No. 10, Division of Geography and Environmental Management, University of Northumbria at Newcastle.

Pain, R.H. (1997) 'Whither women's fear? Perceptions of sexual violence in public and private space', *International Review of Victimology*, **4**, 297–312.

Pantazis, C. (2000) 'Fear of crime, vulnerability and poverty', *British Journal of Criminology*, **40**, 414–436.

Pearce, P.L. (1982) 'Perceived changes in holiday destinations', *Annals of Tourism Research*, **9**, 145–164.

Pizam, A. and Mansfeld, Y. (1996) *Tourism, Crime, and International Security Issues*, Chichester: Wiley.

Prior, D. (2009) 'The "problem" of anti-social behaviour and the policy knowledge base: analysing the power/knowledge relationship', *Critical Social Policy*, **29** (1), 5–23.

Reuters (2009) 'South Africa's crime wave' *Analysis*, US edn, www.reuters.com/, accessed 22 January 2010.

Rountree, P.W. and Land, K.C. (1996) 'Perceived risk versus fear of crime: empirical evidence of conceptually distinct reactions in survey data', *Journal of Research in Crime and Deliquency*, **33** (2), 147–180.

Sacco, V.F and Glackman, W. (1987) 'Vulnerability, locus of control and worry about crime', *Canadian Journal of Community Mental Health*, **6** (1), 99–111.

Schutz, A. (1970) *Reflections on the Problem of Relevance*, New Haven, CT: Yale University Press.

Schutz, A. (1972) *The Phenomenology of the Social World*, trans. by G. Walsh and F. Lehnert, London: Heinemann.

Schutz, A. and Luckmann, T. (1974) *Structures of the Life-World*, trans. by R.M. Zaner and H.T. Engelhardt Jr, London: Heinemann.

Selby, H., Gaffney, A. and Hirschfield, A. (2003) 'Fear of crime and the elderly in Knowsley', unpublished report, Environmental Criminology Research Unit (ECRU), University of Liverpool.

Selby, M. (1995) 'Tourism and urban regeneration: the role of place image', unpublished MSc dissertation, Department of Management Studies, University of Surrey.

Selby, M. (2004) *Understanding Urban Tourism: Image, Culture, Experience*, London: I B Tauris.

Selby, M. (2004a) 'Consuming cities: conceptualising and researching urban tourist knowledge', *Tourism Geographies*, **6** (2), May, 186–207.

Shields, R. (1992) *Lifestyle Shopping: the Study of Consumption*, London: Routledge.

Smith, D. (2009) 'Crime fears grow as South Africa readies for football World Cup. *The Guardian*, 22 September 2009.

Sonmez, S.F. (1998) 'Tourism, terrorism and political instability', *Annals of Tourism Research*, **25** (2), 416–456.

Sontag, S. (1978) *Illness as Metaphor*, New York: Farrar Straus & Giroux.

Taylor, I., Evans, K. and Fraser, P. (1996) *A Tale of Two Cities: Global Change, Local Feeling and Everyday Life in the North of England. A Study in Manchester and Sheffield*, London: Routledge.

Taylor, J., Twigg, L. and Mohan, J. (2001) 'Investigating perceptions of anti-social behaviour and neighbourhood ethnic heterogeneity in the British Crime Survey', *Transactions of Institute of British Geographers*, **35** (1), 59–75.

Taylor, R. B. (2001) *Breaking Away form Broken Windows: Baltimore Neighborhoods and the Nationwide Fight Against Crime, Grime, Fear and Decline*, New York: Westview.

Taylor, R. B. and Hale, M. (1986) 'Testing alternative models of fear of crime', *Journal of Criminal Law and Criminology*, **77** (1), 151–189.

Starmer-Smith, C. Telegraph (2008) 'Crime puts tourists off S. Africa', *Daily Telegraph*, 2 February 2008.

Time Magazine (2009) 'Can Rio's crime problem be solved before Olympics?', 21 October 2009, www.time.com/world/acrticle, accessed on 22 January 2010

Tripadvisor (2010a) 'Acapulco', http://www.tripadvisor.co.uk/Tourism-g150787-Acapulco_Pacific_Coast-Vacations.html, accessed on 16 January 2010.

Tripadvisor (2010b) 'What has happened to Acapulco?', http://www.tripadvisor.co.uk/ShowTopic-g150787-i177-k3227727-What_has_happened_to_Acapulco-Acapulco_Pacific_Coast.html, accessed on 16 January 2010.

Tuan, Y.F. (1980) *Landscapes of Fear*, Oxford: Blackwell.

Tulloch, J., Lupton, D., Blood, W., Tulloch, M., Jennett, C. and Enders, M. (1998) *Fear of Crime*, Canberra: Centre for Cultural Risk Research for the NCAVAC Unit for the NCAVAC, Attorney-General's Department.

United Nations Office on Drugs and Crime (2005) Crime and Development in Africa. UNODC. http://www.unodc.org/unodc/en/data-and-analysis/Data-for-Africa-publications.html, accessed on 22 January 2010.

Upson, A. (2006) *Perceptions and Experience of Anti-Social Behaviour: Findings from the 2004/2005 British Crime Survey*, Home Office Online Report 21/06, London: Home Office.

Urry, J. (1995) *Consuming Places*, London: Routledge.

Valentine, G. (1989) 'The geography of women's fear', *Area*, **21** (4), 385–390.

Warr, M. (1997) 'Fear of victimisation and sensitivity to risk'. *Journal of Quantitative Criminology*, **3** (1), 29–46.

Weaver, M. (2009) 'British backpackers face jail in Brazil of alleged insurance scam', *The Guardian*, 29 July 2009.

Whyte, I. and Shaw, S. (1994) 'Women's leisure: an exploratory study of fear of violence as a leisure constraint', *Journal of Applied Recreation Research*, **19** (1), 5–21.

Wilson, J. Q. and Kelling, G.L. (1982) 'Broken windows', *Atlantic Monthly*, **211**, 29–38.

Wood, M. (2004) *Perceptions and Experience of Anti-Social Behaviour: Findings from the 2003/2004 British Crime Survey*, Home Office Online Report 49/04, London: Home Office.

Woodside, A.G. and Lyonski, S. (1990) 'A general model of traveller destination choice', *Annals of Tourism Research*, 17, 432–448.

World Travel Watch (2006) 'Brazil: crime against tourists increasing in Rio de Janeiro', www.worldtravelwatch.com, accessed 12 January 12 2010.

12 Dark Tourism and Sites of Crime

John Lennon

This chapter will:

♦ Explore in detail the relationship between crime and its attraction to visitors

♦ Consider the phenomenom of dark tourism and its relationship with crime with reference to some UK and international case examples

♦ Develop the relationship between crime and visitation by tourists and the response of policy-makers and governments to issues of commemoration and development

♦ Examine the range of responses to crime sites and what they tell us about ourselves through appeal and visitation.

Introduction

Dark tourism (sometimes referred to as thanatourism) has become established in the last decade as a niche tourism area. Death, suffering, visitation and tourism have been interrelated for many centuries (Foley and Lennon, 1996a; Seaton, 1999). Indeed for many years, humans have been attracted to sites and events that are associated with death, disaster, suffering, violence and killing. From ancient Rome and gladiatorial combat to attendance at public executions, sites of death have held a voyeuristic appeal. As previously recorded, the site of the first battle in the American Civil War was sold as a potential tourist site the following day (Lennon and Foley, 2000) and viewing of the battlefield of Waterloo by non-combatants was recorded in 1816 (Seaton, 1999). These sites associated with death and disaster that exert a dark fascination for visitors are frequently linked to crime locations and the perpetration of lawful and unlawful acts. The sheer diversity of forms of dark tourism sites are significant and have been the subject of emergent research (see for example: Foley and Lennon, 1996a; Lennon and Foley, 2000; Seaton, 1996; Seaton and Lennon, 2004; Dann and Seaton, 2006; Ashworth, 1996; Sharkley and Stone, 2009). However the relationship to criminal acts and punishment for crimes is an important one that has received limited direct attention.

The identification of dark sites and their visitation

Dark tourism has generated much more than purely academic interest. The term has entered the mainstream and is a popular subject of media attention. More importantly it is used as a marketing term on sites such as http://thecabinet.com where the category of dark destinations has been in use since 2006. The appeal of a range of global destinations associated with dark acts shows no signs of abatement. Most recently the enduring appeal has been reinforced in New York, Paris and beyond. The Ground Zero site now attracts significantly greater numbers of visitors since the terrorist attacks of 11 September 2001 (Blair, 2002). In Paris, the death site of Diana, Princess of Wales evidenced pilgrimage and visitation following her death and the site of her burial place – Althorpe – achieved significant visitation for the three years following her death. In Africa, sites in Angola, South Africa, Sierra Leon, and Rwanda have all demonstrated the appeal of dark histories to visitors (Rowe, 2007).

Academic interest in these phenomena was intimated in the work of Rojek (1993) and Ashworth (1996) and Foley and Lennon (1996a) introduced the term 'dark tourism' latterly exploring the phenomena as the subject of a monograph (Lennon and Foley, 2000). This has in turn led to considerable interest both in academia, main stream and electronic media. The range of dark sites associated with the phenomena is considerable and varies significantly from Holocaust sites (which can incorporate genocide, mass killing, incarceration and experimentation) to the manufactured Merlin Entertainment operations which recreate tableaux and have very limited historical artefacts. This highly successful company creates 'Dungeon experiences' in Edinburgh, London and York, which feature crime, punishment, disease and a host of dark elements. More broadly, dark tourists can be found at grave sites, crash locations, sites of assassination, and at museums of torture and death. For many of these sites, elements such as visitor management and conservation, interpretation and marketing, retailing and catering all create issues and challenges. Operationally issues of ethical presentation, visitor behaviour, site management, revenue generation, marketing and promotion, all create areas that are fraught with difficulties and frequently the subject of criticism and debate.

Dark tourism has been in existence as an element of tourism for many centuries (Foley and Lennon, 1996a; Seaton, 1996). Fundamentally, we can identify elements of the ancient, the modern and the post-modern in understanding these phenomena. Murder, execution and sites of lawful and unlawful death have served to attract the attention of visitors and residents from ancient times to the current day. Education and the nature of the learning experience are frequently used to justify and explain motivation for development and visitation in the modern world. Indeed, the idea of travel as an education experience of new and previously unvisited destinations is frequently used as a rational argument, associated with discussions of modernity. More recently it is the significance of communications technology, reporting and real-time communication that serves to heighten awareness about 'dark' destinations that may be visited.

In respect of those sites associated with crime interest, tourism demand has undoubtedly grown as a result of media interest and filmic reproduction that is becoming increasingly graphic and rapid growth in pictorial and narrative reportage. Awareness is a function of the all pervasive media we now live with; the real time reportage and the massive expansion of visual records available in electronic form make data available and help to heighten awareness.

Crime and dark tourism

The relationship between crime and dark tourism has rarely been examined overtly. However it is clear that many of the sites identified by authors have a relationship with crime and the results of criminal behaviour. Famous assassination sites, such as the Dallas Book Depository building, Dallas, Texas and the Elm Street location where President John F. Kennedy was assassinated constitute established tourism destinations (Foley and Lennon, 1996b; Lennon and Foley, 2000), that are synonymous with illegal acts. The Holocaust tourism sites of Poland, Germany and elsewhere (Ashworth, 1996; Beech, 2000) are all inherently linked to the genocide perpetrated by the Nazis during the Second World War.

In recent years the significant appeal of the former site of the World Trade Center in New York as a tourist destination (and dark attraction) has now been established. For many it will always be associated with the terrorist attack of 11 September 2001 and it will continue to enjoy visitation for a number of years to come. The precise nature of illegality will of course be tested in the trial of Khalid Sheikh Mohammed and alleged co-conspirators (BBC, 2009). However the site appears to have become part of the tourist itinerary and an element of many tours to the 'site' of New York. This is obviously a function of location, notoriety, empathy with the location as well as more voyeuristic motivations such as curiosity. This destination has become a commoditised element of the New York package. It has become a part of the tourist itinerary and is celebrated in souvenir merchandise and imagery at the site and throughout New York and beyond. Indeed, controversy has not deserted the development of the site and the proposed Museum of the Twin Towers has continued to concern a range of interest groups, the general public and policy-makers. Perhaps the attraction of sites connected with heinous or spectacular crimes is unsurprising given the ongoing fascination with representations of crime and punishment within popular culture (Reiner, 2007).

The appeal of such sites is less to do with the perpetration of an illegal or criminal act but rather a dark fascination we appear to possess with evil and the acts of evil that we can perpetrate. Whether it is a war crime or a murder, a site of mass killing, or an assassination site the appeal remains significant. Such attraction will also cover sites of 'lawful' killing. Execution sites of earlier times and more recent sites of state execution appear on tourist trails from York and London to Chicago and Dublin. The crime and its consequences provide a framework for an act (whether legal or illegal) which in some cases will exert a draw for visitors. It is interesting that death, torture, incarceration all can be demonstrated to have such appeal. However lesser crimes and their consequences will fail to exert such 'pull' on tourists. Minor crimes, sites of theft, fraud, etc. provide limited potential for viewing or visitation and simply fail to attract. Thus it is the nature and extent of the act and how darkly fascinating it is that holds the key to understanding the appeal of crime sites. Similarly, the historical legacy in terms of existing heritage, either real or created that will give a context and destination for exploration that will help catalyse motivation to visit.

For example, sites and locations associated with conflicts and war hold significant appeal (see Lennon and Foley, 2000). In many cases such sites will be intrinsically linked to crimes of war. What is also apparent is that the nature of visitation will be a function of the location and awareness of such sites and how they are perceived by tourist and visitor audiences. Visits to the sites of multiple deaths of civilian casualties of the Iraq war, deemed as criminal acts by some, will be limited by the safety and accessibility of the location and tourists perceptions and judgments on what constitutes a war crime. The recent trial of Slobodan Milošević in The Hague for the brutal suppression of the Kosovars is a good example of this dilemma. His charges were increased to incorporate crimes of genocide in the Bosnian war and crimes against humanity in Croatia yet he still commanded some popular support in his homeland making site commemoration or future interpretation of death sites and graveyards problematic (for further discussion see Brighton, 2003). Furthermore, Iraqi nationals who may have a different perception of what constitutes a war crime may well have limited resources and more pressing priorities than visitation of such sites. This does not diminish their importance but it does limit visitation. Time and chronological distance are important here. In the case of war grave sites there is a clear need for time to pass before the establishment of commemorative or interpretive sites Accordingly, the nature of the site, the accessibility of the location, its association with a crime and the perception and dominant ideological perspective of visitor groups will impact on visitation.

Case studies in dark fascination

Morbid visitation recorded to 25 Cromwell Street, Gloucester, home of Fred and Rosemary West, was no doubt directly connected to the illegal acts of abduction, torture, and murder that were conducted by these perpetrators at this location. Visitors to sites of incarceration such as Robben Island in South Africa are not only considering the heritage of the apartheid era but also viewing the evidence of imprisonment of the victims of unjust laws. The work of Strange and Kempa (2003) on Robben Island and Alcatraz has relevance in this context. The nature of what such sites should commemorate and the narratives and meta narratives offered is most illustrative of the problematic nature of interpretation and the enduring appeal of such sites. Both Robben Island (Cape Town) and Alcatraz (San Francisco) are amongst the leading visitor attractions in these busy tourist destinations. Police Museums that exhibit items of evidence used in the trials also appear to exert a dark fascination for visitors. Indeed, the celebrated London Waxworks, Madame Tussaud's, has continued to draw visitors to its galleries of criminals and murderers more than any other element of the experience (Spedding, 2001).

In the plethora of dark tourism sites there are those that have little or no connection to actual crime such as those associated with fictional characters like Dracula the subject of products as diverse as castle tours (from Scotland to Romania), thematic pizza offers, walking tours and literary holidays. There is little doubt that the vampire legend continues to exert a fascination for the contemporary audience in film, television and writing. Yet, such an appeal is essentially built on a fictitious premise (albeit linked to a historical figure). Other sites that do not demonstrate criminal linkages would include death sites and last resting places. Locations associated with the tragic deaths of the famous such as ; the site of James Dean's fatal accident at Cholame and Elvis Presley's death site in Graceland, Tennessee, exert a fascination that is much less about crime. Indeed, graveyards and last resting places have appealed to visitors for generations. From Highgate Cemetery in London to the celebrated cemeteries of New Orleans tours can be taken and celebrated graves located. Guides will identify grave sites of the famous from Arlington Cemetery in Washington DC, USA to Glasnevin Cemetery in Dublin, Ireland.

Despite these qualifications it is apparent that abduction, murder and killing appear to exert a strong pull for visitors. The potential for criminal investigation to have a negative impact upon tourist visitation is also a concern in Jersey. An investigation into historic child abuse at Haut de la Garenne care home was initially led by chief police investigator, Lenny Harper. His suspension from the investigation on charges of profession misconduct and bullying (from which he was cleared in May 2009) has allegedly been connected to individuals with tourism interests on the island. Concern about the impact on tourism of media coverage of the investigations is thought to have been a factor in his suspension (Bunyan and Rayner, 2008). In a further example; the town of Soham in Cambridgeshire came to public attention in 2001 as the site of the kidnapping of Holly Wells and Jessica Chapman. This event attracted many casual visitors keen to view the location of their disappearance (Seaton and Lennon, 2004). It followed and reaffirmed the attraction of locations such as Dunblane and Lockerbie as sites of tragic and criminal events that serve to attract tourists and visitors (Lennon and Foley, 2000). In the case of Soham some had come to sign books of condolences leave flowers or children's toys at the site. Others had come to simply observe this ordinary small town in the turmoil following the abduction and murder of these two children. Indeed, there were reports of coach tour buses being rerouted to cover this town as part of their travel itinerary. The appeal of such sites would appear to eventually diminish over time yet potential timescales and monitoring of such chronology of interest and motivation to visit certainly merits further research.

The echoes of similar dark homage paid to 25 Cromwell Street, Gloucester, home of the notorious Fred and Rosemary West can also be identified. Following the suicide of her husband whilst in police custody, Rosemary West was given ten life sentences at Winchester Crown Court in November 1995 (Smith, 1995). However the house where so many of the crimes were perpetrated had become a tourist site. The footfall of police officers, forensic specialists and photographers was replaced by visitors to the site where most of the victims were slaughtered and buried. As a consequence, local policy-makers and administrators faced a dilemma of what to do with the house and whether or not to rename the street. Consultation with residents took place and the impact on property prices of those houses and flats in close proximity to Cromwell Street was cited as a major concern (Varley, 1995). The house was eventually demolished and the debris was buried some 25 metres underground to prevent souvenir hunters from pillaging the site. Unsurprisingly, the street was eventually renamed and the area's appeal to visitors has reduced. Such an approach is not new and it reflects how local authorities and policy-makers struggle to find the 'correct' solution for such sites. In Dallas, the Book Depository Building lay vacant for many years and the lobby for demolition was very strong before a local conservation society eventually succeeded in developing the building to commemorate the life of the President (see Lennon and Foley, 2000 for further discussion). In the UK, the disguise of another address associated with notorious crime was evident at the home of John Christie at number 10 Rillington Place. This location underwent a name change after the execution of its owner in 1953. Christie, who confessed to the killing of four women including his wife, brought an infamy to the area that local residents and local authorities were keen to erase. Rillington Place became Rushton Mews before being later redeveloped and called Wesley Square (Varley, 1995).

Dark tourism sites can create policy dilemmas for civic and local authorities as these locations have an ability to generate headlines, media coverage and visitation. When the notoriety of the site becomes so significant that resources have to be channelled into redevelopment, the dark fascination such sites exert is confirmed. In 2009 the current Mayor of London, Boris Johnson, experienced the problem of sensitivity and public acceptability of notorious site development. On suggesting that Scotland Yard might develop the items contained in its evidence storage facility to form a new tourist attraction to be titled the Blue Light Museum (MacDonald, 2009) both he and his administration were the subject of vociferous criticism. It was intimated that the proposed museum would include a display dedicated to the Scottish serial killer; Dennis Nilsen, who murdered 15 men in London during the 1970s and 1980s. Nilsen's flat in Muswell Hill, London was where he plied his victims with alcohol and then strangled them. He stored bodies in his home under floorboards and when he ran out of room he both burned body parts in his garden and boiled human remains in his kitchen. The proposed display was scheduled to include the cooking utensils utilised, the weapons, a stove and parts of the bathroom in which he murdered his victims. Outrage from the public, and most pointedly a former victim who survived an assault by Nilsen, has led to significant publicity around the acceptability of display and interpretation of such artefacts.

It is interesting to note that along with the Nilsen artefacts the Metropolitan Police holds information and artefacts from 850 cases dating from 1829. This includes material relating to Jack the Ripper and Dr Crippen in an area of Scotland Yard known as the Black Museum. This site is currently not open to the public although police sources acknowledge the potential appeal of the material (Lennon and Foley, 2000).

It would appear that the boundary between acceptable and unacceptable interpretation of criminal acts is indistinct. Critical in this process is the passage of time. Whilst there are close relatives of victims still alive, and whilst the public memory of such incidents remains vivid, the seeming celebration of such events may be too raw for public sensibilities. In 1995, when controversy raged around the fate of 25 Cromwell Street in Gloucester and the media recorded concerns with the ethical acceptability of such morbid visitation, in nearby Nottingham a £3.5 million crime and punishment attraction was being opened (Cramer, 1995). Featuring graphic representation of incarceration, punishment and culminating in an execution themed interpretation area this educative and historical recreation was deemed an acceptable use of UK Lottery funds.

This issue of social and political acceptable and unacceptable commemoration reoccurred with the home of the recently convicted Josef Fritzl of Amstetten, Austria. This was centred upon the dwelling place in Ybbstrasse where Fritzl imprisoned and raped his daughter more than 3000 times. Following his incarceration in 2008, the house had remained a sealed crime scene, guarded by police. Despite this the town of Amstetten has seen an influx of visitors keen to view the location where Austria's most notorious recent criminal had lived. This sprawling 66-room property with its 450 sq ft dungeon (wherein Fritzl's daughter was held) now presents a development dilemma for the local authorities. Fritzl was convicted of murder, rape, slavery, incest, false imprisonment and coercion and received life imprisonment in a secure psychiatric facility. Furthermore, he has been declared bankrupt with debts of more than £3 million. This means that his creditors are likely to demand that the house (his estates' most valuable asset) is sold. The concern of the local authority is that if the house went to the open market it could become a 'house of horrors' type museum attracting significant numbers of dark tourists (Rayner and Gammell, 2009).The Council are considering a compulsory purchase of the site with a view to demolition. As the Mayor of Amstetten, Herbert Katzengruber noted: 'A dark chapter of our town's history has finally been closed. The people of Amstetten now want to be left in peace' (Rayner and Gammell, 2009: 3). The belief that the town's association with this notorious criminal has to be seen as a closed chapter is essentially the driver of policy in this area. Demolition of the property risks a further damages claim from Fritzl's creditors against the local authority but that is seen as preferable to commemoration or interpretation of the site. As a council spokesman recorded: 'The fate of the house has not yet been decided. But we are determined that whatever happens, it will never become a commercial venture offering guided tours of the cellar' (Rayner and Gammell, 2009: 4).

Clearly the actions and comments of the authorities reveals a real fear of stigmatisation of the location, loss of civic reputation, reduced appeal of the destination for investment, etc. if it remains associated with this dark chapter of its history. Whether in the UK or Austria, similar concerns have been recorded and can be highlighted. Indeed, the situation in Amstetten echoes concerns expressed some three years earlier in 2006 in a similar case of kidnap, rape, imprisonment and coercion, also in Austria. Natascha Kampusch, an Austrian teenager was kidnapped and imprisoned in a cellar in Strasshof, near Vienna from 1998 until her escape in 2006. Her kidnapper, Wolfgang Priklopil, had his house seized by the local authority who were determined it should not become a dark attraction. Indeed, the house was later sold to the victim, Natascha Kampusch, for a nominal fee who also expressed concern about its potential appeal. As Kampusch related in relation to the house, 'I don't need it, I don't particularly want it but I don't want anybody trying to turn it into some kind of sick museum' (Rayner and Gammell, 2009: 4).

Sites of crime and decisions about their development thus remain emotionally charged and ethically complex. However, they can also be indicative of political and ideological imperatives at a local and national level. The recent furore in the Republic of Ireland over a proposed museum of child abuse is a further contemporary example of the concern and moral panic such development can catalyse (Jamieson, 2009). This followed a suggestion by an Irish Government Minister, Ruari Quinn, TD that following the extensive proof of child abuse linked to the Roman Catholic Church in Ireland, as detailed extensively in the Ryan Report (2009), that a child abuse museum would be an appropriate development for Ireland's capital to ensure this shameful episode and its perpetrators would not be forgotten. The development proposed was made more context-specific by the proposed location in the former Christian Brothers School at Parnell Square, Dublin. The Christian Brothers and their education establishments were frequently cited as locations where child abuse was commonplace and this particular site in Dublin was no exception. If such a museum were to be established the nature and content of interpretation would be undoubtedly controversial. Yet the scale of this problem at a national level in Ireland is an important factor in understanding why this development remains unlikely to proceed. The Royal College of Surgeons and the Dublin Rape Crisis Centre recently published the major investigative report, *Sexual Abuse and Violence in Ireland* (2009) with funding from the Irish Government that indicated a staggering abuse problem at a national scale. According to the report some 25% of the Irish adult population had suffered some form of abuse, predominantly in a domestic context. Furthermore, some 3% of child abuse in Ireland is attributable to members of the clergy. Whilst that 3% remains completely unacceptable, the exclusive focus of the media on Church related abuse means that the wider national problem goes largely unreported. The museum proposal sought to rectify this.

On the other side of the world in Cambodia, the sites associated with the murderous rule of the Khmer Rouge (1976–79) have evidenced similar development issues and the influence of government. After the temple complex of Angkor Wat in Siem Reap, the most visited sites are those associated with the dark past of this country. Indeed, Cambodia's history will always be overshadowed by the impact of this barbaric regime who dominated the nation with one of the most extreme regimes ever witnessed. Following the defeat of the Khmer Rouge in 1979 Cambodia was devastated. Approximately one third of the population were dead; of the 550 registered doctors only 48 had survived; of the 11,000 recorded university students only 450 remained; and of the 106,000 secondary school students only 5300 survived (Dunlop, 2005). The nation's infrastructure was devastated and just under 70% of temples had been destroyed. Mass graves populate the country and the Choeung Ek site in Phnom Penh records evidence of 19,440 mass graves and 167 former security offices/prisons throughout the country. The mass graves contain the bodies of those deliberately executed. They do not contain or record the young, the old or the sick who died along the road in the forced evacuations, nor those who died from malnutrition, forced labour, paucity of medicines or other causes. During the period of Khmer Rouge rule it is widely acknowledged that between 1.5 and 2 million people died as a result of the Khmer Rouge policies. The exact figure may never be known and accounts differ, see Jackson (1989), CIA (1980) and Vickery (1984) for contrasting assessment. Yet as a percentage of population (estimated at 7.3m in 1975) this was arguably amongst the worst genocide in world history.

Cambodia was thus faced with a tragic past and the difficulties associated with the management and operation of such sites of atrocity and crimes against humanity that have tourist appeal. The brutality of the Khmer Rouge regime merits documentation yet as discussed above, such sites bring with them many challenges in terms of memorialisation, conservation and commercial operation (for useful discussion of a number of such sites see Ashworth and Hartmann (2005)).

Interpretation and development at S-21 a key site of the Khmer Rouge period (1975-9)

Key elements of heritage interpretation of the Khmer Rouge period in Cambodia are located in S-21 Tuol Sleng Museum of Genocidal Crime (a former prison) and Choeung Ek (known as the Killing Field and an execution site). The former will be examined as the extent and quality of interpretation is limited to short narrative panels in either Khmer or poorly translated English. Historical coverage and narrative in interpretive panels remains limited and a range of photographic and diagrammatic information is either untitled, unexplained or both. In addition both sites are in decay. These structures were of relatively poor construction quality and having seen little maintenance since 1979, they are declining rapidly. Objects and buildings are at risk and deterioration of documentation of the incarcerations and executions at Tuol Sleng is a serious concern. Tuol Sleng, just south of Phnom Penh is a former secondary school the use of which was changed in 1976 by the Khmer Rouge. It became a prison (known as S-21) to detain and torture individuals accused of opposing the regime (Chhang and Kosal, 2005). The prisoners and victims of the S-21 facility Tuol Sleng were estimated at 10,499 to which should be added over 2000 children who were also killed here (Chhang and Kosal 2005). Other authors suggest that detailed review of documentation held at S-21 indicate closer to 20,000 executions (Chandler, 1999; Dunlop 2005). On average the prison held between 1200–1500 prisoners. The regime and the nature of incarceration were brutal and the shackles and torture instruments used by the guards are exhibited in the museum. This site is important because after capture by the invading North Vietnamese army it was found to contain the most definitively documented evidence of execution and torture. The documents maintained at Tuol Sleng provide the evidence that within Democratic Kampuchea there was widespread and systematic torture, extra-judicial execution, specific programmes of genocide against religious and ethnic groups as well as the partial decimation of the people of Cambodia (Hawk, 1989). The records and confessions extracted by torture provide inarguable evidence of the nature of brutality and genocide committed by the Khmer Rouge regime.

Entry to the site is low key and the property lacks a formal boundary fence allowing uncontrolled access from the street and surrounding buildings. The admission charge of US$2 is officially a charge for the information and orientation guide since Tuol Sleng has been forbidden by the Cambodian Government to charge for admission. Indeed, since 1979 the museum has faced continual financial crisis. It is starved of government funding and is not permitted to generate its own revenues. In comparison entrance to the Angkor Wat Temple complex is in excess of US$30. This has impacted significantly on conservation efforts and is the primary reason for the limited interpretation (for further discussions see Lennon, 2009). The narrative of the sites is incomplete and the historical evidence is decaying. Primary objects and evidence of genocide are in danger and there is little assistance from central government or heritage agencies to prevent such loss. This same government has resisted the current ongoing trial of Khmer Rouge leaders and it should be noted that the current premier is a former low-ranking Khmer Rouge soldier. The site is popular, attracting over 60,000 visitors per year, yet is clearly regarded as a problem and an embarrassment by the government of Cambodia.

The visitor experiences such sites as part of an increasingly commoditised itinerary of other attractions and activities. In such a context, the enormity of the criminal genocide perpetrated in this site is neither appropriately interpreted, appreciated nor understood. In this sense, tourism attractions and heritage elements such as

S-21 provide the signposts and records of the criminal past. The deterioration of evidence and artefacts and the weakness of the interpretation at such sites can be viewed as acts with political and ideological intent. The non-interpretation of these crimes, their partial obliteration or simply focusing public expenditure in other directions all constitutes political and ideological actions. The extent to which partial interpretation, limited conservation and selectivity combine to veil such criminal acts is a concern. Habermas (1970) has commented on the impossibility of non-ideological interpretation and it is accepted that neutrality and accuracy remain elusive concepts from a curatorial and interpretive standpoint. However, when such narrative is absent, crimes of genocide ignored and primary evidence is at peril, the nature and cause of such selective interpretation becomes transparent.

S21 has changed and altered over time, the authenticity of site, object utilisation and narrative panel or guided interpretation have altered and changed over time. The wooden building at the entry point which was the location for prisoner photographic identification is now a guide rest area and administrative office. The former guard offices are now part of the gift shop and in early 2007, the museum announced the intention of planting a garden for contemplation at the entrance of the site. As these incremental changes occur and the complexities of how these sites (and others like it) were key to the Khmer Rouge maintenance of power remain uninterpreted. This history is being eroded and is fading. While Tuol Sleng has become a tourist stop for visitors; it is not a place where those visitors will learn or appreciate the important and tragic past of this nation. It is ironic that as the internationally funded trial of Khmer Rouge leaders continues, the site that was the source of incriminating evidence remains starved of funds. Cambodia is a place where the evidence of the crimes of a generation is maintained in a visitor attraction against the wishes of the state.

Conclusions

Criminal activity and particularly murder in any location is a serious concern and Gibson (2006) notes that in general it will cause business to reduce. Specifically, aspects such as shopping and other tourism behaviours, excursions, visiting restaurants and bars will be reduced due to fears over personal safety. However as has been argued above serial murder sites can stimulate public interest and catalyse visitation. Gibson (2006) documents a range of cases highlighting the proven appeal of such sites and he has explored traditional tourist behaviours and impacts. Specifically he identifies various activities that can be catalysed from visitation to murder sites, including travel, sightseeing, entertainment, dining, accommodation, photography and retail spend. Clearly, crimes that demonstrate the darker side of human nature can similarly stimulate increased visitation and economic activity. However, the development of such dark sites that are associated with criminal acts, perpetrators and victims are problematic in a number of respects, including the following:

♦ *Destination reputation*: Policy-makers and local administrators continually demonstrate significant reactions in political terms to the stigma associated with destinations that have evidenced criminal events that in turn have attracted consumer interest and generated visitation. This may be observed in the case of the disappearance of Madelaine McCann at Praia D'Ora in Portugal and in the Haut de la Garenne child abuse and murder allegations in Jersey.

♦ *Ethics of development*: Such sites create dilemmas of development and acceptability. In some cases local administrations will take action to prevent development via compulsory purchase, objections to planning and licensing and in extreme (but not unusual) cases demolition.

♦ *Interpretation*: The content, imagery and narrative used to interpret such dark sites is seen as controversial in some cases and questionable in many (for further discussion see Ashworth and Hartman, 2005; Lennon, 2009).

♦ *Attraction management*: Where commercial imperatives and management of visitation become issues the requirement for sensitivity and understanding can often be subsumed for revenue generation and return on investment.

♦ *Dominant ideologies and government policy and practice*: the interpretation of artefacts and the exhibition of materials is an inherently ideological practice. Content and descriptors are not value-free and in some cases, the very ethos and existence of a site will be threatened if it fails to conform to a political perspective on the past (Lennon, 2009). However it is also apparent that crime sites that have dark associations will also threaten reputation and provide policy-makers and government administrators with real development dilemmas (for example this was definitely the case with the Texas Book Depository building in Dallas). In the most extreme examples, sites will be levelled or wholly transformed.

Until governments and policy-makers are comfortable in dealing with the nature and content of such sites, their histories and the attraction of crime-associated locations, then we will continue to see them dealt with in an arbitrary and at times, irrational, way. These sites represent the record, the context and in some cases, the evidence of crime. Their conservation, educational potential and dark appeal deserves comprehension and a voice.

References

Ashworth, G. (1996) 'Holocaust tourism and Jewish culture: the lessons of Krakow-Kazimierz', in M. Robinson, N. Evans and O.P. Callaghan (eds), *Tourism and Cultural Change*, Sunderland: Business Education Publishers, pp.1–12.

Ashworth, G. and Hartmann, R. (2005) *Horror and Human Tragedy Revisited: The Management of Sites of Atrocities for Tourism*, New York: Cognizant Communications Corporation.

BBC (2009) '9/11 trial ignites row' see http://news.bbc.co.uk/1/hi/world/americas/8360018.stm accessed December 2009.

Beech J (2000) 'The enigma of holocaust sites as tourist attractions – the case of Buchenwald', *Managing Leisure*, 5, 29–41.

Beech, J. (2001) 'The marketing of slavery heritage in the United Kingdom', *International Journal of Hospitality and Tourism Administration*, 2, (3&4), 85-106.

Blair, J. (2002) 'Tragedy turns to tourism at Ground Zero', *New York Times*, 29 June

Blom, T. (2000) 'Morbid tourism; a postmodern market niche with an example from Althorpe', *Norwegian Journal of Geography*, **54** (1), 29–36.

Brighton, S. (2003) 'Milošević on trial: the dilemma of political justice', see http://www.bbc.co.uk/history/recent/milosevic_trial_03 accessed November 2009

Bunyan, N. and Rayner, G. (2008) 'Jersey police chief suspended as claims of child murders ripped up', http://www.telegraph.co.uk accessed November 2009.

Chhang and Kosal (2005) *Genocide Museum Tuol Sleng (Former Khmer Rouge S-21 Prison), Phnom Penh*. Government of Cambodia, Tuol Sleng Museum and Documentation Centre of Cambodia.

CIA (Central Intelligence Agency) (1980) *Kampuchea: A Demographic Catastrophe*, Washington DC: US Government Printing Office.

Cohen, E. (1988) 'Authenticity and commoditization in tourism', *Annals of Tourism Research*, **15** (3), 371–386.

Cole, T. (1999) *Images of the Holocaust: the Myth of the 'Shoah Business'*, London: Gerald Duckworth.

Cole, T. (2000) *Selling the Holocaust: from Auschwitz to Schindler, how History is Bought, Packaged and Sold*, London: Routledge and Kegan Paul.

Cramer, J. (1995) 'Life of crime', *Leisure Opportunities*, April, 134, 44–45.

Dann, G. and Seaton, A. (eds) (2006) *Slavery, Contested Heritage and Thanatourism*, Binghampton, NY: Haworth Hospitality Press.

Dunlop, N. (2005) *The Lost Executioner*, London: Bloomsbury.

Foley, M. and Lennon, J. (1996a) 'Editorial: heart of darkness', *International Journal of Heritage Studies*, 2, (4), 195–197.

Foley, M. and Lennon, J. (1996b) 'JFK and dark tourism: a fascination with assassination', *International Journal of Heritage Studies*, 2 (4), 198–211.

Gibson, D.C. (2006) 'The relationship between serial murder and the American tourism industry', *Journal of Travel and Tourism Marketing*, **20** (1), 45–60.

Habermas, J. (1970) *Towards a Rational Society*, London: Heinemann Educational Books.

Hawk, D. (1989) 'The photographic record', in K.D. Jackson (ed.), *Cambodia 1975–78: Rendezvous with Death*, Princeton: Princeton University Press, pp. 208–214.

Jackson, K. D. (ed.) (1989) *Cambodia 1975–78: Rendezvous with Death*, Princeton: Princeton University Press.

Jamieson, L. (2009) 'The Ryan Report: an abuse museum for Dublin'. in *Studies*, http://studiesirishreview.wordpress.com, accessed 7 September 2009.

Lennon, J. and Foley, M. (2000) *Dark Tourism: The attraction of death and disaster*. Andover, UK: Cengage Learning.

Lennon, J. (2009) 'Tragedy and heritage in peril: the case of Cambodia', *Tourism Recreational Research*, 34 (1), 35–44.

MacDonald, S. (2009) 'Nilsen victim attacks museum', *Sunday Times*, 10 May.

Rayner, G. and Gammell, C. (2009) 'Josef Fritzl: fears house of horrors could become ghoulish tourist attraction', *The Times*, 20 March.

Reiner, R. (2007) 'Media-made criminality: the representation of crime in the media', in M. Maguire, R. Morgan and R. Reiner (eds), *The Oxford Handbook of Criminology*, Oxford: Oxford University Press. pp. 302-335.

Rojek, C. (1993) *Ways of Escape*, Basingstoke: Macmillan.

Rowe, M. (2007) 'Intrepid travellers break new ground', *Daily Telegraph*, 20 October.

Royal College of Surgeons and Dublin Rape Crisis Centre (2009) *Sexual Abuse and Violence in Ireland*, Dublin: Royal College of Surgeons.

Ryan Report (2009) *The Commission to Inquire into Child Abuse*, Dublin: Government of Ireland.

Seaton, A.V. (1996) 'Guided by the dark: from thanatopsis to thanatourism', *International Journal of Heritage Studies*, 2 (4), 234–244.

Seaton, A.V. (1999) 'War and thanatourism: Waterloo 1815–1914', *Annals of Tourism Research*, 26 (1), 130–158.

Seaton, A.V. (2009) 'Purposeful otherness: approaches to the management of thanatourism', in R. Sharkley and P. Stone (eds), *The Darker Side of Travel*, London: Routledge.

Seaton, A.V. and Lennon, J.J. (2004) 'Moral panics, ulterior motives and alterior desires: thanatourism in the 21st century', in T. Singh (ed.), *New Horizons in Tourism: Strange Experiences and Stranger Practices*, Wallingford: CABI Publishing, pp. 63–82.

Sharkley, R. and Stone, P. (eds) (2009) *The Darker Side of Travel*, London: Routledge.

Smith, J. (1995) 'Does she belong in this company?', *Independent on Sunday*, 26 November

Spedding, K. (2001) 'Madam Tussauds: a review of the millennium', unpublished BA dissertation, University of Luton.

Strangem C. and Kempa, M. (2003) 'Shades of dark tourism: Alcatraz and Robben Island', *Annals of Tourism Research*, 30 (2), 386–405.

Varley, N. (1995) 'New name for Cromwell Street?, *Independent on Sunday*, 26 November.

Vickery, M. (1984) 'Democratic Kampuchea: themes and variations', in D. Chandler (ed.), *Cambodia 1975-1982*, Boston, MA: South End Press, pp. 178–198.

13 Conclusions: Mapping a Research Agenda

David Botterill and Trevor Jones

We began this book with a review of the development of two hitherto relatively separate domains of study that we feel have much to learn from each other. To date, scholarly work on the social phenomena of crime and tourism have largely eschewed cross-disciplinary engagement. The chapters that followed have attempted to bring together the scant research literature that does exist on the subjects of crime and tourism, whilst examining different forms of victimisation against tourists, various types of offending or deviant behaviour by tourists, and responses to crimes by/against tourists by the authorities. Given the paucity of available literature, it is inevitable that these chapters have relied primarily on writing from the distinct perspectives of criminology or tourism studies respectively, depending on the subject expertise of the author. However, many contributing authors have bravely accepted our challenge to attempt to step into each others' world and open up the crime and tourism nexus. To all our contributors we owe a considerable debt of gratitude for beginning what we hope will be an ongoing and productive dialogue between these subject domains. It is our intention in this final chapter to outline briefly the markers of a research agenda for new scholarship in the two subjects and for potential areas of research collaboration.

In the course of the book's production, a compelling argument has emerged that draws our two subject domains closer. It was not our intention, but the structure of the book aids us in making this argument. While Chapters 2 through 8 of the book are grounded in a largely orthodox view of both crime and tourism, in Chapters 9 to 12 we confront the shifting sands inspired by the actuarial turn in criminology and the critical turn in tourism studies. The argument here is that because criminal acts in a tourism context may be, on the criminological hand, only of peripheral interest and, on the tourism hand, best dismissed as externalities and quickly recovered from, the conceptual shift to embrace contemporary preoccupations with 'risk' and the 'fear of crime' shakes up these older certainties in both subjects. This is best demonstrated in Chapters 9 (Hughes), 10 (Jones) and 11 (Selby *et al.*) and we more fully explore the meaning of these shifts or 'turns' below in our discussion of prospects of cross-disciplinary research.

We think that the chapters in this volume suggest a number of areas for potentially fruitful exchange between the two subject areas. We divide these into three main categories: conceptual/theoretical development, new avenues for empirical enquiry, and policy-oriented research. These divisions are analytical rather than absolute, as in practice of course, the categories merge into one another.

Theoretical/conceptual development

As we outlined in Chapter 1, in so far as the study of tourism often involves examination of behaviours and activities that occur in contrasting legal and cultural contexts, Tourism studies inevitably brings out the transient nature of criminology's core concept. Indeed, it illustrates that an important aspect of the 'problem of crime' is the concept of 'crime' itself, which brings together diverse social practices such as trafficking heroine, homicide, credit card fraud, burglary and sexual assault, collapsed into a single category. Considerations of tourism shines light on this conceptual challenge both in exposing the shifting sands of legal definitions of 'crime', as well as in highlighting the limited conceptual gaze with regard to particular forms of socially harmful behaviour. As social constructionist perspectives have highlighted, 'crime' is legally and culturally contingent, and is the outcome of complex social processes involving the 'deviant', 'controllers' and the social audience more generally. The chapters on time share selling (Bott), drug tourism (Shiner) and sex tourism by paedophiles (Montgomery) demonstrate in stark terms the variable nature of crime and deviance relating to variations in cultural mores about what is and is not acceptable, national differences in legal rules about what behaviours require regulation by the criminal law, and contrasting approaches in the enforcement of legal rules.

Although criminology has of course been reflexive about the slippery nature of its core subject matter, it continues to be criticised on grounds of an overly narrow focus on social harms as defined in the criminal law. A consideration of the literature on crimes in relation to tourism quickly demonstrates an important conceptual limitation of such narrow criminological approaches. Using Walklate's (1996) metaphorical classification of types of crime, it is really only 'crimes of the streets' that have formed the focus of scholarly attention, and this by a very few authors who have crossed the disciplinary divide. This work is summarised comprehensively in the chapters of Rob Mawby and Paul Brunt. Both authors noted that the majority of the extant research is based on official statistics or victimisation surveys. Such approaches explore conventional legal categories of crime, and are based on implicitly individualistic assumptions such as intent, culpability, responsibility and guilt. In effect, such conceptualisations of the 'crime problem' define out what in practice are often greater social harms caused by the misdeeds of corporations or governments, or more generally, systemic social harms that arise out of the processes of capitalistic production. Studies of 'white collar crime'

(Nelken, 2007), corporate crimes and harms (Tombs and Whyte, 2007), and more generally, 'crimes of the state' (Cohen, 2002) remain relatively rare within mainstream criminology. The domain of tourism, given its configuration as an area of significance for both corporations and national/local governments, provides potentially fertile ground for further conceptual and empirical development in the wider study of social harms, whether or not defined formally as 'crimes', and the possible responses to them. We shall consider some of these specific possibilities for such development in the next section on areas for joint empirical enquiry by tourism and criminological scholars.

Another area of potential conceptual interplay between tourism studies and criminology concerns the growing contemporary focus upon 'risk' and security, identified in particular in the chapters on tourism destination image (Selby *et al.*), governing security (Jones), and crime prevention (Hughes). In different ways, these chapters all highlighted the growing tendency for contemporary social life to be organised around attempts to predict and prevent future harms, rather than simply to detect and punish past wrongs. Whilst such arguments have become commonplace within social science generally (Beck, 1992), it seems that they have a particular resonance for the intersection between criminology and tourism studies. This work has had important implications in the field of criminology, informing a burgeoning literature on the governance of security, the emergence of crime prevention and community safety, as well as shifting approaches in the management of offenders. The study of risk in the context of tourism is clearly an important and growing area, with a focus upon effective risk management with regard to a range of possible future harms. The challenge for researchers in both tourism studies and criminology is to explore how the tourism-crime nexus may help further our understanding of the complex ways in which 'risk' plays itself out in the organisation of contemporary social life.

Even without moving beyond conventional notions of crime, the intersection of criminology and tourism studies offers the prospect for refinements in conceptual developments on a different level, in terms of the formulation and testing of theoretical explanations of particular forms of crimes by and against tourists. For example, Mawby's chapters (2 and 3) provide the outline of an initial explanatory model for both property crimes and violent crimes, and one that needs to be tested with more empirical evidence. Studies of particular forms of offending and victimisation by and against tourists offer the possibilities of contributions to further theoretical hypotheses about the causes and effects of such phenomena.

Avenues for further empirical enquiry

Conceptual/theoretical developments should both inform and be informed by rigorous empirical enquiry. Putting together this volume has brought into sharp relief the gaps in the available empirical evidence to inform and test theoretical advances. In particular, we could find very little extant literature referring to either of the two remaining categories of crime suggested by Walklate. For example, it is unlikely that the business of tourism should be any less immune to the prevalence of 'crimes of the suites' than other sectors of the corporate world yet very few researchers have ventured into this area of investigation. We are indebted to Esther Bott for her exposé of the practices of the timeshare industry in Tenerife (Chapter 7) and for demonstrating what it takes to investigate some uncomfortable aspects of what is often lauded as a rapidly expanding global phenomenon in the business of tourism. As we have already suggested, conceptual development beyond the narrow concept of 'crime' would be informed by a greater empirical focus on social harms arising from the activities of tourist corporations (for example, private cruise operators or the developers of tourist 'enclaves') and the damaging social impacts of the relative under-regulation of corporate misdeeds such as the violation of health and safety laws (for example, in its impacts of safety standards for visitors and tourist industry workers in the 'tourist spaces' discussed in Jones' chapter). In addition, we would have liked to have included a chapter on corporate jurisprudence with particular relation to 'crime of the suites' in relation to the tourist sector. High-profile cases involving breaches of health and safety legislation, food hygiene regulation, employment law, etc. are all important areas for future enquiry. All such examples provide critical incidents that should open up an entirely new perspective on the 'business of tourism'.

Of equal, if not more emotive, significance is the relative absence in research literature relating to tourism of consideration of the third of Walklate's categories, 'crime behind closed doors' (Walklate, 1996: 296). In Chapter 1 we observed that the general lack of attention to studies of crime in mainstream tourism studies might be a result of a sort of ideological myopia vested within the tourism academy. Seduced by the ideology of the holiday as pleasurable, the definition of what is constituted as legitimate tourism omits the darker aspects of human behaviour, except when it becomes part of the tourist gaze as Lennon reminds us in Chapter 12. Consequentially, the prospects of engaging with 'crimes behind closed doors' is literally 'bracketed out' of the collective consciousness of the tourism academy. We think this is a major omission that needs to be addressed. As argued above in respect of corporate crime, holidays are not, by definition, immune from criminal acts. Domestic violence, sexual abuse and cruelty are not constrained by situation, and indeed, limited evidence suggests that certain forms of domestic abuse may be in some ways positively related to aspects of leisure or tourism. There is strong evidence that domestic violence accounts for a significant proportion of all violent crime. About 28 per cent of women in England and Wales have experienced domestic abuse after the age of 16, approximating to 4.5 million female victims of domestic abuse (Walker *et al.*, 2009). It is important to ask whether 'crimes behind closed doors' are more likely to occur during holiday periods and be more difficult to counteract precisely because they contradict the twin ideologies of the home and the holiday and occur away from recourse to 'normal' law enforcement interventions. Periods of 'free time' in society have often excited moral panic about human behaviour and leisure studies researchers have documented historical and contemporary examples that would provide a useful reference point for the tourism academy. In the South Wales community where we both live, local police forces mount public relations campaigns warning of the increased risks of alcohol related domestic violence during the annual Six Nations rugby tournament. Emotions intensify around the support for the national team game and the expectations of a Welsh victory spark sometimes violent reaction, sometimes on the streets, but according to the police evidence more likely in the home. Just how much the expectations (and disappointments) of a holiday and the extended intensity of intimacy afforded by the 'free time' of the holiday might contribute to 'crimes behind closed doors' is a black box not yet opened by scholars in either criminology or tourism studies. It needs to be.

We noted in Chapter 1 that by its very nature, tourism studies demands a comparative perspective, and one that has to date been rather absent within academic criminology. The need for more empirical research in this area is perhaps particularly acute in the area of cross-national responses to tourist crime. Heather Montgomery's chapter on sex tourism and that of Spapens on cross-border policing raise important cross-disciplinary themes that need to be addressed by future empirical research. Whilst this applies to both crimes 'of the suites' and 'of the streets', it is perhaps no better demonstrated than in relation to 'crimes behind closed doors'. Here, the lack of visibility of the acts, the omnipresent and sometimes ambivalent power relations between perpetrator and victim, confusion over the reporting of domestic abuse when in a foreign country, and unfamiliarity with (and suspicion of) foreign police force reaction to domestic crime reporting all point, in our view, to a complex picture that needs more careful unravelling.

A further area of potentially fruitful collaboration between tourism studies and criminology concerns the regulation of leisure activities in the so-called 'night-time economy' (NTE). Recent years have seen the emergence of paradoxical approach to governing leisure activities in many British city centres. On the one hand, such approaches are based upon the liberalisation of drinking regulations with a view to promoting increased leisure expenditure – primarily upon alcohol consumption. On the other hand, there are enhanced expectations placed upon the police (and other authorities) to deal with the immediate consequences of alcohol related crime and disorder, as well as the immediate and longer-term health implications. This paradox has already been subject to important criminological enquiry (see, for example, Hobbs *et al.*, 2003) and we had hoped to include a chapter on the phenomenon of 'sanctioned deviance' in the new sites of leisure in towns and city centres. Unfortunately, we did not succeed in commissioning such a chapter in the present volume, but this remains an important area of potential collaboration between criminology and tourism studies. The moves to reposition British cities as liminal places of leisure consumption and the consequent investigations of the night-time economy we refer to above are predated by the development of many thousands of tourist resorts around the world. However, we know very little about the governance of security in both recent (beyond the UK) and established sites of 'sanctioned deviance' and this is surely an area where tourism scholars and criminologists should collaborate in the future.

Lessons for policy research

As the discussion in Chapter 1 indicated, the dialogue between tourism studies and criminology should be of significant interest to policy-makers in a variety of arenas, given the potential importance of crime (and the threat of crime) to the tourist industry, to governments of countries/regions where tourism forms a major contribution to economic wellbeing, and to individual tourists themselves.

In the first instance, it is clear that the tourist industry and governmental authorities need more rigorous evidence about patterns of offending by and victimisation against tourists, and possible explanations for such developments, in order to better inform policy and practice. Perhaps the initial concern here will inevitably relate to self-interest, and, for the tourist business in particular, the concern with 'loss reduction'. But such evidence is also an important precondition for more enlightened interventions that go beyond the immediate demands of commercial self-interest, and speak to loftier ideals relating to broader corporate and governmental responsibility to promote equitable and effective arrangements for governing safety. As Hughes records in Chapter 9, approaches to crime prevention have grown significantly over the past 40 years. Writing from a British standpoint, his analysis includes the recent creation of 'local', multi-agency community safety partnerships. From a tourism studies perspective it would be interesting to know if tourism destinations across the UK present any uniquely different community safety issues or indeed whether there is any recognition of the influx of domestic and international tourists visitors upon the work of the partnerships. More significantly perhaps, Hughes comments that such locally-based approaches naturally miss the reduction of risks for British residents travelling abroad. He concludes that the reduction of crime risks for British residents abroad will be dependent on the tourism-receiving localities and regions carrying out similar community safety processes. Consequentially, the opportunities for comparative research between tourist generating and receiving regions of the world in respect of crime prevention practices are considerable and, we would add, carry significant policy implications.

In particular, the importance of this cross-subject work needs to be better and more vigorously communicated to the leadership of the tourism industry whom, in turn, need to more fully engage with destination governments on the underlying causes of property and violent crime. A culture of reactive measures pervades sectors of the tourism industry, usually involving an embargo on the offending destinations and a switch of tourist gaze through changes to destination itineraries. Such self-interested decision-making calls into the question the long-term commitment of the tourism industry to building sustainable economic and social contributions to many of the poorer regions of the world. The ease with which the industry can switch its attentions and favours causes resentment among local populations and their political leaders and defines the industry as failing to aspire to the 21st century mantra of corporate social responsibility. A recent example of this corporate behaviour is the move to strike-off Antigua and Nassau as ports of call for some cruise line companies operating in the Caribbean (Starmer-Smith, 2010). Given the vital importance of tourism within some governmental agendas, it is important also to raise the profile of applied research on tourism and crime to demonstrate to governmental authorities the nature and pattern of crimes by and against tourists, and indicate the most just and effective methods of regulating such incidents.

Concluding comments

Space precludes a more detailed discussion of the numerous possible avenues of future co-operation between tourism studies and criminology in contributing to theoretical, empirical and policy-related advances in research. The above examples are intended to be illustrative rather than comprehensive. But what they all demonstrate is that the potential overlaps in the research interests of the two subject communities are numerous. In an introductory volume such as this one, it is only possible to touch upon some of these overlaps. But we hope to have shown that the tentative dialogue that we have begun here, is a conversation that should continue to develop, to the benefit of both subject communities.

References

Beck, U. (1992) *The Risk Society: Towards a New Modernity*, London: Sage

Cohen, S. (2002) 'Human rights and crimes of the state: the culture of denial', in E. McLaughlin, J. Muncie and G. Hughes (eds), *Criminological Perspectives*, 2nd edn, London: Sage.

Hobbs, D., Hadfield, P., Lister, S.C. and Winlow, S. (2003) *Bouncers: Violence and Governance in the Night-Time Economy*, Oxford: Oxford University Press

Nelken, D. (2007) 'White collar and corporate crime', in M. Maguire, R. Morgan and R. Reiner (eds), *The Oxford Handbook of Criminology*, 4th edn, Oxford: Oxford University Press. pp. 733-770.

Starmer-Smith, C. (2010) 'Rising crime takes Antigua off cruise routes', *Daily Telegraph*, 6 February.

Tombs, S. and Whyte, D. (2007) *Safety Crimes*, Cullompton: Willan

Walker, A., Flatley, J., Kershaw, C. and Moon, D. (2009) *Crime in England and Wales 2008/09: Findings from the British Crime Survey and Police Recorded Crime (Volume 1)*, Home Office Statistical Bulletin, No. 11/09, London: Home Office.

Walklate, S. (1996) 'Community and crime prevention' in E. McLaughlin and J. Muncie (eds), *Controlling Crime*, London, Sage.

Index